Helping Skills for Working with College Students

In a sea of books teaching counseling and helping skills to others, *Helping Skills for Working with College Students* stands out as clear frontrunner in terms of its accessible and well-researched writing style. This book is an excellent resource for those new to student affairs or looking to improve their helping skills with those in crisis, in or out of the classroom. The text explores the boundaries of help offered by paraprofessional staff and faculty while offering poignant and timely suggestions on how best to support today's college students.

—**Brian Van Brunt,** Senior Vice President for Professional Program Development at the National Center for Higher Education Risk Management (NCHERM), USA

A primary role of student affairs professionals is to help college students dealing with developmental transitions and coping with emotional difficulties. Becoming an effective helping professional requires the complex integration of intrapersonal, interpersonal, and professional awareness and knowledge. For graduate students preparing to become student affairs practitioners, this textbook provides the skills necessary to facilitate the helping process and understand how to respond to student concerns and crises, including how to make referrals to appropriate campus or community resources. Focusing on counseling concepts and applications essential for effective student affairs practice, this book develops the conceptual frameworks, basic counseling skills, interventions, and techniques that are necessary for student affairs practitioners to be effective, compliant, and ethical in their helping and advising roles. Rich in pedagogical features, this textbook includes questions for reflection, theory to practice exercises, case studies, and examples from the field.

Monica Galloway Burke is Associate Professor of Counseling and Student Affairs at Western Kentucky University, USA.

Jill Duba Sauerheber is Professor and Department Head of Counseling and Student Affairs at Western Kentucky University, USA.

Aaron W. Hughey is Professor of Counseling and Student Affairs and Coordinator of the Student Affairs graduate program at Western Kentucky University, USA.

Karl Laves is Associate Director of the Counseling and Testing Center at Western Kentucky University, USA.

Helping Skills for Working with College Students

Applying Counseling Theory to Student Affairs Practice

Monica Galloway Burke,
Jill Duba Sauerheber,
Aaron W. Hughey, and
Karl Laves

Routledge
Taylor & Francis Group

NEW YORK AND LONDON

First published 2017
by Routledge
711 Third Avenue, New York, NY 10017

and by Routledge
2 Park Square, Milton Park, Abingdon, Oxon, OX14 4RN

Routledge is an imprint of the Taylor & Francis Group, an informa business

Library of Congress Cataloging-in-Publication Data
Names: Burke, Monica Galloway.
Title: Helping skills for working with college students : applying
    counseling theory to student affairs practice / Monica Galloway
    Burke [and three others].
Description: New York, NY : Routledge, 2017. | Includes bibliographical
    references and index.
Identifiers: LCCN 2016005002 | ISBN 9781138122369 (hardback) |
    ISBN 9781138122376 (pbk.) | ISBN 9781315650531 (ebook)
Subjects: LCSH: Student affairs administrators. | Student affairs services.
Classification: LCC LB2342.9 .B87 2017 | DDC 371.4—dc23
LC record available at http://lccn.loc.gov/2016005002

ISBN: 978-1-138-12236-9 (hbk)
ISBN: 978-1-138-12237-6 (pbk)
ISBN: 978-1-315-65053-1 (ebk)

Typeset in Perpetua and Bell Gothic
by Apex CoVantage, LLC

Contents

Preface

Never has the importance of higher education been more pronounced or acute with respect to our individual and collective future. As technology and globalization continue to transform the economic, cultural, and political landscape, extending one's education beyond the secondary realm is increasingly seen as the only viable strategy for achieving and sustaining a heightened quality of life. Those students entering our institutions are a product of this transformation and in a very real sense, they share a common bond forged by their exposure to a society that has been rapidly evolving for the past several decades.

Today's college students truly have the potential to change the world. The world they inhabit is substantively different from that of previous generations. One of the defining characteristics of contemporary students is the level of emotional difficulties they tend to exhibit. Whereas college has always been a somewhat stressful experience for many, today's students are arriving on campus with a myriad of complex issues and concerns. The better equipped staff are to accurately recognize and evaluate their state of mind and concerns, the better able they will be to adequately respond to the needs of the students they serve.

A fundamental tenet underlying the philosophy and intent of the authors of this book is that human relations skills are just as important as practical proficiency when it comes to helping today's college students reach their full potential. The student affairs profession is as much about realizing human potential as it is about administration; the two emphases are inextricably intertwined and complement each other. In our roles as educators, practitioners, and helping professionals in student affairs and mental health, the authors understand the relevance of helping skills to effectively support and respond to the needs of students in higher education. We also acknowledge becoming an effective helping professional in student affairs requires the complex integration of intrapersonal and interpersonal awareness, knowledge, and skills. Our goal is to provide a foundation for the development of helping skills for working with college students and to convey information about the basic counseling concepts and applications essential for effective student affairs practice.

This book is designed to provide student affairs professionals at all levels with the knowledge and skills they increasingly need to respond more effectively to the challenges and needs of students. It can also be used in graduate preparation courses designed to prepare student affairs professionals; for professional development and informational sessions or workshops for faculty and staff; and for trainings and workshops with student staff in residence halls or peer mentors.

The content in this book is designed to flow logically and each chapter is designed to support and reinforce the other chapters in order to present a comprehensive scaffolding from which student affairs professionals can be effective in their interactions with students. The book also includes skills practice activities, narratives, recommendations, and exercises throughout to provide context for the reader.

Chapter 1, "The Helping Role in Student Affairs," sets the stage for what follows by giving the reader a context for defining what helping means with respect to today's college students. The authors present an overview of what it means to provide the kind of assistance and support today's college students need.

Chapter 2, "Personal and Professional Responsibilities," is intended to help student affairs professionals understand the moral and ethical parameters and responsibilities that should guide their practice. Included in the discussion are specific guidelines and suggestions for practice that should help professionals be more cognizant of their inherent need and obligation to always put interests of the student first. Additionally, there is an examination of multicultural competence and why student affairs professionals in helping roles must develop awareness, knowledge, and skills necessary to create an affirming environment for all students.

Chapter 3, "Helping Skills," provides a solid foundation and practice exercises in the basic counseling and communication skills that must be mastered in order to empathetically respond to students' needs in a holistic way. Specifically, these include active listening, questioning, paraphrasing, reflection of feeling, interpretation, and summarization.

Chapter 4, "Moving Toward Action," provides concrete examples of evidence-based methods for moving students toward problem solving, self-understanding, and goal setting. Using narratives and recommendations from practitioners, the chapter also reviews self-disclosure and advice giving as well as mindfulness and expressive arts approaches to assist students in exploring difficult emotions and engaging in self-reflection.

Chapter 5, "Conflict Resolution," provides an all-inclusive look at how interpersonal and organizational conflict develops, progresses, and ultimately how it can be resolved. Important considerations such as maturity level and developmental factors are included as are tangible recommendations for dealing with a variety of conflict situations common to college students and staff members.

Chapter 6, "Helping Students in Distress," focuses on the distress students experience that often manifests itself within the college student population such as those precipitated by mood and anxiety disorders such as anxiety and depression, suicide, eating disorders, as well as substance abuse. Included also are suggestions for making referrals and reporting issues related to students in crisis and recommendations for student affairs professionals to collaborate with counseling resources on campus. Multicultural considerations are also discussed in terms of how they impact approaches to assist all students regardless of cultural backgrounds and identities.

Chapter 7, "Developing Your Helping Philosophy," is designed to provide student affairs professionals with a concise yet operational background in the theoretical orientations that form the backdrop for most helping approaches. It is important that everyone who attempts to actively assist students do so from a systematic perspective, which should be an integral component of a personal helping philosophy. The chapter also provides questions for self-reflection to encourage helping professionals to build and transform their personal philosophical approach.

Finally, Chapter 8, "Helping Yourself: Self-Care and Personal Well-Being," reminds the student affairs professionals that in order to help others, they must first attend to their own physical, psychological, and emotional needs. The importance of balance is stressed, along with the need to develop and maintain a personal wellness plan. Burnout continues to be a problem in student affairs and the related helping professions; therefore, it is imperative that those engaged in student affairs work constantly monitor their own well-being and make appropriate adjustments when their effectiveness is in danger of being compromised by neglecting their personal welfare.

Unique features of this book include short "Thinking About My Practice" questions designed to get the reader to reflect on the concepts and applications discussed; "Voices From the Field" sections written by practitioners who agreed to share their observations, interpretations, insights, and suggestions for practice on a variety of topics; and various "Case Study" and "Applying Your Skills" exercises designed to bring the material to life in a meaningful and illuminating manner. This resource was conceptualized, developed, and written from the vantage point of the practitioner and purposefully designed to be a resource student affairs professionals can use on a daily basis to enhance their competency in dealing with a variety of issues common to the modern college student experience.

Chapter 1

The Helping Role
in Student Affairs

Chances are that sometime within the last few days you helped someone. You engaged in some kind of deliberate interaction in which you provided assistance to someone who believed that the task at hand was difficult to manage or complete alone. Perhaps you helped by doing something, listening, advising, or providing guidance. Maybe you helped by contributing your time or money. It is likely that you did not even think twice about engaging in the help you provided. It may feel just natural to you. As defined by Sheafor, Morales, and Scott (2012), "natural helping is based on a mutual relationship among equals, and the helper draws heavily on intuition and life experience to guide the helping process" (p. 31).

You are reading this book because you are interested in helping others in a professional setting. More specifically, as a student affairs professional, you will be expected to engage in helping skills that are deliberate, appropriate to the setting, and according to the organization's expectations and rules. The help you provide will be founded upon a disciplined approach; your help will focus on the needs of the person who is being helped, requiring "specific knowledge, values, and skills to guide the helping activity" (Sheafor et al., 2012, p. 31). You will help by facilitating the helpee's utilization of resources moving toward specific goals (Parsons, 2011). As Cormier and Cormier (1985) suggest, you will be expected to facilitate "the exploration and resolution of issues and problems presented by a helpee" (p. 2). You can do this effectively by incorporating and using the foundational helping skills that counselors and psychotherapists use (Nelson-Jones, 2012, p. 7). Like licensed professional helpers continuously acquire knowledge about potential clientele, it is essential that student affairs professionals do the same.

CARING FOR STUDENTS IN HIGHER EDUCATION

Student affairs professionals are part of a long lineage of helpers and guiders within the university system. Since institutions of higher education were formed, they were endowed the same rights and responsibilities as parents for the care of the student, encapsulated in the doctrine of in loco parentis, a Latin phrase translated as "in the place of a parent" (Garner, 2009; Nuss, 1996; Thelin, 2004). Essentially, in the absence of the students' parents, college authorities were responsible for the students' physical and moral welfare and training (Gott v. Berea College, 1913), allowing "the institution to exert almost untrammeled authority over students' lives" (Kaplin & Lee, 2007, p. 16). Student services performed this prescribed care and were expected to "relieve administrators and faculties of problems of discipline" (American Council on Education Studies, 1937, p. 2). In 1937, the Student Personnel Point of View noted that the duties of student services professionals were to engage in "educational counseling, vocational counseling . . . student health, social programs" as well as a number of other administrative duties (American Council on Education Studies, 1937, pp. 39–40). Expanded in 1949, the revision included a focus on the development of students as well-rounded persons centering on their well-rounded development physically, socially, emotionally, and spiritually, as well as intellectually; viewing the student as a responsible participant in his or her own development; and recognizing the individual differences in backgrounds, abilities, and goals (American Council on Education Studies, 1949).

The concept of in loco parentis began to collapse as students began advocating for their rights, including more decision-making power related to their academics and education (Bickel & Lake, 1999). The university administration generally responded by relinquishing its parental role over students and regarding them as young adults entitled to their own rights (Lee, 2011). With these changes, the focus of student affairs administrators shifted from a personnel concentration to a student development orientation. This change was observed by Nevitt Sanford (1968) who posited that college students should be at the center of a college's activities and go through significant personal growth and development, much of which is influenced by the college environment itself (inside and outside of the classroom), and for growth and personal development to occur, a student needs to have a challenge/support balance.

THE CURRENT CHAPTER IN STUDENT AFFAIRS

While the expectations of the student affairs professionals have slightly changed since the 1970s, the issues that they will encounter, assist with, and the environment in which they will do so has increasingly expanded. It has been asserted that today's generation of college students is more psychologically distressed than previous generations of college attendees (Twenge et al., 2010). In fact, in the article, "Students Under Pressure" (Novotney, 2014), it is noted that students who may not have attended college previously due to mental health issues can now attend thanks to better treatment approaches, new medications, and preventative interventions in high school such as wraparound services and individualized education plans in primary and secondary education. While this is good news, it also infers that institutions need to be prepared to carry on these preventative interventions or maintenance; and the facts support this.

Today, we see that the role of student affairs professionals has changed little from 30 years ago. They are still expected to assist students in balancing the emotional and academic demands of college life, to promote student learning and personal development, and to create a campus environment that is inviting to diverse individuals (Creamer, Winston, & Miller, 2001). They are advisors, mentors, group facilitators, and advocates. Student affairs professionals assist students with academic concerns, relationship issues, work–life balance, identity development, career exploration, depression, anxiety, and other concerns. In his or her respective roles, a student affairs practitioner can focus on something as straightforward as meeting a student's basic needs (e.g., explanation of a scholarship application process, getting student identification or parking decal, room assignments in residence hall) to facilitating situations that promote student development (e.g., facilitating leadership development activities, conflict resolution with a roommate, academic advising or tutoring), or addressing a student's emotional and mental well-being (e.g., working with a student expressing suicidal ideations or deep sadness, a student who is experiencing an unexpected family crisis). These responsibilities are often found in functional areas in student affairs and higher education such as financial aid, academic advising, judicial affairs, diversity/multicultural affairs, disability services, international student affairs, adult learner services, campus housing residents, athletics, health and wellness services, and first-generation college student programs.

In summary, a primary role of student affairs professionals is to help college students with a wide range of problems, transitions, concerns, and coping. They are "key agents who support students' personal and emotional development" as well as "provide important support and validation and contribute to students feeling recognized and included within the campus community" (Higher Education Research Institute, 2014, pp. 2–3). Whether it is a small-scale or large-scale problem or the issue is a continuous, unexpected, or life-altering crisis, students from all walks of life will often need the help of a student affairs professional in multiple ways during college. Consequently, helping skills are essential to effective student affairs practice to address students' psychological and emotional needs, assist with their developmental transitions and emotional difficulties, and promote students' personal well-being.

HELPING SKILLS IN STUDENT AFFAIRS PRACTICE

Students seek out staff and faculty in times of needs with concerns and dilemmas. Although not professional counselors, students come to them for advice, guidance, coaching, and mentoring. Consider the story of Colleen, a struggling sophomore who is stressed, anxious, experiencing academic difficulty, struggling from a traumatic experience, and seeking understanding.

VOICES FROM THE FIELD

Shared Story: Where Do I Belong?

Colin Cannonier

Colleen, a sophomore, is thousands of miles away from where she grew up in the state of Washington. While her current grade point average is slightly below that of the grade point average of her peers, she appears to possess a sufficiently high IQ which predisposes her to performing well in one of the more challenging undergraduate business courses. She is enrolled at a medium-sized reputable private university where she is hoping to pursue a career in the entertainment and recording music industry. Recently, I have noticed that Colleen has been struggling academically, specifically as it relates to attendance and a number of coursework assignments. She informed me that she has been impacted by a traumatic event. The assault has significant implications extending well beyond the jurisdictions of the university whose resources she is already utilizing. Colleen is cognizant of the need to catch up on material due to missed classes. She described the assault as occurring a few months ago during the middle of final exams. It involves a close friend and as a result of this association, she is conflicted on what and the extent of measures to be taken. To be clear, Colleen had been ignoring the incident for some time, in part with the hope that it might go away, and also it was her hope that her "close friend" would eliminate certain behaviors and actions that led to the assault in the first place. As it turns out, the alleged perpetrator briefly complied but has begun participating in the same activities that led to the assault, even though these behaviors, to her knowledge, have been sanctioned. Further, there is at least one other person with knowledge of the assault and whom Colleen refers to as a friend. This "other friend" has sided with the perpetrator and is of the opinion that Colleen is to blame for the circumstances surrounding the incident. They are no longer on speaking terms.

The stress of all this has triggered her anxiety levels to the point where she spends a consummate amount of time and effort in trying to avoid falling back into certain habits which present another set of harmful issues. Colleen suffers from an eating disorder that she was slowly coming to terms with prior to the physical provocation. Indeed, she was receiving treatment in her first year in college. She has depressive episodes, which in the past she was reluctant to confront as an illness affecting her. Her sleep is often obstructed by flashbacks and she experiences panic attacks around the opposite sex or anyone who predisposes to certain kinds of behaviors, reminiscent of those that led to her being a victim. A variety of physical ailments have become common which include severe stomach aches, anxiety-related tremors or shakes, stress as well as jolts of breathing discomfort. While she is undergoing therapy, including medical care, she finds it a constant challenge to summon the energy to undertake those once-regular activities associated with preparing for classes.

What would you say to Colleen? What would you do to begin the helping process? What would you do to put her at ease and begin the conversation? How would you create a climate that includes genuineness and trust? What will you do to ensure that she feels free to explore her feelings and the presenting conflicts? How do you demonstrate that you are authentic and engaging in active, responsive listening? How do you assess her coping strategies, existence of a support system, and goals? With whom would you consult or refer if needed?

Student issues, such as Colleen's, can be multifaceted and require basic skills for understanding, support, and wellness. To accomplish tasks and goals related to student success and wellness, student affairs professionals should possess effective helping skills and use these skills when communicating with students. These basic helping skills to assist students in need can be viewed through the structures of Egan's (2002) three-stage Skilled Helper model.

Stage I: *What's going on?* The goal is to build a trusting relationship, which requires genuineness and empathy, and to help the student explore his or her situation. You help the student to clarify the key issues and work with the student to identify and clarify problems and opportunities as well as assess the student's resources. This stage includes basic helping skills such as active listening, questioning, paraphrasing, reflection, and summarizing which are covered in more detail in Chapter 3.

Stage II: *What solutions make sense for you?* You encourage the student to think about whether there is another way of looking at the issue and with goal setting. This can be difficult because when we are immersed in a situation, it can be difficult to see things from a different angle. You help the student determine outcomes and assist in his or her exploration of options and possible goals. You find out what the student's *preferred picture* would look like. Moving the student toward a goal and action and conflict resolution are discussed in Chapter 4 and Chapter 5.

Stage III: *What do you need to do to get what you need or want?* This step involves helping students develop strategies for accomplishing goals. You help the student with action planning and assess his or her available resources to cope with current problems and if needed, assist the student in learning of new skills to get what he or she wants or needs. Basically, you support the student to look at how he or she might help himself or herself and getting the student to consider who might help or hinder in making changes.

According to Egan (2014), helping is about the collaborative work between the helper and the help seeker to produce favorable outcomes and then, to help the helpee "become agents of change in their own lives" (p. 8). As such, the student affairs professional's goal is to help the student reflect, engage in problem solving, and develop an action strategy that can support his or her goals and objectives. Egan also noted that the three stages overlap and interact with one another as a person works to manage programs and helping is not as logical as the model, just as life itself is not always logical.

BECOMING A HELPER IN STUDENT AFFAIRS

If we have kept your attention thus far, you have made it to the exciting news. As a student affairs professional, you will have many opportunities to work in the trenches, to be the first contact with students who are struggling with developmental transitions and emotional difficulties. Due to student affairs professionals' visibility, approachability, and openness, students will seek them out for assistance with a wide range of problems and concerns (Pope, Reynolds, & Mueller, 2004). Reiterated by Schuh, Jones, Harper, and Associates (2010), "student affairs professionals have endless opportunities to support, help, and offer suggestions to students on a daily basis" (p. 399) and their visibility on campus makes student affairs practitioners appear more accessible and approachable to students, professors, staff, and on-campus mental health providers. Often, as Winston (2003) suggested, student affairs professionals provide essential support to students making important life decisions even though most of these professionals are not trained as counselors and may not possess the skills necessary to be therapists. They are, in a sense, the brokers; passing along information, building and maintaining alliances, and using interpersonal experiences to advise and guide.

Given the immense impact that student affairs professionals can have on the hundreds of students whom they may encounter each year, it is absolutely imperative that they can and do demonstrate the skills necessary to facilitate the helping process and understand how to respond to student concerns and crises, including how to make referrals to appropriate campus or community resources. As Harper, Wilson, and Associates (2010) asserted, "strong helping skills not only enhance student affairs professionals' ability to provide the best assistance but can also help them identify and communicate the boundaries of their roles" (p. 9).

CONCLUSION

Becoming an effective helping professional in student affairs requires the complex integration of intrapersonal, interpersonal, and professional awareness, knowledge, and skills. Acquiring and improving these skills require effort and "therefore, it is essential that their academic preparation and professional development focus on creating and enhancing essential helping skills that allow them to perform all aspects of their work more effectively" (Reynolds, 2009, p. 21). In the end, it takes an investment in one's professional growth and skills enhancement to improve and become comfortable with using basic counseling skills to address the social/emotional needs of college students. It also requires an honest reflection of your helping philosophy and an investment in your well-being so that you are in a position to effectively assist students.

REFERENCES

American Council on Education Studies. (1937). *The student personnel point of view*. Retrieved from www.myacpa.org/sites/default/files/student-personnel-point-of-view-1937.pdf

American Council on Education Studies. (1949). *The student personnel point of view* (no. 13). Retrieved from www.naspa.org/images/uploads/main/Student_Personnel_Point_of_View_1949.pdf

Bickel, R. D., & Lake, P. F. (1999). *The rights and responsibilities of the modern university*. Durham, NC: Carolina Academic Press.

Cormier, W. H., & Cormier, L. S. (1985). *Interviewing strategies for helpers* (2nd ed.). Belmont, CA: Brooks/Cole Publishing Company.

Creamer, D. G., Winston, Jr., R. B., & Miller, T. K. (2001). The professional student affairs administrator: Roles and functions. In R. B. Winston, Jr., D. G. Creamer, & T. K. Miller (Eds.), *The professional student affairs administrator: Educator, leader, and manager* (pp. 3–38). New York, NY: Taylor & Francis.

Egan, G. (2002). *The skilled helper: A problem management and opportunity development approach to helping* (7th ed.). Pacific Grove, CA: Brooks Cole.

Egan, G. (2014). *The skilled helper: A problem management and opportunity development approach to helping* (10th ed.). Belmont, CA: Brooks Cole/Cengage Learning.

Garner, B. A. (Ed.). (2009). *Black's law dictionary* (9th ed.). St. Paul, MN: Thomas Reuters.

Gott v. Berea College, 156 Ky. 376, 161 S.W. 204 (1913).

Harper, R., Wilson, N. L., & Associates. (2010). *More than listening: A casebook for using counseling skills in student affairs work*. Washington, DC: NASPA.

Higher Education Research Institute. (2014). *Findings from the 2014 college senior survey*. Los Angeles: Higher Education Research Institute. Retrieved from www.heri.ucla.edu/briefs/CSS-2014-Brief.pdf

Kaplin, W. A., & Lee, B. (2007). *The law of higher education* (4th ed. Student Version). San Francisco, CA: Jossey-Bass.

Lee, P. (2011). The curious life of in loco parentis in American universities. *Higher Education in Review*, *8*, 65–90.

Nelson-Jones, R. (2012). *Basic counselling skills: A helper's manual* (3rd ed.). Thousand Oaks, CA: SAGE Publications Inc.

Novotney, A. (2014, September). Students under pressure. *Monitor on Psychology*, *45*(8), 37–41.

Nuss, E. (1996). The development of student affairs. In S. Komives & D. Woodard (Eds.), *Student services: A handbook for the profession* (4th ed., pp. 22–42). San Francisco, CA: Jossey-Bass.

Parsons, R. D. (2011). *Fundamentals of the helping process* (2nd ed.). Long Grove, IL: Waveland Press, Inc.

Pope, R. L., Reynolds, A. L., & Mueller, J. A. (2004). *Multicultural competence in student affairs*. San Francisco, CA: Jossey-Bass.

Reynolds, A. L. (2009). *Helping college students: Developing essential support skills for student affairs practice*. San Francisco, CA: Jossey-Bass.

Sanford, N. (1968). *Where colleges fail: A study of student as person*. San Francisco, CA: Jossey-Bass.

Schuh, J. H., Jones, S. R., Harper, S. R., & Associates. (2010). *Student services: A handbook for the profession* (5th ed.). San Francisco, CA: Jossey-Bass.

Sheafor, B. W., Morales, A. T., & Scott, M. (2012). *Social work: A profession of many faces* (12th ed.). Boston, MA: Pearson.

Thelin, J. R. (2004). *A history of American higher education*. Baltimore, MD: Johns Hopkins University Press.

Twenge, J. M., Gentile, B., DeWall, C. N., Ma, D., Lacefield, K., & Schurtz, D. R. (2010). Birth cohort increases in psychopathology among young Americans, 1938–2007: A cross-temporal meta-analysis of the MMPI. *Clinical Psychology Review, 30*(2), 145–154.

Winston, R. B. (2003). Counseling and helping skills. In S. R. Komives & D. B. Woodard (Eds.), *Student services: A handbook for the profession* (4th ed., pp. 84–506). San Francisco, CA: Jossey-Bass.

Chapter 2

Personal and Professional Responsibilities

Since its inception, student affairs has retained a central philosophy of serving the needs of students (Reason & Broido, 2010). As discussed in Chapter 1, student affairs professionals support the needs and development of students through interpersonal experiences, serving as advocates, advisors, role models, mentors, and helpers. In these roles, student affairs professionals work closely in supporting students in their needs and growth. For this reason, in both their personal and professional lives and relationships, it is essential that student affairs professionals are knowledgeable about their personal responsibilities and the professional standards related to student affairs practice and maintain as well as enhance their professional competence. Professional standards serve as a basis for professionals to self-monitor their practice and continue to enhance themselves (Arminio, 2009). Meeting professional standards helps assure student affairs professionals of the integrity and soundness of the professional practices with which they are engaging (Komives & Arminio, 2011). Becoming a professional is a developmental process whereby, "people selectively acquire the values and attitudes, the interests, skills and knowledge—in short, the culture—current in the groups of which they are, or seek to become a member" (Merton, Reader, & Kendal, 1957).

PROFESSIONAL AND PERSONAL RESPONSIBILITY

As a student affairs professional, you develop a professional responsibility between you and the students you help. Professional responsibility implies obligation and standards, defined by a profession, in how services are performed (Redmount, 1978/1979). According to Pescosolido and Aminzade (1999), in discussing the idea of professional responsibility, there are three distinct levels. First, there is the moral-philosophical level which involves the practitioner wrestling with moral choice and ethical standards in dealing with the everyday, real-life situations. This level includes the personal responsibility of the individual professional, considering both the range and the nature of his or her ethical responsibilities, and how he or she works through situational dilemmas using moral and ethical principles. For example, your decisions and actions regarding a relationship with a student is a consideration at the moral-philosophical level (e.g., a hall director is engaged in a relationship with a student who resides in his or her residence hall or a group advisor asking a student in the group to go out on a date). The second level includes social responsibility of a profession to address ethical dilemmas and set standards for professionals' duties. Social responsibility is based on values such as honesty, respect, fairness, the avoidance of harm, and justice, and it requires responsibility to those persons and interests who will be impacted by one's actions (Fitzpatrick & Gauthier, 2001). In student affairs, these values and standards of practice are outlined through professional associations—American College Personnel Association (ACPA) and National Association of Student Personnel Administrators (NASPA). Professional organizations "seek to advance understanding, recognition, and knowledge in the field; to develop and promulgate standards for professional practice" (Nuss, 2003, p. 493). The third level addresses the societal responsibility to assist practitioners by providing publicly defined socioethical responsibilities of practice as they address the cultural, legal, organizational, and political expectations. As the work of student affairs professionals extends beyond the campus community and includes various stakeholders, the professional must be cognizant of any associated consequences and maintain high ethical standards as well as anticipate or avoid political actions that could pose as challenging.

Student affairs professionals need to be concerned about three levels of professional responsibility; essentially, there are three questions that should always be asked when dealing with an issue or concern that includes a moral dimension. In most situations, there is an array of options available to the student affairs professional and the student who is experiencing the dilemma. Part of the responsibility of the professional involves helping the student to see what those options are and then how to go about evaluating them to determine the most appropriate course of action given the circumstances unique to that situation. Effective decision making is one of the keys to successfully negotiating the challenges associated with college as well as life in general; student affairs professionals have an inherent responsibility to help students develop this competency to the maximum extent possible.

There is a personal dimension to professional responsibility. First, you are personally responsible for your actions and acting responsibly. At all times, you should exercise good judgment and take responsibility for your actions. Furthermore, pairing of the two principles of nonmaleficence ("doing no harm") and beneficence ("benefiting others") equate to "acting responsibly," which can link to the character traits of caring (being concerned with the welfare of others); citizenship (behaving appropriately as members of a community); and responsibility (making sound choices and being held accountable for those choices) (Humphrey, Janosik, & Creamer, 2004). Additionally, within our professional responsibilities, student affairs professionals are still solely responsible for their choices. In essence, student affairs professionals are free to make their own personal choices regarding their private lives, but need to remember that these personal choices can have a profound impact on their professional lives as well (Steinman, Richardson, & McEnroe, 1998, p. 26).

Second, you are personally responsible for gaining knowledge and professional development to provide quality service to the students you assist. Therefore, student affairs professionals have a responsibility to actively seek for ways to increase knowledge and improve skills as this enhances their qualifications. As maintained by Carpenter and Stimpson (2007), "Given that student affairs work constitutes an area of professional and scholarly practice, it follows that there exists a rigorous and continuous preparation process for a practitioner to be, and stay, fully qualified" (p. 273). Professional development is essential for a student affairs professional to build his or her professional toolkit and furthermore, "tasks of seeking professional development and demonstrating professionalism fall on the professional, with support from professional associations, supervisors, and colleagues (Arminio, 2011, p. 479). Professional grounding also includes proactively preparing yourself to address ethical dilemmas, which requires an acquisition of knowledge about ethics and standards as well as self-reflection.

Third, professionals who work closely with students have a personal responsibility to evaluate their self-awareness and any issues that might interfere with their ability to effectively help. For example, as you are human, there will be days in which your personal concerns and problems are at the forefront of your mind or your level of patience is low; therefore, you may not be at your best to offer your full attention. You must also continue to self-reflect, educate yourself, and renew yourself (Steinman et al., 1998). There is, nonetheless, an assumption that student affairs professionals are "generally well-intentioned but are also fallible and continue to grow" (Hamrick & Benjamin, 2009, p. 6). So ask yourself: What situation or persons would make me uncomfortable or anxious to work with in a professional role? Next, reflect on ways you can address this concern and work effectively with that population or issue.

Fourth, student affairs professionals "should exemplify the very conduct that they expect of their colleagues and students" (Humphrey et al., 2004, p. 689). In regard to their professional conduct, boundaries with students should also be a consideration for student affairs professionals. In meeting the needs of students, student affairs professionals have numerous interactions with students and often develop close relationships with the students they assist and advise. These relationships should always be maintained at a professional level, even if you are friendly and close to a student. When I (first author) was in an administrative role in student affairs, I had an appointment with a student. As he entered the office, I walked out of my office into the reception area and another female staff member walks up to him, gives him a hug, and slowly rubs on his chest while smiling and commenting about how nice it felt. The student smiled, nodded to the other students in the reception area, and walked into my office. During that meeting, he did not say anything but a few days later, he came to visit me in my office and at that time, informed me that he was shocked when the student affairs staff member touched him on his chest and made a comment, believing this was inappropriate behavior. As a student affairs professional, you have a responsibility to conduct yourself in a professional manner at all times, especially in your relationships with students.

Confidentiality is also an important factor in student affairs as students often share personal stories and feelings to student affairs professionals. However, unlike licensed/professional counselors, student affairs professionals do not have privileged communication. Therefore, what a student shares with you is not protected by legal standards. Regardless, student affairs professionals must respect privacy and maintain confidentiality (Council for the Advancement of Standards in Higher Education, 2015, p. 33). However, in cases where there is a duty to warn (suicide and threat/danger to others) and harassment or abuse (i.e., Title IX, sexual assault, and plans/thoughts related to violence), be sure to follow established procedures and guidelines.

Personal and professional behavior can impact the effectiveness of student affairs professionals. As a helping professional, the student affairs professional should try to act in accordance with the professional standards and ethical principles. Komives (1992) identified maturity, which includes the fact that a professional can act on personal and professional values, as a desirable professional behavior and attitude. Being aware of your personal and professional responsibilities and principles can provide you with a foundation for your professional practice and help you make sense of situations, especially if you must defend your decision and feel at peace with those decisions.

THINKING ABOUT MY PRACTICE

What are your boundaries regarding relationships with students? How close is too close?

How can you effectively advise a student without letting your personal experiences interfere with the information you share with the student or any suggestions you offer?

What can you do to maintain your knowledge about policies and laws related to college students?

PROFESSIONAL COMPETENCE

Professional competencies are skills needed to enact professional practice (Weidman, Twale, & Stein, 2001). A competency can be defined as "a combination of skills, abilities, and knowledge needed to perform a specific task" (Jones &

Voorhees, 2002, p. vii). Basically, competencies are "how we ought to act" based on commonly held values (Young, 2003, p. 97). Student affairs professionals should work diligently to develop professional competencies. Competences are embedded components of professional roles and developing competencies is an ongoing "experiential process of knowing, being and doing" (Komives & Woodard, 2003, p. 421).

The report on Professional Competency Areas for student affairs professionals, developed jointly in 2010 by ACPA (American College Personnel Association) and NASPA (National Association of Student Personnel Administrators), outlined professional competency areas for the field of student affairs, "intended to define the broad professional knowledge, skills, and for some competencies, attitudes expected of student affairs professionals, regardless of their area of specialization or positional role within the field" (ACPA/NASPA, 2010, p. 4). Furthermore, for the enhancement of program quality and excellence as well as for professionals to better serve students, the Council for the Advancement of Standards in Higher Education (CAS) created seven shared ethical principles—autonomy (involves individual rights), nonmalfeasance (not hurting others), beneficence (concerns helping others), justice (ideal of being fair), fidelity (relates to matters of loyalty and truthfulness), veracity, and affiliation—for student affairs professionals to abide by in their professional practice (Council for the Advancement of Standards in Higher Education, 2015). Practitioners should consider these ethical principles when challenged to resolve an ethical dilemma (Canon, 1996; Kitchener, 1985). Because these principles deal with helping students, student affairs professionals must apply these ethical principles in the context of their daily responsibilities and duties. As a professional in student affairs, you need to understand that there are complexities that demand skills and knowledge, including ethical codes obligated to the field of practice (Loewenberg & Dolgoff, 1992).

Ethics

Ethics is concerned with determining what acts or behaviors are "right" or "ought to be done/not done" (Winston & Saunders, 1991). Student affairs practitioners must determine what is right or what ought to be done within legal and institutional policy parameters. Furthermore, ethical behavior is critical to the well-being of the student affairs profession and student affairs professionals should possess a sound understanding of the ethics.

One of the areas included as a competency in the *Professional Competency Areas for Student Affairs Practitioners* (ACPA/NASPA, 2010) is related to ethical professional practice which "pertains to the knowledge, skills, and attitudes needed to understand and apply ethical standards to one's work" (p. 12), focusing specifically on the integration of ethics into all aspects of self and professional practice. In addition, the *Council for the Advancement of Standards (CAS) in Higher Education*

Professional Standards for Higher Education (CAS, 2015) is a guide for quality practice in student affairs. Outlined by CAS (2015), student affairs professionals must:

- employ ethical decision making in the performance of their duties;
- inform users of programs and services of ethical obligations and limitations emanating from codes and laws or from licensure requirements;
- recognize and avoid conflicts of interest that could adversely influence their judgment or objectivity and, when unavoidable, recuse themselves from the situation;
- perform their duties within the scope of their position, training, expertise, and competence;
- make referrals when issues presented exceed the scope of the position.

(p. 33)

Basically, "Ethical beliefs and belief systems are intended to serve as guides to action in confusing and difficult circumstances" (Fried, 1997, p. 5). Professional ethical standards and principles are potential guides for student affairs professionals in ambiguous circumstances where there is no clear right course of action or where there may be multiple right choices (Nash, 1997). Ethical statements, codes, and standards have been promoted by professional associations for student affairs professionals to guide their process to make ethical decisions (i.e., American College Personnel Association, National Association of Student Personnel Administrators). Winston (2001) reports that many student affairs professionals are only vaguely familiar with these codes and many do not use them in their daily practice.

An increased understanding of ethics and ethical principles is relevant as "Oftentimes practitioners are faced with ethical problems that involve so many different people, factors, and perspectives that it can become quite convoluted" (Humphrey et al., 2004, p. 684). Sundberg and Fried (1997) pointed out that "making ethical choices and thinking through ethical issues are at the very core of our work as student affairs professionals" (p. 67). At some point in their career, student affairs professionals can encounter a situation or choice that could pose a challenge to them. Interestingly, professionals often find it challenging to uphold student affairs standards, especially those of an ethical nature (Janosik, 2007; Whitt & Blimling, 2000). I (first author) often suggest "the bell, book, and candle" model in making ethical decisions, especially challenging ones.

- The Bell: Do bells or warning buzzers go off as you consider your choice of actions?
- The Book: Does your decision violate any laws or codes in policies or the statute or ordinance books?

- The Candle: Will your decision withstand the light of day or spotlight of publicity (http://business.josephsoninstitute.org/blog/2010/11/18/when-ethical-principles-conflict/)?

There are also models for ethical decision making to guide ethical decision making for persons in student affairs (see Humphrey et al., 2004; Janosik, 2007; Janosik et al., 2004; Kitchener, 1985).

As emphasized by Barr, McClellan, and Sandeen (2014), "How we make our decision is just as important as the decision we make" (p. 30). The first question a student affairs professional should always ask when considering what course of action to pursue in a given situation is, of course, "Is it legal?" (Robinson & Moulton, 2005). This is the most fundamental consideration and should serve as a reference point when trying to decide how a particular situation should be handled. As such, the student affairs professional has an obligation to know all the applicable laws that might apply to the circumstances being faced by the student. If the issue involves sexual assault, for example, the student affairs professional should be fully aware of what constitutes illegal behavior (both in the initial incident as well as the potential response). The professional should then use this information to help guide the student toward a response that is well within the legal parameters applicable to his or her circumstances. So, the answer to this question should always be "Yes."

The second question that should always be asked is, "Is it ethical?" (Robinson & Moulton, 2005). In many situations, an option can be well within the legal limits but outside the scope of what is considered ethical. The law tends to be rather straightforward and involves behaviors that could lead to arrest or even incarceration. Ethics has more to do with the responsibility that one individual has toward another and whether or not one's actions cause harm to another person. For example, lying to a student in order to absolve one's responsibility for a given incident may not be illegal, but it could certainly be considered unethical. Teaching students to behave in an ethical manner is one of the primary responsibilities of student affairs professionals as they are often in the best position to help cultivate this way of thinking. Again, the answer to this question should always be "Yes."

Finally, the third question that should always be asked in any situation where multiple options are being considered is "Is it appropriate?" (Henke, Langstraat, Mackie, & Morgan, 2013). Of all the three questions that should be posed in problematic situations, this is perhaps the most challenging as the answer often involves the cultural and organizational norms associated with a given area. There are some standards of conduct, for instance, that might be considered entirely appropriate at a publically funded state university but not at a small, religiously affiliated college. In order for the student affairs professionals to be able to assist students in answering this final question, they must be intimately aware of the community and institutional context in which the situation has occurred. As has been the case with the previous questions, the correct answer to this final question should always be "Yes."

To illustrate the importance of these three questions, consider the following scenario. A student from a large, metropolitan city on the West Coast decides to attend a small, liberal arts college in the Midwest. He is subsequently employed in the student activities office where part of his job responsibilities is to help provide programming for the student body. The student likes uncensored hip-hop music and routinely plays it in his office. Many of the songs are saturated with language some at the institution would consider obscene. One of his fellow students is offended by the music and asks him not to play this kind of music where others can hear it. The student who is fond of hip-hop feels that it is his right to listen to whatever kind of music he wants to in his own office and comes to you, the director of student activities, for some advice on how to handle this request.

In processing his options, three questions are asked. First, is it against the law to play this kind of music? No, playing hip-hop is not against the law so he has passed the first test. Second, is it unethical to play this kind of music? This could be more ambiguous. Although it may not violate any ethical codes in a strict sense, some might consider it to be unethical based on their personal beliefs. Even though the answer to this question might not be as clear-cut, let's assume that after discussing the matter in some depth, it was determined that it was not unethical. Finally, is it inappropriate? In this situation, at this school, and in this context, playing this kind of music in this setting where others can hear, it is probably not appropriate. Therefore, the student should be advised not to play his music "out loud" when others are in the office. If the student wants to listen to this genre, he could probably do so with ear buds. There are always options that meet all three criteria.

Ethics is at the core of student affairs since student affairs professionals see ethical struggles play themselves out in different ways (e.g., making choices between competing interests; ensuring that they create a fair, welcoming environment for all students; deciding between two undesirable alternatives; being torn between doing the right thing and acting in their own self-interests; and being in a challenging position in observing unfair behavior of a supervisor toward a colleague) (Humphrey et al., 2004). For example, one ethical dilemma faced early in my (first author) student affairs career was having to choose between doing what I felt was the right thing to do (to not negatively impact someone else) and doing what I was asked to do by the leader of the division, assuming that it could be attached to keeping my job. The ordeal of making the decision caused me great discomfort, and the thoughts regarding the consequences of the options were nerve-racking and challenging, but there was one undeniable truth—I had to make a choice. I chose to do what I believed was right; however, there were consequences I had to endure because of this choice (which is a potential reality). In making my decision, I weighed the pros and cons and evaluated what degree of positive and negative would come from each choice.

While the concepts of balance and weight (i.e., evaluating pros and cons) provide more tools for ethical dilemma resolution, Kitchener (2000) maintained that there is still likelihood that some ethical dilemmas might not be resolvable. For example, some circumstances might be too complicated or information might not be completely known. Student affairs professionals must also be able to defend their choices in resolving ethical dilemmas (Canon, 1996; Kitchener, 1985). Ask yourself: Can I defend my action in a court of law? It's not a happy thought, but it is a realistic one. In addition, when facing an ethical dilemma, it should also be acknowledged that professional codes often will not provide an answer (Blimling, 1998; Kitchener, 1985). It is important for student affairs professionals to note that, at times, personal and professional standards are inadequate to resolve complex situations involving two competing ethical principles and, therefore, should then turn to professional codes for guidance.

It is difficult to be fully prepared for ethical dilemmas and the challenges that accompany them. Therefore, student affairs professionals should be reflective, gather all information that is available, and consider all options (Kitchener, 2000). Student affairs professionals also must not run away from challenging circumstances because not making a decision is, in essence, making a decision; have the knowledge of the situation and codes as well as a commitment to make a choice and follow through to the end (Blimling, 1998; Winston & Saunders, 1991). It is also judicious to confer with professional peers, especially those with more experience and an understanding of the lay of the land when facing an ethical dilemma. Consulting with respected colleagues can help you make decisions that are professionally and ethically sound (MacKinnon & Associates, 2004). Talking to someone about the dilemma can potentially provide you with an expanded perspective and a new way to see things.

Professional Responsibility in Helping

In student affairs, you have a unique relationship with the students you help. As student affairs professionals are often close to the students they help, socially and emotionally, a potential for ethical problems exist. The welfare of the student is utmost in the helping relationship and accordingly, requires ethical conduct. Subsequently, competence, trust, and ethical conduct must be present to have an effective helping relationship with students. Pope, Reynolds, and Mueller (2004) specify helping competencies such as communication and microcounseling skills, conflict management, problem solving, empathy and positive regard, self-awareness, ethical integrity, knowledge of related theories, and building effective relationships. Throughout the book, these competencies are discussed in more detail.

Above all, you should ensure the emotional safety for the student throughout the relationship and refrain from all forms of dual relationships, including emotional, sexual, and business involvement (Steinman et al., 1998). To be effective, student affairs professionals must be knowledgeable about personal and professional responsibilities, ethics, professional standards, and competencies needed to be an effective helping professional. This knowledge extends to working with students from diverse cultures.

MULTICULTURAL COMPETENCE

College campuses have become increasingly diverse, and consequently, pluralism and inclusion have emerged as a foremost value of student affairs (Reason & Broido, 2010; Young, 2003). Cultures exist on various levels on a college campus, and multicultural issues can inspire or unsettle a campus community. For example, protests at the University of Missouri in the fall semester of 2015 were related to racism, students feeling uncomfortable on campus, and an indictment of administrators' apathy and inaction. What accompanied the protest were threats against Black students circulating on social media, difficult conversations about racism on campus, and the termination of the top two campus leaders. At the core of this situation was the fact that multicultural issues presented by students were not adequately addressed and a lack of cultural consideration for all students in the campus community.

Kuh and Whitt (1997) defined culture as,

> The collective, mutually shaping patterns of norms, values, practices, beliefs, and assumptions that guide the behaviors of individuals and groups in an institute of higher education and provide a frame of reference within which to interpret the meaning of events and actions on and off campus.
>
> (p. 127)

Student affairs professionals should be aware of the power of the internal and external dimensions associated with cultural identities for students, such as race, sex, gender, ability, class, and religion, in our society and apply considerations that take care not to perpetuate any marginalization. While adhering to ethical responsibility and practices, student affairs professionals need to be more aware of their limitations and possess cultural skills to serve diverse students in the most productive way to facilitate rapport and provide support.

Developing Multicultural Competence

Developing multicultural competence, which includes awareness, knowledge, and skills (Sue, Arredondo, & McDavis, 1994), is necessary for student affairs professionals for their work in culturally diverse campus environments. In part, the helping process should be approached from the context of the personal culture of the student (Sue & Sue, 2007). The skills required to work productively with individuals and groups who come from varying cultural backgrounds can be difficult to acquire. Nonetheless, multiculturally competent student affairs professionals devote time and energy to supporting and nurturing all students regardless of their cultural background. They are also cognizant of how cultural issues affect the campus community, students, and relationships. Pope et al. (2004) explained the concept of multicultural competence as "those awareness, knowledge and skills that are needed to work effectively across cultural groups, and to work with complex diversity issues" (p. xiv).

Awareness in multicultural competence "entails the awareness of one's own assumptions, biases and values; an understanding of the worldview of others; information about various cultural groups; and developing appropriate intervention strategies and techniques" (Pope et al., 2004, p. 9). In a helping role, cultural self-awareness is a must. Student affairs professionals should reflect upon and analyze their personal beliefs, biases, fears, worldview and attitudes, including the sources, and how these influence their perspectives. They should also avoid having a narrow and rigid view of the world and cultural backgrounds while using their own cultural group as a reference and standard of normality (Hays & Erford, 2014). Check your biases and stereotypes, develop a positive orientation toward multicultural perspectives, and recognize ways in which personal biases and values can affect how you develop a helping relationship with students who are culturally different. The ability to be self-aware and evaluate your biases, stereotypes, worldview, and multicultural experiences are vital components in developing your multicultural competence and this process requires an honest evaluation on your part. To work on your self-awareness, you can engage in journaling or self-reflection and self-assessment activities. Take the opportunity to honestly reflect on and assess what it means to be a person in an underrepresented and/or marginalized group in our society; how power, privilege, and discrimination shape perspectives; how your own identity formation has shaped your worldview; and how your cultural background and perspective influence your helping style. Some questions for you to reflect on include:

1. What is the foundation of your personal and social identities? Reflect on your internal and external cultural dimensions (i.e., your age, gender, ability, ethnicity, race, community in which you grew up, religion, marital history, parental status, educational background, occupation/work experience and career, political affiliation, recreational and personal habits, socioeconomic status/social class—currently and growing up—including observations through any changes, and past/current geographic location). What role do these play in your life, your motivation, and your social belonging? One way to achieve this is for you to identify your personal, social, and cultural

identities (i.e., elements of self that are primarily intrapersonal and connected to your life experiences; grown from your involvement in social groups with which you are interpersonally committed; and what contributes to your social belonging), focusing on the identities that are most salient for you at this specific time in your life. For example, a person could list athletic, dog lover, lover of reading, frequent traveler, member of a Greek organization, student affairs professional, daughter/son, sibling, woman, and multiracial. Next, honestly reflect on why you selected the elements you believe are most salient for you and why they are most relevant at this time of your life. How might these identities influence and inform your helping style? Which of these is most salient to you at this time? Which identities do you not think about often? Think about if/how these identities inform your approach to your duties and choices.

2. What is your perspective regarding your cultural foundation? Reflect on the following:
   a) What is your definition of family?
   b) What specific values were held by your family of origin and community (e.g., religion, education, work, food, or family)?
   c) What views were held about diversity in your family? Are your views the same, similar, or dissimilar at this time? How?
   d) How was your family impacted by diversity issues of gender, nationality, race, sexuality, disability, or religion?
   e) How is your current "family" culture similar to or different from your family of origin?
   f) What are the gender roles and gender role expectations in your family of origin? Are your views the same, similar, or dissimilar at this time? How?

3. How do you define privilege? How has "privilege" eased or made life more difficult for your family? What are your thoughts about the connection between privilege and power?

4. How has change in the social and cultural nature of society at large influenced your cultural experience?

5. Describe how your cultural self-understanding will enable you to be a culturally effective student affairs professional.

6. What are some personal biases and limitations that may hinder you? What cultural assumptions do you have?

7. How will your communication values and skills impact your role as a competent multicultural student affairs professional?

8. Considering the nature of your cultural experience, describe strengths you will bring to your role as student affairs/higher education professional.

Student affairs professionals must also acquire information and knowledge regarding different cultural groups and social identities (e.g., difference and identities in U.S. society related to race, ethnicity, social class, sex/gender, sexuality, religion, and disability) when working with students on campus. This acquisition of knowledge and understanding increases a student affairs professional's ability "to have empathy for the experiences, feelings, and concerns" of culturally diverse students (Pope et al., 2004, p. 87) and to carefully apply acquired knowledge about cultural groups in the helping relationship (Pope et al., 2004). It is also important to remember that culture and identities can be complex and compounded issues can exist. For example, the identity of a Black student who grew up in a Caribbean country was primarily based on a national or geographic origin prior to attending college in the United States and will now be defined solely by his or her race in the United States (T.B. Smith, 2004). Furthermore, the student could view sociopolitical and sociocultural issues differently from a Black student who grew up in the United States and therefore, student affairs professionals should be aware of their assumptions in working with diverse students.

Cultural Knowledge

Student affairs professionals should also acquire knowledge and remain abreast on cultural issues (e.g., oppression, social justice, sociopolitical matters) and current news that impact diverse college students. Reynolds and Pope (2003) suggested that student affairs professionals increase content knowledge about important culturally related terms and concepts as well. To increase content knowledge, there should be familiarization with terms and concepts related to social and cultural diversity. Although not an exhaustive listing, the following is illustrative of intracultural and intercultural cultural terms and concepts that should be a part of student affairs professionals' knowledge base. Additionally, there are several books and articles related to these topics that you can use to increase your understanding, knowledge, and awareness through research and reading.

Acculturation and Enculturation

Dimensions of cultural identity include enculturation and acculturation. Acculturation, defined by Kim and Omizo (2005) as adapting to the normative process of the dominant culture, results in culture learning which contributes to an individual developing multicultural competency in a diverse world (Flaskerud, 2007). It includes the adaptation of the beliefs, traits, and behaviors of a dominant culture by a person of a minority group who has significant contact with the dominant group and while assuming new ways and behaviors of a culture different from one's culture of origin, the individual retains some beliefs and attributes of his or her native culture (Schmidt, 2006). As acculturation is a process of adapting to a cultural change, Poyrazli, Kavanaugh, Baker, and Al-Timimi (2004) believed acculturation encompasses social, physiological, and psychological aspects. Acculturation occurs when immigrants come to a new country and when a person migrates within a society that consists of multiple cultures (Schmidt, 2006). It is suggested that the four acculturation strategies (assimilation, integration, separation, and marginalization) differ greatly from one another, apply to individual preferences, and individuals may select different acculturation strategies at different times depending upon the environment they are in as they try various acculturation strategies before choosing one they find most fitting (Berry & Sam, 1997). Whereas acculturation refers to the meeting of at least two different cultures, by contrast, enculturation can occur within one dominant culture (McAuliffe & Associates, 2013). Enculturation refers to the process of a person becoming a member of a cultural group, combining "both formal and informal relationships to convey knowledge, history, language, awareness, and other aspects of a particular culture to the individual" (Schmidt, 2006, p. 6). Everyone is enculturated and through this process of learning and acquiring competence, develops a cognitive map, the terms of reference for acting in the world (McAuliffe & Associates, 2013). Adjusting to a new environment occurs for all incoming students in college, both domestic and international. For example, a student who comes from a small, racially similar, rural community and attends college in a large, racially diverse, urban environment could go through the process of acculturation just as a student coming from a Caribbean country, Canada, or Australia. Student affairs professionals must be sure to move beyond biases, cultural conditioning, and stereotypes when working with students who are living in a different culture from the one that is familiar to them and try to understand what cultural aspects are relevant to them as they matriculate.

Bicultural Identity and Biculturalism

Increasingly, individuals identify with two or more cultures and report bicultural identification (e.g., Chinese and American), organizing their cultural identities in different ways (Mok & Morris, 2012). A bicultural individual often balances participating in a dominant culture in one environment (e.g., at work or school) while fully embracing his or her cultural identity in another (e.g., a religious community or at home) (McAuliffe & Associates, 2013). Biculturalism refers to the two cultural traditions, best understood as the interaction between dominant and nondominant cultures in the United States, that minorities inherit (Sue & Sue, 2008). Furthermore, biculturalism represents a person's comfort and proficiency with both one's heritage culture and the culture of the country or region in which one has settled (Schwartz & Unger, 2010). For example, a Chinese American student might eat hamburgers together with traditional Chinese vegetables and mix in social groups that include both Chinese and American friends (Schwartz &

Unger, 2010). To effectively work with diverse students, student affairs professionals need to comprehend the influences of cultural and contextual forces and the possible conflicts and stress that may arise from balancing two cultural identities.

Collectivism and Individualism

It is important for student affairs professionals to understand the basic differences between individualistic and collectivist cultures as these contrasting worldviews are related to relevant considerations for students such as aspirations, development, independence, and perspectives. Collectivism is described as "the belief that the group is more important than individuals are because everyone is part of a group, tribe, family, or other type of unit" (Schmidt, 2006, p. 10). At the core of collectivism, an assumption exists that groups bind and mutually obligate individuals (Oyserman, Coon, & Kemmelmeier, 2002). Inherently, there is a value on interdependence more so than on independence. For example, Dennis and Giangreco (1996) noted how decision making might differ in many Hispanic families in which control of important decisions remains with the parents (or grandparents) until the child reaches adulthood or marries and moves away from the family. On the other hand, individualism is focused on rights above duties, a concern for oneself and immediate family, an emphasis on personal autonomy and self-fulfillment, and the basing of one's identity on one's personal accomplishments (Hofstede, 1980). An individualistic culture emphasizes and prefers personal individual development (Schmidt, 2006) where a person may be allowed or encouraged to make choices based on what is best for him or her as opposed to what is best for the group.

Cultural and Social Capital

Social capital includes one's social networks and connections that also function as currency to obtain additional capital to maintain or increase one's status (Winkle-Wagner, 2010). Social capital is described as "the aggregate of the actual or potential resources that are linked to possession of a durable network of more or less institutionalized relationships of mutual acquaintance and recognition" (Bourdieu, 1986, p. 248). This includes the sum of the actual and potential resources embedded within, available through, and derived from a network of social relationships (Nahapiet & Ghoshal, 1998). The social capital metaphor is that the people who do better are somehow better connected (Burt, 2001). Essentially, recognizing that social networks have value, it is not what you know but who you know and who knows you. On the other hand, cultural capital is the nonfinancial currency, including skills, abilities, tastes, preferences, and norms, that enables social mobility. Bourdieu (1986) defined cultural capital as the cultural resources that

23

allow individuals from any background to gain access to power. Cultural capital is a resource, such as extensive knowledge of a topic such as art, mannerisms, and etiquette; practices that have high status values; and educational credentials that can advance access to power for the individuals who possess it (Horvat, 2003). Cultural resources can include, for example, a person's educational attainment, parental educational attainment, intellect, style of speech, family name, and dress. For example, a person who is well traveled, well read, speaks more than one language, has earned a degree from an Ivy League institution, and is articulate would be considered to possess more cultural capital in our society. In its embodied form, cultural capital is a "competence" or skill that cannot be separated from its "bearer" (Bourdieu, 1986). For instance, understanding social and cultural capital can be useful in recognizing the needs and experiences of low-income students who are the first in their families to attend college as a student affairs professional assists them in managing an unfamiliar environment by providing them with relevant information, guidance, and support. To connect and engage with students as well as provide support to students in a culturally relevant, affirming, and meaningful way, student affairs professionals should understand that students bring social and cultural capital to college with them and can also acquire this capital, to some extent, during college.

Cultural Bias, Prejudice, and Discrimination

People classify themselves within various groups (based on age, race, organizational affiliation, etc.) and these categories help people to define their environment. Consequently, people are commonly defined as other on the basis of race or ethnicity, gender, religion, sexual orientation, socioeconomic status, age, and physical or mental ability with each form having oppression associated with it: racism, sexism, religious oppression/anti-Semitism, heterosexism, classism, ageism, and ableism (McIntosh, 1990). This otherness and categorizations can be accompanied by stereotypes, prejudice, and discrimination. Prejudice, defined as prematurely holding a belief or attitude without appropriate examination or consideration of actual data, can be positive or negative and is based on stereotyped views and accompanying emotions (Hays & Erford, 2014). Social identity theory explains how prejudice can develop from intergroup relations involving identification with the in-group and negative attitudes toward the out-group (Nesdale & Flesser, 2001). Prejudice differs from discrimination which refers to covert and overt behaviors based on generalizations held about individuals based on their cultural group memberships (Hays & Erford, 2014). Cultural bias involves a prejudice or highlighted distinction in viewpoint that suggests a preference of one culture over another and introduces one group's accepted behavior as valued and distinguishable from another lesser-valued societal group (Yingst, 2011). In their helping role, student affairs professionals should note that "There is no sanctuary from cultural bias" (Corey, Corey, Corey, & Callanan, 2015, p. 106). Therefore, student affairs professionals should not underestimate the influence of cultural bias on their helping role and worldview. Moreover, they should monitor when they label people, ignoring the uniqueness of an individual by putting all members of a particular group in the same box. To work effectively with all students, student affairs professionals should focus on similarities and not give in to the thought of *us* versus *them*.

Cultural, Racial, and Ethnic Identity

Cultural, racial, and ethnic identity are critical parts of our social contexts and how we identify ourselves personally and socially. In fact, cultural identity and cultural experiences alter how individuals view their world (Berry, 2005). Brock and Tulasiewicz (1985) explained that cultural identity "is used to designate a distinctive way of life—a lived culture within political, economic or more specific educational and social structures" (p. 3). Furthermore, it is noted that cultural identity may change through acculturation or adaptation (Jun, 2010). Racial identity is defined by Helms (1990) as a sense of group or collective identity based on a person's perception that he or she shares a common heritage with a particular racial group. However, as race is a social construct in our society (Helms & Cook, 1999), "racial identity is a surface-level manifestation based on what we look like yet has deep implications in how we are treated" (Chávez & Guido-DiBrito, 1999, p. 40). According to Cross (1991), dissimilar to cultural identity or ethnic identity, racial identity is typically shaped by oppressive and racist experiences. Ethnic identity development is an essential human need that provides a sense of belonging and historical continuity and creates a foundation on which a person builds self-concept (Charlesworth, 2000). Described as dynamic, multidimensional, and changing over time, ethnic identity is considered a basis for a person's behavior (Phinney, 1990) and ethnic identity development consists of an individual's movement toward a highly conscious identification with his or her own cultural values, behaviors, beliefs, and traditions (Chávez & Guido-DiBrito, 1999, p. 41). Tajfel (1981) defined ethnic identity as a part of a person's self-concept which is derived from his or her knowledge of membership in a social group (or groups) combined with the value and emotional significance attached to that group membership (Tajfel, 1981). To be effective in establishing and maintaining helping relationships, student affairs professionals must create affirming environments by being nonjudgmental and respectful of multiple perspectives connected to a person's cultural, racial, and ethnic identity. As students of color encounter feelings of social isolation, alienation and marginalization, stereotyping, invisibility, difficulty with acculturation, and discriminatory treatment by faculty and staff (Ponterotto, Casas, Suzuki, & Alexander, 2001), it is also important that student affairs

25

professionals diligently work to enhance their awareness, knowledge, and skills so that they can ensure students of color feel worthy and safe.

Culture

Culture, as defined by Sue and Sue (1990), encompasses the thoughts, beliefs, practices, and behaviors of a person(s) in the areas of history, religion, social organization, economic organization, political organization, and collective production. Additionally, culture which "refers to social groups that are identified by race, ethnicity, gender, class, sexual orientation, and religion" is pervasive in people's lives (McAuliffe & Associates, 2013, p. 11). In our society, culture shapes how people perceive their world and function within it; influences a person's personal and group values, attitudes, and perceptions; and helps us to understand how people interpret their environment (Geertz, 1973; Jandt, 2013; Markus, Mullally, & Kitayama, 1997; McAuliffe & Associates, 2013). As individuals in our society, we identify with a particular culture—for example, racial, ethnic, cultural, gender, sexual, national, linguistic, regional, indigenous, and religious—from which we gain a sense of belonging. Since "our perception and thought processes are not independent of the cultural environment" (Jandt, 2013, p. 59), student affairs professionals should be aware of the role culture plays in their lives as well as others. In helping a student, student affairs professionals must also consider a student's perspective of the world and avoid cultural encapsulation, which refers to "a narrow and rigid view of the world and other cultural groups using one's own cultural groups as a reference" (p. 6) and as a standard of normality (Hays & Erford, 2014). Due to the relevance of culture in people's lives, student affairs professionals need to take active steps to be cognizant of their own culture, beliefs, and values.

Dominant and Subordinate Culture

Within culture, there are dominant and subordinate cultures. Dominant culture refers to the "social practices and representations that affirm the central values, interests, and concerns of the social class in control of the material and symbolic wealth of society" (Darder, Baltodano, & Torres, 2003, p. 65). In U.S. society, there is a group considered dominant, which is systematically advantaged by the society because of group membership, and a group considered subordinate (targeted), which is systematically disadvantaged (Tatum, 2000). Associated with dominance is power (e.g., political power, economic power, organizational power) and "when people hold membership in a dominant group, they automatically have privilege bestowed upon them by association" (Schmidt, 2006, p. 18). The dominant group holds the power and authority in society relative to the subordinates and determines how that power and authority may be acceptably used, sets the parameters within which the subordinates operate, and has the greatest influence in determining the structure of the society (Tatum, 2000). Accordingly, those individuals in the sub-ordinate culture are well aware of the structure of society, disadvantages, and limi-tations associated with not being in the dominant group. Consequently, a social group can be excluded from the mainstream of the society placing members of that group legally or socially on the "margins" of the society, referred to as marginaliza-tion (Cushner, McClelland, & Safford, 2003). A marginalized person is one who has suffered discrimination and oppression and those who have been marginalized could be skeptical and distrustful of others, especially those in a dominant position; therefore, it is important that student affairs professionals not assume things about the experiences of persons in a subordinate group (Allyn & Bacon, 2004). Student affairs professionals should increase their awareness of the impact of various aspects of the dominant culture on an individual in a subordinate culture.

Identity Abrasion

An identity abrasion is an attack on one's self-identity through conscious or uncon-scious offensives that hurts everyone and the pain is perpetuated when the victim is taunted for being "overly sensitive," causing injuries on both sides (Ely, Meyer-son, & Davidson, 2011). It refers to "psychological twinges that one experiences when feeling put down or affronted—injuries to one's self-image" (Davidson, 2011, p. 138). Ely, Meyerson, and Davidson (2006) noted that an identity abrasion constitutes the perception that one's selfness has been attacked by another person, whether it is true or not. For example, a White student is talking with a student of color and says, "I am so tired of most of the scholarships at the university being taken by minority students which takes away from deserving and hardworking stu-dents." For students of color, this statement can trigger hurt feelings, resentment, and distrust, wanting to defend his or her position. A consequence of an identity abrasion is that it can cause a person to behave defensively and disengage in cross-difference relationships, pushing two people apart as the perceived assault is not discussed for fear of judgment and people tend to reinforce and protect their image as good, well-meaning individuals (Davidson, 2011). To connect to, engage, and support students in a culturally relevant, affirming, and meaningful way, stu-dent affairs professionals need to understand that students bring cultural capital and beliefs with them to college. This understanding and effective helping skills are needed to create opportunities for students to engage in difficult, constructive conversations and conflict resolution when identity abrasions occur.

Microaggressions

Microaggressions are the brief and everyday slights, insults, indignities, and deni-grating messages sent to people of color by well-intentioned White people who are unaware of the hidden messages being communicated (Sue, 2010). Perpetrators of microaggressions are often unaware that they are engaging in such communications when interacting with racial/ethnic minorities. Microaggressions appear in three forms: microassaults (conscious and intentional discriminatory actions such as using racial epithets); microinsults (verbal, nonverbal, and environmental communications that subtly convey rudeness and insensitivity that demean a person's racial heritage or identity such as a guest asking a well-dressed person of color in a hotel to get towels for them, assuming the person of color is part of the housekeeping staff); and microinvalidations (communications that subtly exclude, negate, or nullify the thoughts, feelings, or experiential reality of a person of color such as when an Asian American, born and raised in the United States, is complimented for speaking good English). In a helping relationship, people of color who experience microaggressions could need what Sue, Capodilupo, and Holder (2008) refer to as a "sanity check," validation that the microaggression occurred, which is effective in helping to mitigate the effects of microaggressions (Nadal, Griffin, Wong, Hamit, & Rasmus, 2014; Sue et al., 2008). Furthermore, experiencing racial microaggressions, which communicates an underlying underachieving message, threatens individuals' potential to achieve any goals that they may have (Torres, Driscoll, & Burrow, 2010).

Personal and Social Identity

Tajfel and Turner (1979) asserted that a person has not one personal identity, but rather several identities that correspond to a person's membership within social circles. Personal identity is seen as one's fundamental sense of self, the synthesis of various elements into a whole—as well as those aspects of the self that are consistent over time and place (Dunkel, 2005). It refers to self-knowledge that derives from an individual's unique attributes (e.g., special talents, peculiar tastes, related to physical appearance) (Turner, 1982). Social identity theory involves people who tend to classify themselves and others into various social categories and involves three primary concepts of categorization (people categorize themselves, others, and groups using concepts and language to make sense of their social environment), identification (individuals identify with social groups), and comparison (cognitive process of noticing and realizing that differences and similarities between oneself and other people exist as well as groups comparing themselves to other groups) (Schmidt, 2006). An individual belongs to certain groups together with some emotional and value significance to him or her related to group membership (Tajfel, 1972). For example, a Latina student may view herself as a woman when confronted with sexist remarks or behavior, but as Latina when confronted with racial prejudice or harassment. As asserted by Deaux (1993), "social identities are those roles or membership categories that a person claims as representative" (p. 6) and there is a motive for positive social identity, which is presumed to drive the social comparison process and the search for positive in-group distinctiveness (Tajfel, 1978). For example, a student who belongs to a Greek fraternity or sorority is aware of the common in-group identification, including the preferred appropriate behavior, practices, values, customs, traditions, and norms of the group. The student also compares the group to out-groups and is aware of the group's distinctiveness and how others may perceive his or her membership in the group. In addition, personal identity and social identity continually evolve and impact one another as well as an individual's interactions with others (Schwartz, Montgomery, & Briones, 2006). It is important that student affairs professionals not overlook this fact as they work with college students.

Privilege and Social Injustice

Student affairs professionals should enhance their understanding about the concepts of privilege and social justice and the factors that reinforce privilege—e.g., power, meritocracy, the isms, and loss of individualism. Privilege refers to any advantage that is unearned, exclusive, and socially conferred (Johnson, 2006). As stressed by Derald Wang Sue (Sue & Sue, 2008), making the invisible visible should be the goal of helping professionals (p. 25). As discussed by McIntosh (1990) and Johnson (2006), the "luxury of obliviousness" includes a lack of awareness of one's advantages as a member of the dominant group and the freedom to live unaware of the effect. The luxury of obliviousness can also, unfortunately, allow a student affairs professional to uphold the core beliefs about egalitarianism, the idea that everyone is equal, and to not question individualism, the idea that individuals only have to work hard enough in order to achieve (Ancis & Szymanski, 2001). Lacking awareness and understanding about privileges and social justice can be associated with having denial about prejudice realities and discrimination. You should enhance your understanding about privileges and social injustice in order to show empathy toward culturally diverse students. In your work with students, you cannot afford to be in denial about privilege, especially due to your potential influence and professional duties. Exhibiting denial and resistance can include denying that privilege exists; blaming the victim; renaming the issue; claiming that everyone prefers things the way they are; thinking that good intentions cannot result in something bad; labeling yourself as a good person and simply becoming a concerned observer; and taking a "sick and tired" stance regarding the topics such as privilege and oppression in society (Johnson, 2006).

Racial Battle Fatigue

The consistent expectation and encounters with racism, discrimination, stereotypes, and prejudice can potentially create negative psychological impacts on an individual's well-being. Racial battle fatigue (RBF), a theoretical concept, is described as a person of color's reaction to the troubling conditions that occur from dealing with racism on a daily basis (W.A. Smith, 2004). As an interdisciplinary theoretical framework, RBF considers the increased levels of psychosocial stressors and subsequent psychological (e.g., frustration, shock, anger, disappointment, resentment, hopelessness), physiological (e.g., headache, backache, "butterflies," teeth grinding, high blood pressure, insomnia), and behavioral responses (e.g., stereotype threat, John Henryism, social withdrawal, self-doubt, and a dramatic change in diet) of fighting racial microaggressions in mundane, extreme, environmental stress (MEES) (W.A. Smith, 2004). For student affairs professionals, there needs to be an awareness of the effects of RBF not only as it relates to students, but to persons of color who are student affairs professionals as well.

Sex and Gender

Sex and gender are often used interchangeably, even though they are not the same thing (McAuliffe & Associates, 2013). Sex refers to a person's biological status and is typically categorized as male, female, or intersex, including a number of indicators (i.e., sex chromosomes, gonads, internal reproductive organs, and external genitalia) whereas gender refers to the attitudes, feelings, and behaviors associated with a person's biological sex (American Psychological Association, 2012). In essence, "gender is not innately related to an individual's biological sex, but is constructed socially, within the family and society" (McAuliffe & Associates, 2013, p. 386), the social expression of sex. Some relevant terms and concepts related to gender include gender roles, gender role stereotypes, gender typing, gender role standard, gender role conflict, and gender polarization. Associated with the concept of gender is gender identity, which refers to the sex that a person identifies with and his or her awareness and acceptance of his or her biological nature as male or female (T. B. Smith et al., 2004). Furthermore, gender identity can be considered as a continuum rather than a dichotomy (American Counseling Association, 2009). Sexual identity refers to the sexual orientation with which a person identifies and sexual orientation refers to the sex of the person to whom a person is attracted to sexually (American Counseling Association, 2009). Therefore, a person "may identify as heterosexual, gay, lesbian, bisexual, or questioning, to name a few" (Hays & Erford, 2014, p. 8). A person who views his or her gender as inconsistent from the biological sex he or she was assigned at birth and may live full or part-time as the other sex is considered transgender, an umbrella term (Lawrence, 2007). Some relevant terms and concepts associated with sexual identity include heterosexism, homophobia, transphobia, transsexual, cross-dresser, and biphobia. Furthermore, many LGBT persons have multiple identities and thus, some may experience oppression based on the intersection of their sexual orientation and other minority statuses (i.e., race, ethnicity, gender, ability, and social class) which can be challenging (McAuliffe & Associates, 2013). For example, a Black female student from a lower socioeconomic status who identifies as a lesbian and lives in a small town located in a rural area has multiple identities and should be seen beyond singularized categories of identity. Issues involving two or more identifiable minority statuses can be complex. In addition, there are demands surrounding a person being both a visible and invisible minority which can cause stress (Greene & Boyd-Franklin, 1996). To be effective in their helping role, it is necessary for student affairs professionals to be aware of issues and challenges associated with gay, lesbian, bisexual, and transgender students as well as coming out. Furthermore, student affairs professionals must be aware of the relevant issues related to "multiple minorities" (Sue & Sue, 2013) and understand the complexities of multiple identities and the effect of the multiple minority status on a person's self-concept, well-being, and perspective.

Stereotypes and Stereotype Threat

Stereotypes are defined as learned expectations that are oversimplified and uncritical generalizations about individuals who are identified as belonging to a specific group (Corey et al., 2015). Stereotypes could hinder the ability of student affairs professionals to form supportive, sincere, and effective helping relationships with all students. In addition, awareness of negative stereotypes can psychologically threaten an individual, an occurrence known as stereotype threat (Steele & Aronson, 1995), which could impact college students' performance, engagement, and well-being. Stereotype threat refers to "being at risk of confirming, as self-characteristic, a negative stereotype about one's group" (Steele & Aronson, 1995, p. 797). A person in a subordinate group wants to represent himself or herself and the group in a positive manner. For example, a student could believe that the poor behavior or bad choices of another student who is in the same social group makes all members of the group look bad. Situations that a person experiences that increase the salience of the stereotyped group identity can increase vulnerability to stereotype threat. In the college environment, stereotype threat can impact the academic and social experiences of students of color and their academic performance in a situation that invokes a stereotype-based expectation of poor performance. Unfortunately, the long-term effects of stereotype threat might contribute to educational and social inequality (Good, Aronson, & Harder, 2008). Potential consequences of stereotype threat include decreased effort, anxiety, negative cognitions, lowered performance expectations, distraction, narrowed attention, self-consciousness, and withdrawal of effort or over-effort (Steele & Aronson, 1995; Steele, Spencer, & Aronson, 2002).

Worldview

Human beings are born into this world with the capacity to perceive events and draw conclusions about those experiences that help define a person's worldview (Schmidt, 2006). Worldview is defined as a composite of demographic, socioeconomic, and cultural influences that shape the way an individual perceives the world (Ponterotto et al., 2001). Essentially, it is how an individual conceptualizes his or her relationships with the world (Hays & Erford, 2014) and also includes a person's values, beliefs, and assumptions about life aspects such as his or her perspectives of past and present events and outlook about the future (Baruth & Manning, 2012). In their helping role, it is the responsibility of the student affairs professionals to recognize that their worldview and the worldview of the student are present in the helping relationship. For example, a student affairs professional who believes that being on time is a high value behavior and being late, even by a minute, is disrespectful might have an issue with a student who believes it is more important to genuinely listen to the problem of and help a loved one in need even if it means being a few minutes late for an appointment. Because the difference in worldviews can lead to miscommunication and misunderstanding, it is necessary for student affairs professionals to accept the validity of alternative worldviews to engage and support diverse students. Additionally, student affairs professionals should be aware that understanding their own worldview and those of other cultures can facilitate communication and foster the helping relationship.

Using these concepts as a foundation, student affairs professionals can use their knowledge and understanding to assist students who experience any psychological, psychosocial, and physiological stressors. To develop your multicultural knowledge, you could attend a conference related to diversity, participate in a webinar or workshop; converse with a colleague who is proficient in issues related to diversity to get different perspectives; immerse yourself in various cultural experiences; or read literature to increase awareness competency. Subsequently, with acquired awareness and cultural knowledge, student affairs professionals should learn to be more responsive, appropriate, and culturally sensitive in their interventions and efforts (Pope et al., 2004). Underlying the use of these multicultural skills is the development of culturally interpersonal relationships and the use of appropriate intercultural communication skills, verbal and nonverbal. There must be an appreciation for cultural differences, and to function effectively as a helping professional in student affairs, you must "know and respect specific cultural differences and realize how cultural values operate in the helping process" (Corey & Corey, 1998, p. 197).

MANAGING DIFFICULT DIALOGUES AS A PROFESSIONAL

As a student affairs professional, there could also be times you encounter a student's cultural assumptions, misunderstandings, and subtle or blatant affronts. Experiencing physiological and psychological stressors, whether it is overt or covert, has an effect on a person's well-being and energy, which can impact a professional's ability to be accepting and desire to work with certain students. As in the case *Yes, It's Me*, a student affairs professional discusses dealing with microaggressive exchanges in her professional role.

VOICES FROM THE FIELD

Sharing a Story: Yes, It's Me

Dr. U. Monique Robinson-Nichols

Being an African American senior student affairs administrator working at a top 20 predominantly White institution can present many challenges. For example, I am constantly managing others' perceptions. Routinely, I have students stop in my door (I have no administrative assistant) and ask to speak to the "Dean" and when I say "Yes, may I help you?," I sense that they have to take a minute to reconcile their cognitive dissonance. I have had several students respond "Do you know when she will be in?" Of course, I answer "I am she." Some recover quickly, and others seem a little dazed. This behavior is not only confined to students. Parents who have spoken to me on the phone oftentimes are taken aback when they actually meet me. It is just something in their expression and in their stance, which says "Mmm . . . it never occurred to me that you might be African American."

I mentally gird myself for these type of reactions so that I can still be cordial and professional. Being an African American higher education administrator requires resilience. Racial battle fatigue (W. A. Smith, 2004) requires constantly renewing your spirit against the constant barrage of slights, insults, and stereotypes. You must always check-in with yourself and say "Did I hear that correctly?" or "Is that how they meant it?" Self-care and an extensive network of allies are key in assuring a sense of positivity despite the plethora of microaggressions student affairs professionals of color can face.

Some general strategies professionals can use to cope with and address any experiences related to cultural inequities and microaggressive exchanges include the following:

- Have a support network as these healthy relationships can support you when you experience the stressors.
- Have allies and mentors who can provide sensible advice and a willingness to listen.
- Focus on maintaining a healthy self-concept, spend a minimal amount of time dwelling on an incident and giving it power.
- Have self-awareness as you remind yourself about who you are beyond the surface.

- Engage in physical and psychological care.
- Focus on positive reappraisal by putting things into perspective.
- Undertake positive self-talk and steadfastness to rise above so as to not be limited or constrained by an incident.

Becoming a Culturally Competent Professional

Student affairs professionals should be prepared to effectively work with diverse students and address issues related to diversity. In the end, a culturally competent student affairs professional lets the diverse student tell his or her story as the professional listens and values the student's context. Acknowledging the positive impact of emotional and social support, student affairs professionals should actively support diverse students by understanding and addressing their struggles and obstacles and see beyond their worldview and assumptions. Listen and be open to the stories of those most disempowered and do not allow your emotional reactions to negate their voices because you become defensive (Sue & Sue, 2008). Howard-Hamilton (2000) suggested that certain behaviors should manifest when a culturally competent staff is working with a student, proposing that a culturally competent staff member:

- Is comfortable with and understands own racial identity;
- Is comfortable with own cultural identity (ies);
- Understands own bias and checks assumptions;
- Is willing to ask questions about diversity and suspends judgment;
- Understands limits of own expertise and consults with students;
- Sets a climate for dialogue, disagreement, reflection, challenge, and support;
- Develops realistic learning goals and objectives;
- Follows up with students;
- Enrolls in multicultural courses or workshops regularly; and
- Shares ideas and issues with a multiculturally competent mentor.

(pp. 69–70)

Cultural differences can affect a helping relationship, and student affairs professionals need to understand that cultural barriers could also exist, which would impact the helping relationship. Your knowledge and self-awareness can put you in a position to assess any issues and work to incorporate the multicultural competencies into your practice. Developing multicultural competence and learning how to apply the associated knowledge, awareness, and skills will take effort, time, and practice. It also requires that you remain open-minded, reflective, and flexible in order to grow and develop as an effective student affairs professional.

CONCLUSION

Student affairs professionals must have a lucid understanding about personal responsibilities, professional responsibilities, standards, ethics, and related competencies, especially in their roles as a helper. Understanding these concepts and gaining these competencies are pertinent in the decision-making process and the helping role of student affairs professionals. It is also necessary that student affairs professionals gain knowledge about multicultural concepts and competencies as well as strive to enhance their awareness, knowledge, and skills to work effectively with all students regardless of their cultural backgrounds.

REFERENCES

ACPA/NASPA. (2010). *ACPA and NASPA professional competency areas for student affairs practitioners.* Washington, DC: Joint publication of ACPA and NASPA.

Allyn & Bacon. (2004). *Diversity issues in group counseling* [PowerPoint slides]. Retrieved from www.ablongman.com/helpingprofessions/coun/ppt/group/diversityissuesingroupcounseling.ppt

American Counseling Association. (2009). *The ACA encyclopedia of counseling.* Alexandria, VA: Author.

American Psychological Association. (2012, January). Guidelines for psychological practice with lesbian, gay, and bisexual clients. *American Psychologist, 67*(1), 10–42.

Ancis, J. R., & Szymanski, D. M. (2001). Awareness of white privilege among white counseling trainees. *The Counseling Psychologist, 29*(4), 548–569.

Arminio, J. (2009). Applying professional standards. In G. S. McClellan, J. Stringer, & Associates (Eds.), *The handbook of student affairs administration* (3rd ed., pp. 187–205). San Francisco, CA: Jossey-Bass.

Arminio, J. (2011). Professionalism. In J. H. Schuh, S. R. Jones, S. R. Harper, & Associates (Eds.), *Student services: A handbook for the profession* (5th ed., pp. 468–481). San Francisco, CA: Jossey-Bass.

Barr, M. J., McClellan, G. S., & Sandeen, A. (2014). *Making change happen in student affairs: Challenges and strategies for professionals.* San Francisco, CA: Jossey-Bass.

Baruth, L. G., & Manning, M. L. (2012). *Multicultural counseling and psychotherapy: A lifespan approach* (5th ed.). Upper Saddle River, NJ: Pearson.

Berry, J. W. (2005). Acculturation: Living successfully in two cultures. *International Journal of Intercultural Relations, 29*, 697–712.

Berry, J. W., & Sam, D. L. (1997). Acculturation and adaptation. In J. W. Berry, M. H. Segall, & C. Kagitcibasi (Eds.), *Handbook of cross-cultural psychology: Social behavior and applications* (pp. 291–326). Needham Heights, MA: Allyn & Bacon.

Blimling, G. S. (1998). Navigating the changing climate of moral and ethical issues in student affairs. In D. L. Cooper & J. M. Lancaster (Eds.), *Beyond law and policy: Reaffirming the role of student affairs* (pp. 65–75). New Directions for Student Services, No. 82. San Francisco, CA: Jossey-Bass.

Bourdieu, P. (1986). The forms of capital. In J. G. Richardson (Ed.), *Handbook of theory and research for the sociology of education* (pp. 241–258). New York, NY: Greenwood.

Brock, C., & Tulasiewicz, W. (1985). The concept of identity: Editors' introduction. In C. Brock & W. Tulasiewicz (Eds.), *Cultural identity & educational policy* (pp. 1–10). London, England: Croom Helm.

Burt, R. S. (2001). Structural holes versus network closure as social capital. In N. Lin, K. Cook, & R. S. Burt (Eds.), *Social capital: Theory and research* (pp. 31–56). New York, NY: Aldine de Gruyte.

Canon, H. J. (1996). Ethical standards and principles. In S. R. Komives, D. B. Woodard, Jr., & Associates (Eds.), *Student services: A handbook for the profession* (3rd ed., pp. 106–125). San Francisco, CA: Jossey-Bass.

Carpenter, S., & Stimpson, M. T. (2007). Professionalism, scholarly practice, and professional development in student affairs. *NASPA Journal, 44*(2), 265–284.

Charlesworth, R. (2000). *Understanding child development*. Albany, NY: Delmar Thomson Learning.

Chávez, A. F., & Guido-DiBrito, F. (1999). Racial and ethnic identity and development. In C. Clark & R. Caffarella (Eds.), *An update on adult development theory: New ways of thinking about the life course* (pp. 39–48). New Directions for Adult and Continuing Education, No. 84. San Francisco, CA: Jossey-Bass.

Corey, M. S., & Corey, G. (1998). *Becoming a helper* (3rd ed.). Belmont, CA: Brooks/Cole.

Corey, G., Corey, M. S., Corey, C., & Callanan, P. (2015). *Issues and ethics in helping professions* (9th ed.). Stamford, CT: Cengage.

Council for the Advancement of Standards in Higher Education. (2015). *CAS Professional Standards for Higher Education* (9th ed.). Washington, DC: Author.

Cross, W. (1991). *Shades of black: Diversity in African American identity*. Philadelphia, PA: Temple University Press.

Cushner, K. H., McClelland, A., & Safford, P. (2003). *Human diversity in education: An integrative approach* (4th ed.). New York, NY: McGraw-Hill.

Darder, A., Baltodano, M., & Torres, R. D. (Eds.). (2003). *The critical pedagogy reader*. New York, NY: Routledge.

Davidson, M. N. (2011). *The end of diversity as we know it: Why diversity efforts fail and how leveraging difference can succeed*. San Francisco, CA: Berrett-Koehler Publishing.

Deaux, K. (1993). Reconstructing social identity. *Personality and Social Psychology Bulletin, 19*, 4–12.

Dennis, R., & Giangreco, M. F. (1996). Creating conversation: Reflections on cultural sensitivity in family interviewing. *Exceptional Children, 63*, 103–116.

Dunkel, C. S. (2005). The relations between self-continuity and measures of identity. *An International Journal of Theory and Research, 5*, 21–24.

Ely, R. J., Meyerson, D. E., & Davidson, M. N. (2006, September). Rethinking political correctness. *Harvard Business Review, 84*(9), 78–87, 157.

Fitzpatrick, K., & Gauthier, C. (2001). Toward a professional responsibility theory of public relations ethics. *Journal of Mass Media Ethics, 16*(2/3), 193–212.

Flaskerud, J. H. (2007). Cultural competence column: Acculturation. *Issues in Mental Health Nursing, 28*, 543–546.

Fried, J. (1997). Changing ethical frameworks for a multicultural world. In J. Fried (Ed.), *Ethics for today's campus: New perspectives on education, student development, and institutional management* (pp. 5–22). New Directions for Student Services, No. 77. San Francisco, CA: Jossey-Bass.

Geertz, C. (1973). *The interpretation of cultures*. New York, NY: Basic Books.

Good, C., Aronson, J., & Harder, J. (2008). Problems in the pipeline. *Journal of Applied Developmental Psychology, 29*(1), 17–28.

Greene, B., & Boyd-Franklin, N. (1996). African American lesbians: Issues in couples therapy. In J. Laird & R. J. Green (Eds.), *Lesbian and gay men in families: A handbook for therapists* (pp. 251–271). San Francisco, CA: Jossey-Bass.

Hamrick, F. A., & Benjamin, M. (Eds.). (2009). *Maybe I should ... case studies on ethics for student affairs professionals.* Lanham, MD: University Press of America.

Hays, D. G., & Erford, B. T. (2014). *Developing multicultural counseling competence: A systems approach* (2nd ed.). Boston, MA: Pearson.

Helms, J. E. (1990). *Black and White racial identity: Theory, research and practice.* Westport, CT: Praeger Publishers.

Helms, J. E., & Cook, D. A. (1999). *Using race and culture in counseling and psychotherapy.* Boston, MA: Allyn and Bacon.

Henke, H., Langstraat, L., Mackie, A., & Morgan, E. (2013). *Ethics in higher education: A reader for writers.* Southlake, TX: Fountainhead Press.

Hofstede, G. (1980). *Culture's consequences.* Beverly Hills, CA: Sage.

Horvat, E. M. (2003). The interactive effects of race and class in educational research: Theoretical insights from the work of Pierre Bourdieu. *Perspectives on Urban Education, 2*(1), 1–25.

Howard-Hamilton, M. F. (2000). Programming for multicultural competencies. In D. Liddell & J. Lund (Eds.), *Programming approaches that make a difference* (pp. 67–78). New Directions for Student Services, No. 90. San Francisco, CA: Jossey-Bass.

Humphrey, E., Janosik, S. M., & Creamer, D. G. (2004). The role of principles, character, and professional values in ethical decision-making. *NASPA Journal, 41*(4), 675–692.

Jandt, F. E. (2013). *An introduction to intercultural communication: Identities in a global community* (7th ed.). Los Angeles, CA: Sage Publications.

Janosik, S. M. (2007). Common issues in professional behavior. *NASPA Journal, 44*, 285–306.

Janosik, S. M., Creamer, D. G., & Humphrey, E. (2004). An analysis of ethical problems facing student affairs administrators. *NASPA Journal, 41*(2), 356–374.

Johnson, A. G. (2006). *Privilege, power, and difference* (2nd ed.). New York, NY: McGraw-Hill.

Jones, E. A., & Voorhees, R. A. (2002). *Defining and assessing learning: Exploring competency-based initiatives.* Report of the National Postsecondary Education Cooperative Working Group on competency based initiatives in postsecondary education. Retrieved from http://nces.ed.gov/pubs2002/2002159.pdf

Jun, H. (2010). *Social justice, multicultural counseling, and practice: Beyond a conventional approach.* Los Angeles, CA: Sage.

Kim, B. S. K., & Omizo, M. M. (2005). Asian and European American cultural values, collective self-esteem, acculturative stress, cognitive flexibility, and general self-efficacy among Asian American college students. *Journal of Counseling Psychology, 52*(3), 412–419.

Kitchener, K. S. (1985). Ethical principles and ethical decisions in student affairs. In H. J. Canon & R. D. Brown (Eds.), *Applied ethics in student services* (pp. 17–29). New Directions for Student Services, No. 30. San Francisco, CA: Jossey-Bass.

Kitchener, K. S. (2000). *Foundations of ethical practice, research, and teaching in psychology.* Mahwah, NJ: Lawrence Erlbaum Associates.

Komives, S. R. (1992). The middles: Observations on professional competence and autonomy. *National Association of Student Personnel Administrators Journal, 29*, 83–90.

Komives, S. R., & Arminio, J. (2011). Promoting integrity through standards of practice. In R. B. Young (Ed.), *Advancing the integrity of professional practice* (pp. 27–34). New Directions for Student Services, No. 135. San Francisco, CA: Jossey-Bass.

Komives, S. R., & Woodard, D. B. (Eds.). (2003). *Student services: A handbook for the profession* (4th ed.). San Francisco, CA: Jossey-Bass.

Kuh, G. D., & Whitt, E. J. (1997). The invisible tapestry: Culture in American colleges and universities. Culture defined and described. In E. J. Whitt (Ed.), *College student affairs administration* (pp. 125–135). Needham Heights, MA: Simon & Schuster Custom Publishing.

Lawrence, A. A. (2007). Transgender health concerns. In I. H. Meyer & M. E. Northridge (Eds.), *The health of sexual minorities: Public health perspectives on lesbian, gay, bisexual and transgender populations* (pp. 473–505). New York, NY: Springer.

Loewenberg, F. M., & Dolgoff, R. (1992). *Ethical decisions for social work practice* (4th ed.). Itasca, IL: Peacock Publishers, Inc.

MacKinnon, F. J. D., & Associates. (2004). *Rentz's student affairs practice in higher education* (3rd ed.). Springfield, IL: Thomas.

Markus, H. R., Mullally, P. R., & Kitayama, S. (1997). Selfways: Diversity in modes of cultural participation. In U. Neisser & D. Jopling (Eds.), *The conceptual self in context: Culture, experience, self-understanding* (pp. 13–61). New York, NY: Cambridge University Press.

McAuliffe, G. & Associates (2013). *Culturally alert counseling: A comprehensive introduction* (2nd ed.). Los Angeles, CA: Sage.

McIntosh, P. (1990). *Interactive phases of curricular and personal revision with regard to race.* Working paper #219. Wellesley, MA: Wellesley College Center for Research on Women. Retrieved from the ERIC database. (ERIC No. ED336310).

Merton, R. K., Reader, G. G., & Kendal, P. L. (Eds.). (1957). *The student physician: Introductory studies in the sociology of medical education.* Cambridge, MA: Harvard University Press.

Mok, A., & Morris, M. W. (2012). Managing two cultural identities: The malleability of bicultural identity integrations as a function of induced global or local processing. *Personality and Social Psychology Bulletin, 38*(2), 233–246.

Nadal, K. L., Griffin, K. E., Wong, Y., Hamit, S., & Rasmus, M. (2014). The impact of racial microaggressions on mental health: Counseling implications for clients of color. *Journal of Counseling & Development, 92*(1), 57–66.

Nahapiet, J., & Ghoshal, S. (1998). Social capital, intellectual capital, and the organizational advantage. *Academy of Management Review, 23*(2), 242–266.

Nash, R. (1997). Teaching ethics in the student affairs classroom. *NASPA Journal, 35*(1), 3–19.

Nesdale, D., & Flesser, D. (2001). Social identity and the development of children's group attitudes. *Child Development, 72*(2), 506–517.

Nuss, E. (2003). The development of student affairs. In S. Komives, B. Woodard, & Associates (Eds.), *Student services: A handbook for the profession* (4th ed., pp. 65–88). San Francisco, CA: Jossey-Bass.

Oyserman, D., Coon, H. M., & Kemmelmeier, M. (2002). Rethinking individualism and collectivism: Evaluation of theoretical assumptions and meta-analyses. *Psychological Bulletin, 128*(1), 3–72.

Pescosolido, B. A., & Aminzade, R. (Eds.). (1999). *The social worlds of higher education: Handbook for teaching in a new century.* Thousand Oaks, CA: Pine Forge Press.

Phinney, J. (1990). Ethnic identity in adolescents and adults: Review of research. *Psychological Bulletin, 108*, 499–514.

Ponterotto, J. G., Casas, J. M., Suzuki, L. A., & Alexander, C. M. (2001). *Handbook of multicultural counseling.* Thousand Oaks, CA: Sage.

Pope, R. L., Reynolds, A. L., & Mueller, J. A. (2004). *Multicultural competence in student affairs.* San Francisco, CA: Jossey-Bass.

Poyrazli, S., Kavanaugh, P. R., Baker, A., & Al-Timimi, N. (2004). Social support and demographic correlates of acculturative stress in international students. *Journal of College Counseling, 7*, 73–82.

Reason, R. D., & Broido, E. M. (2010). Philosophies and values. In J. H. Schuh, S. R. Jones, S. R. Harper, & Associates (Eds.), *Student services: A handbook for the profession* (5th ed., pp. 80–95). San Francisco, CA: Jossey-Bass.

Redmount, R. S. (1978/1979). New dimensions of professional responsibility. *The Journal of the Legal Profession, 3*, 43–56.

Reynolds, A., & Pope, R. (2003). Multicultural competence in counseling centers. In D. Pope-Davis, H. Coleman, W. Liu, & R. Toporek (Eds.), *Handbook of multicultural competencies in counseling & psychology* (pp. 365–383). Thousand Oaks, CA: SAGE Publications.

Robinson, G., & Moulton, J. (2005). *Ethical problems in higher education.* Lincoln, NE: iUniverse.

Schmidt, J. J. (2006). *Social and cultural foundations of counseling and human services: Multiple influences on self-concept development.* Boston, MA: Allyn & Bacon.

Schwartz, S. J., Montgomery, M. J., & Briones, E. (2006). The role of identity in acculturation among immigrant people: Theoretical propositions, empirical questions, and applied recommendations. *Human Development, 49*, 1–30.

Schwartz, S. J., & Unger, J. B. (2010). Biculturalism and context: What is biculturalism, and when is it adaptive? *Human Development, 53*(1), 26–32.

Smith, T. B. (2004). *Practicing multiculturalism: Affirming diversity in counseling and psychology.* Boston, MA: Allyn & Bacon.

Smith, W. A. (2004). Black faculty coping with racial battle fatigue: The campus racial climate in a post-civil rights era. In D. Cleveland (Ed.), *A long way to go: Conversations about race by African American faculty and graduate students* (pp. 171–190). New York, NY: Peter Lang Publishers.

Steele, C. M., & Aronson, J. (1995). Stereotype threat and the intellectual test performance of African-Americans. *Journal of Personality and Social Psychology, 69*, 797–811.

Steele, C. M., Spencer, S. J., & Aronson, J. (2002). Contending with group image: The psychology of stereotype and social identity threat. In M. Zanna (Ed.), *Advances in experimental social psychology* (Vol. 34, pp. 379–440). New York, NY: Academic Press.

Steinman, S. O., Richardson, N. F., & McEnroe, T. (1998). *The ethical decision-making manual for helping professionals.* Belmont, CA: Brooks/Cole.

Sue, D. W. (2010). *Microaggressions in everyday life: Race, gender, and sexual orientation.* Hoboken, NJ: John Wiley & Sons.

Sue, D. W., Arredondo, P., & McDavis, R. J. (1994). Multicultural counseling competencies and standards: A call to the profession. *Journal of Counseling and Development, 70*, 477–486.

Sue, D. W., Capodilupo, C., & Holder, A. (2008). Racial microaggressions in the life experiences of Black Americans. *Professional Psychology: Research and Practice, 39*, 329–336.

Sue, D. W., & Sue, D. (1990). *Counseling the culturally different: Theory and practice* (2nd ed.). New York, NY: Wiley.

Sue, D. W., & Sue, D. (2007). *Counseling the culturally different: Theory and practice* (5th ed.). New York, NY: Wiley.

Sue, D. W., & Sue, D. (2008). *Counseling the culturally diverse.* Hoboken, NJ: John Wiley & Sons.

Sue, D. W., & Sue, D. (2013). *Counseling the culturally diverse: Theory & practice* (6th ed.). New York, NY: John Wiley & Sons, Inc.

Sundberg, D. C., & Fried, J. (1997). Ethical dialogues on campus. In J. Fried (Ed.), *Ethics for today's campus: New perspectives on education, student development, and institutional management* (pp. 67–79). New Directions for Student Services, No. 77. San Francisco, CA: Jossey-Bass.

Tajfel, H. (1972). Social categorization. English manuscript of 'La catégorisation sociale.' In S. Moscovici (Ed.), *Introduction à la Psychologie Sociale* (Vol. 1, pp. 272–302). Paris, France: Larousse.

Tajfel, H. (1978). *Differentiation between social groups: Studies in the social psychology of intergroup relations.* London, England: Academic Press.

Tajfel, H. (1981). *Human groups and social categories.* Cambridge, England: Cambridge University Press.

Tajfel, H., & Turner, J. C. (1979). An integrative theory of intergroup conflict. In W. G. Austin & S. Worchel (Eds.), *The social psychology of intergroup relations* (pp. 33–47). Monterey, CA: Brooks/Cole.

Tatum, B. D. (2000). The complexity of identity: "Who am I?" In M. Adams, W. J. Blumenfeld, H. W. Hackman, X. Zuniga, & M. L. Peters, (Eds.), *Readings for diversity and social justice: An anthology on racism, sexism, anti-Semitism, heterosexism, classism and ableism* (pp. 9–14). New York, NY: Routledge.

Torres, L., Driscoll, M. W., & Burrow, A. L. (2010). Racial microaggressions and psychological functioning among highly achieving African-Americans: A mixed methods approach. *Journal of Social and Clinical Psychology, 29*(10), 1074–1099.

Turner, J. C. (1982). Towards a cognitive redefinition of the social group. In H. Tajfel (Ed.), *Social identity and intergroup relations* (pp. 15–40). Cambridge, England: Cambridge University Press.

Voorhees, R. A. (2001). Competency-based learning models: A necessary future. In R. A. Voorhees (Ed.), *Measuring what matters: Competency-based learning models in higher education* (pp. 5–13). New Directions for Institutional Research, No. 110. San Francisco, CA: Jossey-Bass.

Weidman, J. C., Twale, D. J., & Stein, E. L. (2001). *Socialization of graduate and professional students in higher education: A perilous passage?* ASHE-ERIC Higher Education Report, 28. San Francisco, CA: Jossey-Bass.

Whitt, E. J., & Blimling, G. S. (2000). Applying professional standards and principles of good practice in student affairs. In M. J. Barr, M. K. Desler, & Associates (Eds.), *The handbook of student affairs administration* (2nd ed., pp. 612–628). San Francisco, CA: Jossey-Bass.

Winkle-Wagner, R. (2010). Cultural capital: The promises and pitfalls in educational research. *ASHE Higher Education Report, 36*(1), 1–144. Retrieved from Academic Search Complete database (EBSCOhost).

Winston, Jr., R. B. (2001). *Standards of professional practice: A survey of NASPA members' opinions.* Unpublished paper, Washington, DC: National Association of Student Personnel Administrators.

Winston, R., & Saunders, S. (1991). Ethical professional practice in student affairs. In T. Miller & R. Winston (Eds.), *Administration and leadership in student affairs: Actualizing student development in higher education* (2nd ed., pp. 309–329). Muncie, IN: Accelerated Development.

Yingst, III, T. E. (2011). Cultural bias. In S. Goldstein & J. A. Naglieri (Eds.), *Encyclopedia of child behavior and development* (p. 446). New York, NY: Springer Science and Business Media, LLC.

Young, R. B. (2003). Philosophies and values guiding the student affairs profession. In S. R. Komives, D. B. Woodard, Jr., & Associates (Eds.), *Student services: A handbook for the profession* (4th ed., pp. 89–106). San Francisco, CA: Jossey-Bass.

Chapter 3

Helping Skills

In Chapter 1, helping was discussed as a primary role of student affairs professionals to help college students adjust to, cope with, and move through a wide range of problems and concerns; and accordingly, helping skills are essential to effective student affairs practice. This chapter goes a step further and provides an overview of basic microskills, the basic foundational skills involved in effective helping relationships, including practice examples and activities. In order to effectively help students, it is imperative for student affairs professionals to learn and demonstrate the basic helping skills necessary to facilitate the helping process; understand how to respond to student concerns and crises, including how to make referrals to appropriate campus or community resources; and feel comfortable with supporting students through the problem-solving process. This process begins with learning basic helping skills and practicing to gain competency as well as participating in honest self-reflection and self-assessment (Clark, 2009). First, you must be actively involved in learning microskills to gain competency (Meier & Davis, 2005). Moreover, it is important to note that helping skills will come naturally with practice and time.

FIRST THINGS FIRST

Because of student affairs professionals' high level of contact with students (Burkard, Cole, Ott, & Stoflet, 2005), possessing helping skills is a must to effectively provide students with coping skills and with the context for making decisions to resolve dilemmas and create positive relationships and environments for students (Long, 2012). Becoming an effective helping professional in student affairs requires the complex integration of intrapersonal, interpersonal, and professional awareness, knowledge, and skills which includes the following:

- Accept the student as an individual and deal with the student as such.
- Recognize that in a helping relationship, you should be thinking and brainstorming *with* the student and not *for* him or her.

- Understand that all decision making should rest with the student you are helping. See your role as a guide through the process. If you consistently solve the problem for the student, you are not helping him or her to develop problem-solving skills of his or her own. Consequently, the student can begin to become dependent on you when he or she has problems.
- Acknowledge that your role is to help students solve their own problems by providing encouragement, support, and challenge.
- Rather than assuming you know students' feelings and thoughts, strive to understand their worldview.
- Recognize that your assumptions about others and their beliefs or cultures will interfere with your ability to help them.
- Having boundaries with students is necessary (e.g., not having a drink at the bar with the student to talk over his or her problem or not telling one student about an issue or incident in the life of another student).

Whether meeting with the student once or over a period of time, helping skills play an important role. Notably, interactions with the student are a powerful tool in the helping relationship and, therefore, building rapport and creating an environment in which the student feels secure are essential. A student, the helpee, is more likely to achieve goals when a positive relationship exists between the student and the student affairs professional, the helper. The quality of the relationship "needs to be of primary concern to all seeking to develop their helping skills," (Parsons, 2011, p. 4).

BASIC SKILLS FOR HELPING

As basic helping skills can be used to enhance your communication with students and enable you to effectively build rapport and engage students, it is necessary for student affairs professionals to develop and practice these skills. Helping skills are basic verbal and nonverbal skills that are essential for establishing and maintaining rapport, form the basis of effective communication, and provide a solid foundation for helping (Okun, 2002). The concepts discussed in this chapter focus on the core conditions needed to build rapport and establish a helping relationship with a student as well as encourage the student to talk. In addition, the skills, strategies, and techniques associated with the helping process are discussed. Of course, each student and situation will be different because "in reality there is no hard-and-fast, cookbook approach that can be used in each and every helping encounter" (Parsons, 2011, p. 47). The approaches outlined, once incorporated into your student affairs practice, can serve as a basis to provide both helpful and meaningful support to students.

Core Conditions of the Helping Relationship

In establishing a positive relationship and demonstrating care, a student affairs professional must possess listening and attending skills. Fundamentally, central to the helping process is the presence of accurate empathy or understanding of the helpee's perspective, positive regard, respect, and genuineness, as these conditions establish the parameters of the helping relationship (Corey & Corey, 2011; Cormier & Hackney, 1999).

Empathy and Understanding

Being present and thoughtfully responding to what a student is experiencing are important ingredients in the helping process and can be communicated through genuineness and achieved through sympathy and empathy. Understandably, there is often ambiguity between the terms *empathy* and *sympathy*. Sympathy is an expression of feeling sorrow or concern for a distressed person, rather than feeling the same emotion (Meier & Davis, 2011). Empathy focuses on communicating a sense of caring and understanding regarding another person's experiences (Egan, 1994). For example, if a student informs you that he or she is sad and feeling adrift because the student's mother recently passed away, a helper conveying sympathy could say: "Trying to get through the loss of a parent can be difficult." On the other hand, if the helper is expressing empathy, the helper could say: "I know it's difficult to get through the loss of a parent because I have lost my mother." Learning to understand requires skillful listening, sensing the feelings of another person, and the capacity to switch from your own set of experiences to another as seen through that person's eyes (Cormier & Hackney, 1999). Once you have a sense of understanding, you must verbally express it with proper warmth and acceptance.

Positive Regard

For a positive relationship to exist, the student affairs professional must convey positive regard, which is an "overall sense of protection, support or acceptance, no matter what is divulged" (Karusu, 1992, p. 36), and must be cognitively and emotionally present. In showing positive regard, an expression of appreciation of a person as unique and worthwhile should be present (Cormier & Hackney, 1999). This regard also means that the helper must respect a person's values, perspectives, feelings, wishes, and thoughts without conditions and exhibit warmth. Thinking or saying that "I will only accept you if you behave in a way I believe is appropriate" is not demonstrating positive regard. You should not expect a student to meet a specific expectation, request, or requirement to receive your acceptance and warmth. Helping someone without prejudice, with respect for the person's uniqueness, and with a recognition that the person is self-determining can be difficult as we all have values and opinions, are fallible, have personal limits, and few of us are without our own pain and shame (Mearns & Thorne, 1988; Wilkins, 2000). For example, if a student affairs professional has experienced a recent break-up due to a cheating partner, he or she may not be as accepting of a student who is upset because the student's partner is breaking up with him or her because of cheating. This possibility compels a need for student affairs professionals to engage in an honest self-assessment of their values, worldviews, and biases as these could filter out in the helping process and hinder acceptance. Although difficult, student affairs professionals must put forth the effort to ensure that they communicate respect and warmth in an unbiased manner to be effective and supportive.

Genuineness

As in establishing any relationship, genuineness and respect go a long way. If you have ever interacted with someone who came across as disingenuous, fake, and/or rude, can you recall how you felt? Did you want to continue interacting with that person? In a helping relationship, genuineness encompasses being honest and authentic in communicating with those being helped. Being genuine is behaving without front or façade, being fully aware of one's feelings at that moment, and being able to freely communicate these feelings openly (Rogers, 1956; Shaw, 2004). It is important to note that in communicating feelings openly, a helper's expression of his or her feelings should not take precedence over understanding the other person's feelings (Cormier & Hackney, 1999). You can be true to yourself and yet, connect to the person you are helping. Parsons (2011) described a genuine helper as "one who is open as opposed to defensive, real as opposed to phony" (p. 31). Genuineness also includes congruence between words and behaviors and inner feelings, which requires a need for a helper to be aware of his or her personal feelings rather than "present one attitude, as an outward facade, while actually holding another attitude at a deeper or unconscious level" (Rogers, 1956, p. 995). For example, if a student affairs professional professes that he or she is comfortable helping a student who is gay but the professional's behavior shows uneasiness, this can become a barrier. Therefore, there must be a reasonable level of self-awareness on the part of the helper. It is particularly helpful for student affairs professionals to engage in an honest assessment of their feelings, values, beliefs, and thoughts related to identities and social categories (e.g., appearance, race/ethnicity, political affiliation, class, sexual identification, etc.) as they often work in diverse environments.

45

THINKING ABOUT MY PRACTICE

How do you usually put someone at ease? What skills can you identify?

How do you communicate acceptance and understanding to others? What skills can you identify?

Are you able to suspend your biases and personal values momentarily to see a situation from someone else's perspective? What biases, beliefs, and values (e.g., related to appearance, race/ethnicity, religion, political affiliation, sexuality, etc.) might interfere with you effectively working with someone?

ATTENDING AND LISTENING

Now that the core conditions in establishing an effective helping relationship in a positive environment have been identified, the next step is to focus on the knowledge and skills to facilitate the helping process. The focus will now shift to the attending and listening skills needed to support students in your helping role as a student affairs professional.

Attending Behaviors

We communicate with more than our words. If someone says "I am happy for you" but does not smile while the person's arms are folded and eye contact is not directed at you, would you really believe that the person is happy for you? If our verbal message is incongruent with our nonverbal message, the person with whom we are communicating can be confused, concerned, and become wary. As Ralph Waldo Emerson (1860) penned,

> The eyes of man converse as much as their tongues, with the advantage that the ocular dialect require no dictionary, but is understood the world over. When the eyes say one thing, and the tongue another, a practiced man relies on the language of the first.

> (p. 81)

In other words, if there is a contradiction between verbal and nonverbal messages, we usually believe the nonverbal message (Gazda et al., 1995). This potential outcome is why attending behaviors are important in building a positive environment when working with students; these behaviors show the other person that you are interested in what is being said and paying attention.

Attending behavior, a communication skill, is used to establish a positive environment in a helping relationship, including the use of physical behaviors such as maintaining an open posture, making eye contact, smiling, gesturing, and nodding to convey that the helper is interested in and open to the person being helped (Egan, 1977). In exhibiting attending behavior, "the student affairs professional is alert to individual students and reflects the appearance and behavior of someone who is prepared to listen" (Long, 2012, p. 12). Support can be demonstrated by the words you say, your voice, and body language. According to Cormier and Cormier (1998), attentiveness, which shows that you are following the message of a person's story, is communicated through facial expressions, eye contact, bodily positions and movements, and verbal responses. Attending requires both "a physical stance or position and a psychological orientation" (Wicks, Parson, & Capps, 1993, p. 106).

Considering that your mindset, body language, and ability to actively listen are essential to have meaningful interactions with the students you help, it is important for you to be knowledgeable of attentiveness skills that influence connecting with others. Our eye contact, facial expressions, hand gestures, and body posture show others that we are carefully attending to them (Capuzzi & Gross, 2013; Sharpley & Sagris, 1995). Unlike verbal communication, which is mostly under our voluntary control, nonverbal communication operates at the edge or beyond of conscious awareness (Silverman, Kurtz, & Draper, 2013). Since our attitudes, feelings, and emotions are conveyed nonverbally, it is also imperative to be aware of feelings that may appear, even without you realizing it, through facial expressions, body language, and verbal tone (Weaver, 1972), especially since our gestures and mannerisms are capable of producing feelings and counter-feelings (Routh, 2011). Think about when you are speaking to someone; if we see the person nod his or her head and smile, we can feel encouraged. However, if someone moves his or her eyes around in a circle and sighs, we may not be as enthused to continue the conversation and can possibly not think favorably of the other person at that moment. Understandably, it is important for you to be aware of the impact of and work to enhance your verbal and nonverbal foundational skills, including kinesics—communication with our body such as body language, eye contact, gestures, and facial expressions; proxemics—interaction distances and personal space; and paralanguage—the conveyance of emotion—in establishing and sustaining a helping relationship with students (Wolfgang, 1985).

Kinesics

Body language, "a nonconscious method of communication between people" (Routh, 2011), can influence interpersonal interactions as it is important from the perspective of the receiver and the person conveying the information. In a helping relationship, it is relevant since it can encourage someone to continue to talk with you or discourage the person from continuing with the conversation. To foster an environment of caring and show the person you are taking part in the face-to-face interaction, Gerard Egan (2014) developed the acronym SOLER (Face the helpee Squarely, both metaphorically and literally; adopt an Open, nondefensive posture; Lean forward toward the person to show interest; make good Eye Contact; and stay Relaxed) to describe techniques for orienting one's body to convey nonverbally that the helper is visibly tuning in to the helpee. According to Egan's technique, in face-to-face interactions, it important to be aware of how you posture yourself relative to the person you are helping, with your face square to the other person showing that you are engaging, interested, and actively listening. In addition, to facilitate openness, your arms and legs are uncrossed and you lean toward the other person to indicate that the person's concerns are being heard and understood.

It is also important to look at students while speaking to them because it shows them that you are tuned in to what they are saying. Effective eye contact can signal understanding and provide feedback (Evans, Hearn, Uhlemann, & Ivey, 2008). Cormier and Hackney (1999) suggested that good eye contact lies somewhere between a fixed gaze and frequent breaks in eye contact. Maintaining eye contact shows interest and concern; however, vary the eye contact so as not to stare, which could be perceived as threatening and be a source of distraction to the person you are helping (Parsons & Meyers, 1984). Since a person's eyes can more accurately reflect what the person is truly feeling (Richmond & McCroskey, 2000), noticing another person's eye contact can also help you in developing a sense of that person's emotional state; for example, enabling you to assess if the person is sad or nervous. In the end, try to be natural and culturally aware as to avoid making stereotypical judgments about someone's eye contact (Cormier & Hackney, 1999).

We also "speak" with our bodies and our facial expressions. Gestures can be used to convey your thoughts and feelings in a positive or negative way (Nelson-Jones, 2009). How would you feel if someone pointed his or her index finger close to your face or "rolled his or her eyes" at you? Although a word is not said, a message is sent. Since verbal messages function in conjunction with non-verbal messages, the relevance of facial expressions and gestures in a helping relationship is evident. The face communicates our emotional states, helps us to assess emotional states, reflects interpersonal attitudes, and provides non-verbal feedback to others' comments and actions (Knapp & Hall, 2006). For example, our face can express what we feel even when we do not know what to say to express our feelings (e.g., sorrow at the death of a loved one, happiness for someone's joyous news, flirtation when we like someone). When working with students, you should use your facial expressions to reinforce what you are saying or receiving verbally (e.g., smile when you say that you are proud of them or when they share good news with you); reflect the emotions of students (e.g., look sad when they are sad); be conscious of what your facial expression is conveying; and aware of cultural norms when it comes to facial expressions. Our bodies can also reinforce what we are saying or encourage the person to whom we are speaking and demonstrate our attentiveness. For example, head nods and hand gestures can be used to encourage the other person to talk (Winokuer & Harris, 2016). In fact, a head nod is the most common gesture of listening (Nelson-Jones, 2009). If a student needs encouragement, a simple head nod lets him or her know that you are there with the student in the conversation. On the other hand, negative gestures can display inattentiveness (e.g., clenched hands, rubbing your neck, finger drumming, checking watch, inspecting fingernails) and discourage the student to continue talking to you (Nelson-Jones, 2009). A gesture can also show that you are anxious, tentative, or nervous (e.g., wringing hands, foot tapping, leg bouncing) which could be picked up by the student. As gestures can occur unconsciously or reflectively, you must try to be aware and conscientious of them and ensure that they are used properly to facilitate communication with students.

Proxemics

In student affairs professionals' work with students, face-to-face conversations can sometimes occur in a setting where Egan's suggested stance is not conducive, such as while you sit behind your desk, walk with a student, or stand in a hallway. In these conditions, proximity—the amount of comfortable distance for interactions—and personal space—the region surrounding people which they regard as psychologically theirs (Hall, 1966)—play a significant role. Hall (1966) suggested that the distance within which people feel comfortable when interacting with others is influenced by their relationship (e.g., personal space, from 18 inches to 4 feet, is typical for interactions with family members and good friends; social space, from 4 to 12 feet, is typical for interaction with other people and acquaintances). The proximity of people to one another when they interact sends a message that affects people in different ways (e.g., people could feel discomfort or anxiety if they believe the person to whom they are speaking is too close). Interpersonal distance can also serve as a protective component (Sommer, 1969). What happens when you believe someone has invaded your personal space? Do you avoid the person's gaze or move to put more space between the two of you? We typically find a way to compensate for the discomfort. As Adler and Rodman (1997) contended, we have an unconscious expectation that our personal space will not be violated. In your interaction with students, be aware of and respect their personal space at all times. It is also important to note that you should be aware that an individual's proxemic behavior varies according to situations and is influenced by type of relationship with the student, and social variables, such as culture, subculture, gender, and age (Aiello, 1987). Cultural influences largely control what is considered an optimal "comfort zone" for conversing (Capuzzi & Gross, 2013). Furthermore, regardless of where interactions with students occur, it is worthwhile to mention that you should try not to be distracted (e.g., check emails, text messages, or social media accounts, gaze into the distance, etc.), and maintain your focus.

Paralanguage

Not only are the actual spoken words important but how they are said; this is referred to as paralanguage (Lewis, 2014). Paralanguage refers to other vocal cues that individuals use to communicate (e.g., hesitations, loudness of voice, pauses, volume, pitch rate, silence, a sigh or a gasp). These vocal cues help us attach meaning to spoken words and should be considered in our responses to others (Okun, Fried, & Okun, 1999; Sue & Sue, 2013). Through paralanguage, a person's emotional state, veracity, and sincerity are communicated (Neuliep, 2015). For this reason, a student affairs professional must be aware of not only what he or she says, but how he or she says things in trying to connect to a student he or she is helping. For example, most of us can identify when a speaker is confident or nervous through the speaker's vocal pitch, rate, and pace or whether a speaker is being genuine, cynical, or sarcastic (Neuliep, 2015). Often, it is not what you say but how you say it in interactions with others. A person's tone, pitch, volume, and pace can add meaning to and change the meaning of the person's spoken words. If, for example, you were to give a student bad news, but did it in a hurried, loud voice, how might this be interpreted by the student? What if you were to convey the bad news in an unhurried manner, with a calm voice while displaying appropriate body language? Do you think these messages would be perceived differently?

Attending skills are used to reassure and support students, and the components of verbal and nonverbal serve as supporting behaviors that affect the establishment of a helping relationship. Student affairs professionals need to be aware of their attending behaviors and realize that proxemics (space), kinesics (body), and paralanguage (voice) are important foundations for communicating with students. Additionally, they should become knowledgeable about how race, culture, and gender affect communication styles and interpretation. It is also important for student affairs professionals to notice the verbal and nonverbal messages of students and be aware of their own verbal and nonverbal messages in communicating with and attending to students. Therefore, these behavioral skills need to accompany a student affairs professionals' ability to actively listen.

ACTIVE LISTENING

The most effective way to establish yourself as sincere, trustworthy, respectful, and helpful is to demonstrate to students that you are there for them and understand their plight and feelings, which can be accomplished through active listening. Culley and Bond (2004) described active listening as a means for listening with purpose and responding in such a way that both persons are aware they have been heard and understood. Active listening communicates that you are indeed listening; and that you are paying attention to what the other person is saying, possibly thinking, as well as what the other person is doing (i.e., nonverbal communication which can include body language, expressions, reactions, etc.). It also serves as a way to encourage the helpee to continue telling his or her narrative. Remember, your goal is to understand as much of the story as possible, or better yet, to understand it from the helpee's perspective (as if you were standing in his or her shoes).

Basic active listening skills include the following: encouragement, paraphrasing, summarizing, reflection of feeling, and attending to nonverbal communication (Egan, 1998). Encouraging responses communicates that you are listening and paying attention; they also are a way of encouraging the person to continue talking. Encouragement may take the form of any of the following:

- Head nods.
- "Mmm, hmm."
- "Okay."
- Repetition of a particular word that the person said.

Encouragement should not be mistaken with any of the following:

- Praise such as, "I think you did an excellent job on that!" Praise is typically subjective; the important element is listening for what the helpee thinks about the situation and/or himself or herself.
- "I understand." "Right." "I know." It is highly unlikely that anyone completely understands or "gets" what the other person is saying or his or her experience. For example, even if you experienced a bad break-up, your situation will still have contextual differences. It is best to listen for the helpee's narrative, while suspending judgment rather than falling into the trap of believing your experience matches his or hers.

Have you ever noticed someone smiling when she was telling you about something good that she experienced? Or perhaps you could not help but notice how sad someone's face looked? Maybe you realized just how anxious someone was as you noticed him shaking his leg nervously as he talked to you? If you have ever noticed nonverbal behavior, congratulations, you have this skill down! A speaker's nonverbal behavior gives us additional information about what he or she is trying to say. You can communicate that you are actively listening by simply pointing out this nonverbal behavior. In response to the above three scenarios, you might respond:

- "I can't help but notice how much you are smiling when you talk about this new job!"
- "I can see in your face that you are very sad about what happened."
- "This seems very stressful to you; you are even shaking your leg as you talk about it."

Let's see just how advanced your attention to nonverbal behavior is! Have you ever noticed someone talking about something disturbing while she was smiling? What about a friend who was talking about a failing grade he just received who looks emotionally numb? Often, you will see nonverbal behavior that is seemingly contradictory to the message that is being verbalized. Here are some ways that you can respond:

- "You are talking about a very stressful situation that you are in, yet you are smiling."
- "You mentioned that you failed the history course; and I don't see any emotion in your face."

When you comment on someone's discrepant nonverbal behavior, you are again demonstrating that you are listening *and observing* him or her.

SKILLS OVERVIEW AND PRACTICE

In this section, the focus is on invitational, reflective, and response skills associated with the helping process. These helping skills allow you to respond verbally and put your listening skills in action as well as facilitate the helping process. Okun and Kantrowitz (2015) recommended that your verbal responses allow you:

- to communicate to students that you are truly hearing and understanding them and their perspective;
- to communicate that you can help and are warm, accepting, respectful, and caring;
- to increase the student's self-understanding and self-exploration as well as the student's understanding by focusing on major themes, clarifying inconsistencies, reflecting back the underlying feelings, and synthesizing the apparent and underlying concerns and feelings.

Based on the suggestions of Meier and Davis (2011), as you encourage a student's self-exploration, helpful guidelines include that you avoid advice, premature problem solving, and relying on questions; listen closely to what the person says, listen to metaphors, and pay attention to the nonverbal; be concrete; and keep the focus on the student.

Although not all of the microskills are examined, the skills outlined—questioning, paraphrasing, reflecting, summarizing, and interpreting—can provide you with building blocks to develop your skill set for helping students. The skills can aid you in assisting a student with exploring problems and identifying issues and concerns; prioritizing problems and needs; and establishing possible goals and devising actions. Of course, as your knowledge expands, you will become more comfortable with using the skills. Think of it as how you would learn another language, it will take time and practice.

Note, the information presented in this section was acquired from the various sources: Brammer and McDonald, 2003; Corey and Corey, 2011; Cormier and Hackney, 1999; Cormier and Hackney, 2012; Dillon, 1990; Hill, 2009; Okun and Kantrowitz, 2015; Parsons, 2011.

Questioning: Open and Closed Questions

Questioning allows you to gain information, increase understanding, and explore issues and concerns of the student. Effective questioning can guide the conversation and may assist in the student in telling his or her story. Consider the difference between two versions of the same question.

1. "Do you want to go ahead and complete a roommate agreement?"
2. "How do you feel about completing a roommate agreement?"

As you can see, the first question can be answered with a *yes* or *no*. In contrast, the second question provides an individual with an opportunity to respond in more detail. When using open and closed questions to solicit information from a student, consider the following:

- Have a purpose for each question that you ask.
- Ask only one question at a time.
- Avoid asking too many questions as this could cause the person to see you in an interrogatory role.
- Introduce the question with *what*, *where*, *when*, or *how*. Avoid *why* questions and rephrase the question as *what* or *how*.
- Be comfortable with silence because it is not necessarily a bad thing albeit uncomfortable at times. When you are unsure about what to say, say nothing. Silence can actually allow the student time to process an issue and reflect.

53

Closed Questions: Questions can be answered with few words, multiple choice, or yes/no responses and can be used to gain information, to ask for a repeat of a statement, or to ask if your assessment was accurate. For example:

- Are you going to have the project completed by the deadline?
- Do you drink often?
- When was the last time you felt that way?

Open Questions: Ask when elaboration is needed. The response is not limited to a "yes" or "no" or a one- or two-word response. These questions can focus on thoughts, feelings, reflection, and exploration. Open questions can encourage a student to discuss without restraint and can help you better understand a student's situation. For example:

- Tell me about your relationship with your parents while you were growing up.
- What do you think about moving forward with that option?
- How did you feel when that happened?

On occasion, a student's response will leave you wondering what he or she is trying to say. Rather than guess or assume, using an open question permits you to request clarification in order to gain clarity about vague or ambiguous information. A request for clarification allows the student to rephrase and it also shows the student that you are seeking understanding. Clarification can also be useful when the student is extremely emotional and may not be thinking clearly enough to present details in a coherent manner. For example, a student shares the following with you:

I've been trying to talk to her about it for months, trying to get her to understand my point of view. First, it was small things that I noticed were missing, like trinkets from my jewelry box. Then, it was my pearls and business card case. I also cannot find my favorite t-shirt from my trip to Jamaica which she said she liked a lot. Even when I confronted her, she didn't want to talk about the missing stuff; instead, she wanted to talk about how I hurt her feelings. Not to mention, the music issue. Can you help me with this issue?

For clarification, you could say:

- "I am not quite sure if I am understanding. Could you please describe the situation to me another way?"
- "Could you go through the order of events again for me?"

Practice: *Provide examples of responses for each of the following statements using closed questions.*

1. Statement: "I hate it when a friend of mine criticizes me."
   Example: "Do you have a specific example of when one of your friends has criticized you?"

   Helper:

   _____

   _____

   _____

   _____

2. Statement: "Sometimes, I cannot sleep because I am tense all the time."
   Example: "Has this occurred recently?"

   Helper:

   _____

   _____

   _____

   _____

3. Statement: "I feel as if everyone is against me right now."

   Helper:

   _____

   _____

   _____

   _____

4. Statement: "My boyfriend/girlfriend thinks I'm too fat."

   Helper:

   _____

   _____

   _____

   _____

5. Statement: "Everything in my life is horrible right now."

   Helper:

   _____

   _____

   _____

   _____

6. Statement: "I can't seem to get my assignments done by the deadlines."

   Helper:

   _____

   _____

   _____

   _____

7. Statement: "My mother is constantly questioning me about everything in my life."

   Helper:

   _____

   _____

   _____

   _____

8. Statement: "Sometimes, I get so angry at my roommate."

   Helper:

   _____

   _____

   _____

   _____

Provide examples of responses for each of the following statements using open questions.

1. Statement: "I hate it when a friend of mine criticizes me."
   Example: "What is a specific example of what one of your friends has said to you?"

Helper:

_____

_____

_____

_____

2. Statement: "Sometimes, I cannot sleep because I am tense all the time."
   Example: "Tell me about the last time this happened to you."

   Helper:

_____

_____

_____

_____

3. Statement: "I feel as if everyone is against me right now."

   Helper:

_____

_____

_____

_____

4. Statement: "My boyfriend/girlfriend thinks I'm too fat."

   Helper:

_____

_____

_____

_____

5. Statement: "Everything in my life is horrible right now."

   Helper:

_____

_____

_____

_____

6. Statement: "I can't seem to get my assignments done by the deadlines."

   Helper:

   _____

   _____

   _____

   _____

7. Statement: "My mother is constantly questioning me about everything in my life."

   Helper:

   _____

   _____

   _____

   _____

8. Statement: "Sometimes, I get so angry at my roommate."

   Helper:

   _____

   _____

   _____

   _____

Paraphrasing

Paraphrasing is a summary in your own words of what you were told. It also clarifies content, highlights issues, and shows that you are engaged in the conversation. As a helper, paraphrasing conveys the meaning, tone, feeling, and/or the content of the message communicated by repeating what has been said in somewhat different words. When you use paraphrasing, consider the following:

- It is useful to paraphrase when the student has presented a lot of material and you feel confused.
- It could help the person simplify, pinpoint, and solidify what he or she has said.
- It may encourage elaboration.

- It allows the person to continue speaking without much interruption from you during the conversation.
- It can also be helpful if you want to focus on one aspect of a story.
- It can verify the accuracy of your perceptions.
- It focuses more on the cognitive content of a student's response.
- It can be challenging to reduce or condense a student's story into a few words.

Essentially, paraphrasing involves restating something that the student mentioned. Paraphrases are brief. The purpose is, again, to communicate that you are following. For example, if the student said, "I am really struggling with my roommate. She smokes and when she comes back to the dorm she reeks. I have tried to tell her how much it bothers me but she gets defensive, slams the door and leaves. I don't know what or how else to say it. I feel like I am in a no-win situation. We are only two weeks into the semester!" Your paraphrase might include any of the following:

- "You feel stuck, like you are in a no-win situation."
- "Your roommate's habit really bothers you."

When paraphrasing, note that:

- Paraphrases can be just a few words or one or two brief sentences.
- Do not simply repeat or parrot what the person has said.
- Be sure to pick out the most important content.
- It is good to start the sentence with a stem. For example:
  - "Let me see if I hear you correctly . . ."
  - "As I hear you speak . . ."
  - "As I see things . . ."
  - "You appear touched by . . ."
  - "In other words . . ."

Practice: *Provide examples of responses for each of the following statements using paraphrasing.*

Student 1
"Just this month, I have had to pay an installment on my tuition, purchase four new tires for my car, pay out $280 in application fees for graduate school, and buy a plane ticket to go home for the holidays."

Helper Response:

_____

_____

_____

_____

Student 2

"Lately, I have been running around consistently going to classes, completing assignments and projects, attending meetings, studying, and running errands. It is really hard to find time to do much of anything else."

Helper Response:

_____

_____

_____

_____

Student 3

"I am fighting with my roommate, my peers at work seem to be isolating me lately since I got the promotion, and my best friend is not spending a lot of time with me as she used to since she started dating this new guy."

Helper Response:

_____

_____

_____

_____

Student 4

"Since losing my mother to cancer last semester, I cannot stop thinking about her. I think about how we would talk briefly every night before we went to sleep and have our 'tell me the good news and bad news' reports. I think about how when I was young, we would have our morning coffee, well I actually had hot chocolate, and talk about any topic we could think of. I think about how she consistently encouraged me, even when I knew she did not feel her best. I can't stop thinking about her."

Helper Response:

_____

_____

_____

_____

Student 5

"I have finally broken up with Harold. Putting up with his drama and the way he was treating me was just too much for my nerves and patience. Every time I tried to talk with him about what I was thinking about our relationship and express my feelings, he would shut down or change the subject quickly. Honestly, I am glad that it is over."

Helper Response:

_____

_____

_____

_____

Reflection

Reflection is repeating or rephrasing a student's statements. This could include identifying a person's feelings, stated or inferred. Reflection can be used not only to show that you are listening and understanding, but it can also encourage a person to say more by echoing his or her thoughts. Reflection can also help someone to open up and look at issues in a new and fresh way. A student can feel validated and understood when you accurately convey an understanding of the feelings, thoughts, and concerns. When using reflection:

- Listen for the basic message, considering the content, feeling, and meaning communicated.
- Do not repeat the person's exact words.

Many of us get our thoughts mixed up with our feelings. For example, when someone says, "I feel that I should get over it, but I am not sure," or "I feel like I can do it" the person is actually communicating what he or she *thinks* should or could be done. In fact, there is no feeling about the situation even mentioned. In your active listening, you listen for the actual feeling behind the belief. A reflection of feeling to the above comments might be:

- "You are feeling confused and stuck."
- "You are feeling confident about being able to do it."
- "After the conversation with your academic advisor, you were discouraged."
- "You looked sad when you mentioned your younger sister."

Reflecting feeling allows you to communicate that you are listening and understand the core feelings involved in the person's message by using the same word or phrase equivalent to what the person is conveying to you. A reflection of the student's feelings helps you to connect empathically or sympathetically and bring the emotional message to the forefront of the conversation. A reflection of feeling response can identify the student's emotions, including verbal and nonverbal messages. A reflection of feeling response is a paraphrase of the affective portion of the content. For example, "You feel that your partner ignores you" is a paraphrase, but "You sound upset because you feel that your partner ignores you" is a reflection of feeling. With reflection of feeling:

- Try to capture the *feelings* of words when you are reflecting feeling.
- Think carefully about which words are chosen to communicate feelings. See Table 3.1, "Feeling Words and Emotions."
- Check for accuracy of the reflection of feeling with the person.
- Recognize that cognitive distortions can influence a person's emotions and thought patterns. Burns (1980, 1999) identified looking at things in black and white, overgeneralization, discounting positive accomplishments and events or qualities, jumping to conclusions, blaming self for events beyond one's control, blaming and criticizing others while overlooking ways that one's own attitudes and behavior might contribute to a problem, labeling self with one's shortcomings, focusing on the negative and ignoring the positive, blowing things out of proportion and shrinking importance of things, and emotional reasoning as some ways people distort their thinking. For example, a student receives many positive comments about his or her presentation to a group, but one of the participants says something mildly critical. The person will fixate on this reaction for days and ignore all the positive feedback.

Practice: *Provide examples of responses for each of the following statements using reflection of feeling and meaning.*

Student 1
"My life is going pretty well now that I have reduced my alcohol usage for a month. I have begun to make more friends and my grades have improved significantly. However, I am tired much of the time because I still am not sleeping very well. I think that I slept better when I had a glass or two of wine at bedtime. I do not want to ruin all the progress I have made, but I'm not sure what to do as I really need to get a good night's rest."

Reflection of Feeling Response:

_____

_____

_____

_____

Student 2

"I am sorry that I am so distracted, but I cannot make a decision about what to do about my relationship with one of my longtime friends. Lately, she has become very critical and judgmental when we talk. I am trying to be patient since I understand that she has a lot going on in her life and is stressed about not being able to find a job and her parents' divorce. For example, during our last conversation, she tells me for the first time that she doesn't like my boyfriend and that I am a doormat for him which makes me stupid. This is just one example of her many vitriolic comments I have had to endure over the past two months. Ugh!"

Reflection of Feeling Response:

_____

_____

_____

_____

Student 3

"I just don't know what to think. I really thought that things would be different once I came to college. But it seems like another level of high school. It seems that people's insecurities and pettiness exist here just as much as it did in high school. Last night, I cried as I was falling asleep. It's hard for me to understand what is going on."

Reflection of Feeling Response:

_____

_____

_____

_____

Student 4

"I am about to graduate and I know that I should be happy. I have worked hard to have good grades and spent a lot of time studying. There were many nights I passed up having a good time with friends just to make sure that I was prepared for class or an exam. Now that I am at the end, I don't feel like I thought I would. I am not sure who I am now."

Reflection of Feeling Response:

_____

_____

_____

_____

TABLE 3.1 Feeling Words and Emotions

Sad	Happy	Hurt	Unsure
Blue	Amused	Crushed	Ambiguous
Dejected	Celebratory	Dejected	Ambivalent
Depressed	Ecstatic	Despised	Apprehensive
Discouraged	Elated	Destroyed	Cautious
Dismayed	Enthusiastic	Embarrassed	Discombobulated
Fatigued	Grateful	Hated	Hesitant
Guilty	In high spirits	Insulted	Indecisive
In despair	Joyful	Judged	Insecure
Lonely	Optimistic	Mistreated	Self-doubting
Mournful	Overjoyed	Offended	Tentative
Sorrowful	Thrilled	Rejected	Uncertain
Upset		Slighted	

Confident	Tired	Angry	Anxious
Assured	Blah	Annoyed	Afraid
Brave	Burned out	Bitter	Concerned
Certain	Drained	Enraged	Fearful
Poised	Exhausted	Frustrated	Frightened
Positive	Indifferent	Fuming	Nervous
Secure	Listless	Furious	Pressured
Self-assured	Powerless	Incensed	Stressed
Supported	Weary	Infuriated	Tense
Sure of yourself		Irate	Troubled
		Mad	Uptight
			Worried

Calmed	Refreshed	Enthusiastic	Hopeless
At ease	Encouraged	Ambitious	Defeated
Comforted	Energized	Determined	Dejected
Consoled	Enlivened	Driven	Despairing
Content	Inspired	Eager	Disheartened
Peaceful	Invigorated	Excited	Distressed
Pleased	Recharged	Motivated	Doubtful
Relaxed	Rejuvenated	Passionate	Drained
Solaced	Relaxed	Ready	Inadequate
	Renewed	Willing	Powerless
	Restored		Scared
	Revitalized		Useless
	Revived		Weak
	Strengthened		Worthless
	Vibrant		

Summarization

Summarization is pulling together several ideas or feelings into a succinct, concrete statement, focusing on a general theme and drawing connections between two or more themes. In summarizing what has been said, you cover more of the content of the conversation than you would with paraphrasing.

- Summarization can help with the redirection of the conversation when the student to whom you are speaking talks about several topics without focus or direction and rambles.
- Summarization can be used to recap the conversation and review.
- Summarization can be used to move the conversation to another topic or goal setting.
- Summarization allows the person to whom you are speaking an opportunity to clarify any misinterpretations you have.
- Summarization can be used to begin a follow-up meeting.

A summary is an attempt to capture as much as possible of what the speaker is saying. The purpose is generally the same as paraphrasing; namely, to communicate that you are following and are "actively listening." Consider the above example again. If the student said, "I am really struggling with my roommate. She smokes and when she comes back to the dorm she reeks. I have tried to tell her how much it bothers me but she gets defensive, slams the door and leaves. I don't know what or how else to say it. I feel like I am in a no-win situation. We are only two weeks into the semester!"
Some possible summaries might be:

- "This has been a rough start for you. You have made attempts to communicate to your roommate about her smoking; however, she gets very upset when you do so. You are feeling stuck on where to go next."
- "You really want to work out this situation with your roommate. You would like to find a solution that involves not having to smell secondhand smoke and get along with your roommate."

Look at this interaction between a student and a helping professional:

Student's Comment to Helping Professional

"I come from a family of high-achievers. I am the youngest of four and each of my siblings has completed or is enrolled in professional or post-baccalaureate studies. Getting high grades to get into a good graduate program is of high priority to me, especially since my family keeps reminding me that good grades are key to getting into a good graduate program at a high-quality institution. In addition,

I just started this new job on campus and I feel lost daily because I haven't figured things out. This is so unlike me. Everything in my life feels so unsettled right now. I just don't think that I can handle all of these responsibilities at the same time."

Helping Professional's Response Using Summarization

"There are a number of areas in your life which make you feel overwhelmed with responsibility. So far you've indicated your dissatisfaction with the pressure you feel from your family to have very high grades and get into a quality graduate program and your performance at your new job. Each is contributing to the stress you feel and each presents a degree of responsibility you feel that you must bear, resulting in uncertainty about your ability to cope with those responsibilities."

Do you see the similarity and difference between paraphrasing and summarization?

Practice: *Provide examples of responses for each of the following statements using summarization.*

Student 1

"My mother complains constantly that I have not been a good daughter since I came to college because I do not call her every evening and I am not coming home on the weekends regularly. I call her 3–4 days per week and I go home on the weekends that I do not work. She tells me that she is noticing that I seem to just take and I am never appreciative. This week it has been difficult to concentrate and focus on academics because I am extremely angry at my mother for waking me up early in the morning and laying on the guilt trip. I am also disappointed in my father for not stepping in, simply stating that this is between me and my mother. I have not called her in 4 days because lately, I felt guilty and started blaming myself after our phone conversations. I have even taken on more hours on the weekend at work to avoid her. This situation is causing a lot of stress for me and is taking its toll."

Helper Response:

_____

_____

_____

_____

Student 2

"I have a lot going on this semester. In addition to serving as the treasurer for my sorority and my tutoring job, I have taken on a second major. I thought that the second major would make me more marketable. To stay on track with my original graduation date, I decided to take 18 hours each semester. It's only one more class. Unfortunately, I am finding it more difficult to keep up with all the assignments and projects and in one class, I just cannot seem to catch up. Maybe I am just not as smart as I thought I was."

Helper Response:

_____

_____

_____

_____

Interpretation

Interpretation allows the helper to present a way of thinking about an issue or situation that the student may not have previously considered. It allows you to move beyond what the student has overtly stated or acknowledged and provide a framework of meaning, reason, or explanation for behaviors, thoughts, or feelings so the person can see the situation in a new way. The goal is to connect isolated statements or actions, themes, and/or patterns in the person's behavior or feelings. When offering interpretations, consider the following:

- It can help increase the student's awareness or insight and make a connection between incongruent statements, thoughts, beliefs, emotions, events, or behavior.
- It can validate the ideas of the student.
- It can deepen the student's understanding of himself or herself, his or her decisions, actions, goals, and emotions.
- Be cautioned as it can put the helper in a more authoritative position within the helping relationship and color the student's perception of the helper.
- It is essential to have a rapport and trust with the person for interpretation to be successful.
- Deliver interpretations with empathy or sympathy.
- Have the facts to support your interpretation.
- Allow time for discussion of your interpretation.
- Do not provide too many interpretations during the conversation.
- It is good to use when the student is in a decision-making conflict.

Example:

Student: "I am still arriving late for my first classes of the day. Maybe it's because of my lack of interest. My professors are boring and the content of these required general courses I'm taking are also boring and a waste of time. I mean, really, when will I ever use that information? I lay out my clothes and organize all the items I need for classes the next day and yet, I still arrive late. I have plenty of time to study and prepare myself since I am not involved in anything on campus and have no interest in joining an organization. I keep to myself. I also have the room to myself since my roommate has a boyfriend and is basically living with him off campus. Lucky her! I still have not had anyone show an interest in me. Maybe if she was around in the morning I would be more enthused to wake up in the morning and get my day started. It's a struggle."

Helper: "You said that you are often late for class, even when you prepare everything the night before. Previously, you said it was because you do not like taking the general education courses as you do not see the significance of it. Then, you said it was because you do not find the professors interesting and you are bored in class. Is it possible that your problems with being late are related to you feeling down and alone?"

Practice: *Provide examples of responses for each of the following statements using interpretation*

Student 1

"For my girlfriend's birthday, I spent the morning cleaning her apartment and cooking her favorite meal while she was in class. I rented movies that she told me she wished that she could watch but was too busy to do so. When she came home, I met her at the door with a bouquet of her favorite flowers and a smile. Interestingly, she tells me that my gesture annoyed her because now she felt obligated to take part and she had things to do. She then tells me that some of her classmates invited her out for wings and beer later to celebrate her birthday and she did not want to disappoint them. Therefore, she would not eat a lot of what I prepared because she did not want to be too full. Seriously? Lately, it seems that nothing I do is what she wants. I'm confused. "

Helper Response:

_____

_____

_____

_____

Student 2

"I am so worried to the point I am sick. Well, I am also dealing with morning sickness. However, I am most nervous about telling my parents that I am pregnant. My father grew up in our hometown, is a well-respected businessman, and a deacon at our church. My mother is liked by everyone because she is so sweet and outgoing. Honestly, my parents are really great people. That's why I don't want to tell them that I am pregnant. The thought of disappointing them is weighing so heavy on me. I plan to go home this weekend to tell them. If I am lucky, I might run into a ditch and die."

Helper Response:

_____

_____

_____

_____

CHALLENGES AND NEXT STEPS

For student affairs professionals, helping and advising are considered core competencies essential for effective and ethical practice (Pope, Reynolds, & Mueller, 2004). Because of your helping role, uncertainty and tentativeness can occur. For that reason, when helping a student, it is important for you to realize that you should not worry about saying the "right thing," "screwing up" the student, or thinking that you are interfering in a student's private life. Accept that at times, you will be less than perfect and might make a mistake; therefore, you must set realistic expectations for yourself and know that you are consistently growing and learning.

Although you are a professional, you are not expected to be the expert on all student issues. Consult as needed with colleagues and mental health professionals and know how to refer students to qualified professionals (see Chapter 6). Realize that "All helpers benefit from professional dialogue" (Parsons, 2011, p. 165); therefore, it is beneficial for you to have a mentor and support network to serve as sounding boards and get to know other helping professionals, such as the staff of the counseling center or community mental health professionals. In addition, if you are to adequately meet the needs of students, take the time to be knowledgeable of campus and external resources within the community to assist students as needed.

Practicing helping skills can help you develop as a helper in student affairs and reflect on your growth. Below are suggested activities for group exercises, role plays, and a case study to assist in making you more familiar with the knowledge and skills discussed in this chapter. Use these exercises and activities to practice your helping skills and discuss ways to implement and integrate helping skills when working with college students.

ACTIVITIES FOR PRACTICE AND SKILL DEVELOPMENT

1. Videotape a helping interaction or role play and review it, paying particular attention to helping concepts and skills. In the video, you should display the characteristics and behaviors that can influence and enhance the helping process and your helping skills with an orientation toward wellness and intervention if needed. In your review with a professional peer, discuss and analyze how you demonstrated your ability to establish rapport, paraphrase, reflect the person's feeling and meaning, and assess the problem or concern. Ask yourself and discuss: Did I respond to the student's content and/or feelings? Were there any alternative response(s) I could have made? What were exhibited nonverbal behaviors/responses and what about the student's? How did I demonstrate openness to the student? What do I believe worked well in the interaction and what did not work well?

2. Role play with two other peers in which each member of the trio will take turns playing the role of (1) student, (2) student affairs professional, and (3) an observer. After deciding who will play which roles for the first rotation, the "student" will review the presenting situation for the role play (see "Role Play Scenarios" on pp. 71–75) and begin the role play with the "student affairs professional." After about 8–10 minutes of role play between the "student" and the "student affairs professional," the "observer" will provide feedback to the "student affairs professional." Next, each person will reflect on his or her roles as the "student" and the "student affairs professional." In the group discussion, try to summarize and reflect on the group's experience, including how skills were demonstrated and what was learned about the helping process. Some questions for reflection could include:
    - How did you feel reflecting feelings to the "student"?
    - How comfortable were you with the process?
    - Are there particular feelings that you have difficulty dealing with because of your own discomfort or problems?

3. For a larger group, divide into smaller groups. Each small group will develop a "case" related to a student presenting issues to a student affairs professional and establish discussion questions. After the cases are complete, groups will exchange cases with another group. Each group will discuss the case, paying special attention to how helping skills can be utilized, and respond to the discussion questions. A sample case study, *When Drama Arrives Before Your Morning Coffee*, is provided.

4. Use role play cards (see p. 71 for sample cards) with a team of two in which each individual will take turns practicing each of the helping skills

(i.e., questioning, clarification, summarizing, and paraphrasing) and providing feedback. The role play card provides a brief description of the situation and information that the "student" should convey during the role play.

Applying Your Skills: Role Play Cards

You are a college sophomore who has just broken up with his/her girlfriend/boyfriend after seven months of dating.

Convey

- You are very sad.
- You are also angry.
- It is hard to get out of the bed to attend classes.
- You are not spending as much time with friends since the break-up.
- You are not going out socially anymore because you are embarrassed.
- You are also avoiding alcohol as you are aware that it is a depressant.

You are a student who is uncomfortable with another student in one of your classes. He is always offering to walk with you to your residence hall, following you to your residence hall, and showing up at places you go. He makes you feel uneasy but you admit that he has not done anything to you directly.

Convey

- You barely talk to him in class.
- You were in a group with him for an in-class assignment.
- You have declined his request for a date.
- Your feelings are moving from uncomfortable to now being slightly afraid and unsure.

Role Play Scenarios

In groups of three, decide who will be the helper, who will role play the scenario, and who will be the observer. Rotate until each member of the group has played each role.

I. Appease to Please

You are a 19-year-old sophomore in your second semester in college of the academic year. You have been referred by a faculty member who has noticed that your academic performance has diminished. You follow up with the faculty's recommendation and visit a student affairs professional to discuss your academic performance. You have always flourished academically, completing high school in the top 1% of your graduating class and earned a full scholarship to the university. You do not think there is an issue with your academic performance and do not understand why the faculty member insists that you speak with a staff member. You are only meeting with the professional because you do not want the faculty member to hold it against you.

Offer this information only when the helper asks relevant questions or makes other appropriate response (e.g., appropriate reflection, interpretation, etc.).

- You currently possess a 3.92 GPA.
- You have a major in Biology with a minor in Kinesiology.
- A month ago, you and your boyfriend/girlfriend, whom you dated since the first semester of your freshman year (about 1 ½ years), broke up. The two of you broke up because he/she cheated on you.
- Your father died in a car accident when you were 16.
- Your mother is a high school teacher who wants to retire after you earn a college degree.
- Recently, you are crying a lot and easily, particularly at night. Therefore, you are not feeling rested when you awaken in the morning. This is impacting your ability to pay attention in class, but you believe that you are still on top of things.

II. Lonely for Love

You are a 19-year-old sophomore who has been experiencing a lot of stress for over a year. Primarily, you are always worried about your grades because you want to keep your scholarship and additionally, unlike your friends, you do not have a boyfriend/girlfriend, which makes you lonely. Recently, you have engaged in a couple of sexual relationships because you thought this would help you gain the interest of a partner. However, this has only made you sad and admittedly, you do not like the guys/girls enough to have sex with them. You feel guilty about your actions and you are now avoiding the guys/girls as well as your friends. You are now spending more time alone in your private room.

Offer this information only when the helper asks relevant questions or makes other appropriate response (e.g., appropriate reflection, interpretation, etc.).

- You only had sex with her high school boyfriend/girlfriend on your high school graduation night.

- You and your ex-boyfriend/ex-girlfriend broke up at the end of your freshman year due primarily to distance.
- You maintain a high GPA of 3.98. The scholarship dictates that you maintain at least a 3.25 GPA.

III. Wine Down

You are a senior who is currently drinking alcohol at the end of your day 4–5 times during the week to relax and relieve stress. You are experiencing more stress as you search for a job and you are anxious about the next step in your life. Your mother and father would have a glass of wine each day after work to de-stress as they talked about their day. Therefore, you are not concerned about your drinking. In spite of missing some classes and having more headaches, in your opinion, you do not see a problem with your drinking.

> **Offer this information only when the helper asks relevant questions or makes other appropriate response (e.g., appropriate reflection, interpretation, etc.).**

- You only started drinking once you came to college.
- You typically drink 3 bottles of wine per week.
- Your GPA dropped slightly from the previous semester.
- You dropped out of social organizations to focus on your job search.
- You still hang out with your friends on the weekends, but mostly at bars.

IV. Beyond the Blues

You are a 20 year old who is dealing with a lot of stress and sadness in your life. You are feeling lethargic and not answering your phone. You have a history of suicidal ideations but none at the current moment. However, recently you have thought that you would be better off if you just went to sleep and did not wake up. You feel that everything is coming down on you all at once and feel like your coping skills will not get you through this stressful time.

> **Offer this information only when the helper asks relevant questions or makes other appropriate response (e.g., appropriate reflection, interpretation, etc.).**

- During high school, you went to counseling.
- You recently had an argument with your closest friend and you two have not reconciled yet.
- You did not get accepted into your academic program of choice.

- You recently saw your ex-boyfriend/ex-girlfriend on a date with someone and he/she looked very happy. You wonder why you cannot be happy like him/her and question if something is wrong with you.
- A friend recently gave you marijuana, urging you to use it so that you can feel better. You are thinking about using it.
- You are unsure about what you would like to do after you graduate from college. In addition, your family and neighbors seem to constantly ask you about your next step after college.

V. No Need for a Boiling Rabbit

About a month ago, you went to lunch with a fellow student to discuss a course project. The two of you spoke fairly often for about a month while working on the project. However, since the project has been submitted, the student is calling you, but twice as much. He/she consistently suggests ways for the two of you to meet and expresses that he/she is disappointed or very upset when you do not accept the invitation.

Offer this information only when the helper asks relevant questions or makes other appropriate response (e.g., appropriate reflection, interpretation, etc.).

- You are not returning his/her phone calls.
- You are fearful that he/she will make false allegations against you or possibly seek revenge if you do not continue to be nice to him/her.
- During one of the latest conversations, he/she professed his/her love to you but quickly replied that he/she "was playing around."
- Since he/she has your cell phone number, he/she has started to text a lot as well.
- He/she would often show up at the same places you frequented while you were there. You have since tried to change your routine.
- You closed your personal email account and deactivated social media accounts to avoid him/her.
- When you have mentioned the situation to friends, they have dismissed it, emphasizing that "he/she is just crazy" and will give up soon.
- You find yourself often looking around to see if he/she is near.

VI. Stretched

You are a 20-year-old junior and in addition to being a full-time student and a work-study student in the Admissions Office, you are the president of your fraternity/sorority, a student ambassador for the university, and a senator in student government. You recognize that you are feeling overwhelmed but do not want to let anyone down.

Offer this information only when the helper asks relevant questions or makes other appropriate response (e.g., appropriate reflection, interpretation, etc.).

- Lately, you have been unintentionally vomiting a lot.
- You have lost some weight, but acknowledge that maybe that is a good thing.
- Your parents call you daily for life and school updates.
- Your friends expect you to always be the life of the party in social settings.
- The stress is starting to feel overwhelming.
- You love to run, but have since stopped.
- You are a first-generation college student.

CASE STUDY

When Drama Arrives Before Your Morning Coffee

Setting

Eastman University is a predominantly White public university located in a traditional college town in the South with an enrollment of 16,000 undergraduates. EU is primarily a residential campus with 10,500 students living on campus. Established student organizations on campus involve about 32% of the student population.

Facts

Gloria, a Business and Marketing major, is a 19-year-old sophomore who is a member of a group that you advise, the Eastman Student Activities Council (the ESAC), which provides programs, events, and services to the university community focusing on social, physical, intellectual, and emotional development. She joined her freshman year and was actively involved in all aspects of the organization. This year, she serves as the Coordinator of Marketing and Advertising for the group. Lately, Gloria has missed meetings and a couple of deadlines for submitting materials for advertisements.

Case

As you arrive in your office with your White Chocolate Mocha Frappuccino coffee in hand and review your calendar, you note that today, you have a 2:00 p.m. meeting scheduled with Gloria. She has canceled two meetings prior to this one and she has not responded to your emails or voicemail messages since the semester began. Gloria is responsible for coordinating the marketing campaign for an upcoming concert on April 1 and for managing her committee. However, several members of her committee convey to you that they have not heard from Gloria and are unaware of their assigned duties. Everyone agrees that this behavior seems out of character for Gloria. A couple of the students on the ESAC, Bill and Teddi, report that they have seen Gloria around a few times on campus, in class and in the residence halls and that she seems to be in a sad mood and aloof. Additionally, in the latest ESAC board meeting, many of the members state that Gloria was irritable and appeared weary.

At 8:10 a.m., you receive a phone call from Gloria asking for a date and time to reschedule due to an unexpected conflict. After looking up her class schedule and realizing from the conversation that she is next door having breakfast, you decide to casually walk over and "run into" her. Once you see Gloria, you ask if it is acceptable for you to sit and have breakfast with her and she, seeming reluctant, agrees.

From your conversation with Gloria, you find out:

> Gloria's mother is a single parent who recently began a second job as a cashier at Target (in addition to being a teacher at an elementary school) to assist with the costs of tuition. Although her mother does not complain, Gloria believes that her mother seems more tired and unhappy than before she came to college and that her mother is sacrificing too much of herself.
>
> Gloria states that she is more anxious due to the competitiveness of admission to the Marketing program at Eastman. The minimum GPA requirement for admittance is 2.85. She is worried since her GPA dropped to 2.98 the previous semester.
>
> Gloria has ceased dating and socializing because she has decided that she needs to focus solely on being admitted into the Marketing program and prove to the admissions committee that she is committed and capable. Most of her time is now spent alone studying in her room.
>
> Gloria's roommate, who is also a close friend from high school, has basically moved out and is spending most of her time outside of class with a boyfriend who lives in an apartment off campus.

You inform Gloria that you have noticed that she is not her typical happy self and is not performing at her usual level with the ESAC and that this concerns you. Gloria responds by stating that she is just nervous about getting into the program, doing well, and eventually getting a good job in the marketing field. She emphasizes several times that she has to do well. Additionally, she states that she is feeling a little hopeless at this time because she is tired of dealing with, and worrying about it all, and that on some mornings, it is difficult for her to pull herself out of bed. However, she offsets this statement by explaining that she is just tired because she stays up late and arises early each day. She also informs you that she has decided to withdraw from the ESAC.

What Do You Do Next?

After reviewing the case study, what will/can you do to:

1. Exhibit active listening skills (e.g., appropriately establishing interpersonal contact, paraphrasing, summarizing, questioning, encouraging, avoid interrupting, clarifying)?
2. Establish rapport with the student?
3. Ensure that you use appropriate nonverbal communication?
4. Strategically and simultaneously pursue multiple objectives in conversations with the student?
5. Facilitate problem solving?
6. Facilitate individual decision making and goal setting?
7. Challenge the student effectively?
8. Encourage the student effectively?
9. Suggest referral sources (e.g., other offices, outside agencies, knowledge sources) if needed?
10. If you were this student, what would you expect from the student affairs professional?

CONCLUSION

The purpose of the helping process in student affairs is to work with the students, support them, and guide them with the use of facilitation and helping skills. Through attending behaviors, including core conditions of a helping relationship as well as verbal and nonverbal communication, and listening actively attentively, you can use helping skills to meet the needs of the students you help. Helping skills provide student affairs professionals with a framework that helps them understand the helping process and how to use helping skills in a way that is congruent with their personal style of helping. Furthermore, practicing and enhancing your helping skills can help you grow as a helper in student affairs.

REFERENCES

Adler, R. B., & Rodman, G. (1997). *Understanding human communication*. Fort Worth, TX: Harcourt Brace College Publishers.

Aiello, J. R. (1987). Human spatial behavior. In D. Stokols & I. Airman (Eds.), *Handbook of environmental psychology* (Vol. 1, pp. 389–504). New York, NY: John Wiley.

Brammer, L. M., & McDonald, G. (2003). *The helping relationship: Process and skills* (8th ed.). Englewood Cliffs, NJ: Prentice-Hall.

Burkard, A., Cole, D. C., Ott, M., & Stoflet, T. (2005). Entry-level competencies of new student affairs professionals: A Delphi study. *NASPA Journal, 42*(3), 283–309.

Burns, D. D. (1980). *Feeling good: The new mood therapy*. New York, NY: HarperCollins.

Burns, D. D. (1999). *Feeling good: The new mood therapy* (3rd ed.). New York, NY: Avon Books.

Capuzzi, D., & Gross, D. R. (Eds.). (2013). *Introduction to the counseling profession* (6th ed.). New York, NY: Routledge.

Clark, M. R. (2009). Microcounseling skills. In A. Reynolds (Ed.), *Helping college students: Developing essential support skills for student affairs practice* (pp. 131–167). San Francisco, CA: Jossey-Bass.

Corey, M. S., & Corey, G. (2011). *Becoming a helper* (6th ed.). Belmont, CA: Brooks/Cole.

Cormier, S., & Hackney, H. (1999). *Counseling strategies and interventions* (5th ed.). Boston, MA: Allyn and Bacon.

Cormier, S., & Hackney, H. (2012). *Counseling strategies and interventions* (8th ed.). Boston, MA: Allyn & Bacon.

Cormier, W. H., & Cormier, L. S. (1998). *Interviewing strategies for helpers: Fundamental skills and cognitive behavioral interventions* (2nd ed.). Monterey, CA: Brooks/Cole.

Culley, S., & Bond, T. (2004). *Integrative counselling skills in action* (2nd ed.). London, England: Sage.

Dillon, J. T. (1990). *The practice of questioning*. New York, NY: Routledge.

Egan, G. (1977). *You and me: The skills of communicating and relating to others*. Monterey, CA: Wadsworth Publishing.

Egan, G. (1994). *The skilled helper: A model for systematic helping and interpersonal relating* (5th ed.). Monterey, CA: Brooks/Cole.

Egan, G. (1998). *The skilled helper: A problem-management approach to helping* (6th ed.). Pacific Grove, CA: Brooks/Cole.

Egan, G. (2014). *The skilled helper: A problem management and opportunity development approach to helping* (10th ed.). Belmont, CA: Brooks Cole/Cengage Learning.

Emerson, R. W. (1860). *The conduct of life*. North Charleston, SC: Create Space Independent Publishing Platform.

Evans, D. R., Hearn, M. T., Uhlemann, M. R., & Ivey, A. E. (2008). *Essential interviewing: A programmed approach to effective communication*. Belmont, CA: Brooks/Cole.

Gazda, G. M., Asbury, F. S., Blazer, F., Childers, W. C., Phelps, R. E., & Walters, R. P. (1995). *Human relations development: A manual for educators* (5th ed.). Boston, MA: Allyn and Bacon.

Hall, E. T. (1966). *The hidden dimension*. Garden City, NY: Doubleday.

Hill, C. E. (2009). *Helping skills: Facilitating exploration, insight, and action* (3rd ed.). Washington, DC: American Psychological Association.

Karusu, T. J. (1992). *Wisdom in the practice and psychotherapy*. New York, NY: Basic Books.

Knapp, M., & Hall, J. (2006). *Nonverbal communication in human interaction*. Belmont, CA: Thomson Wadsworth.

Lewis, T. (2014). Communications and team working in perioperative practice. *Journal of Operating Department Practitioners, 2*(3), 139–144.

Long, D. (2012). The foundations of student affairs: A guide to the profession. In L. J. Hinchliffe & M. A. Wong (Eds.), *Environments for student growth and development: Librarians and student affairs in collaboration* (pp. 1–39). Chicago, IL: Association of College & Research Libraries.

Mearns, D., & Thorne, B. (1988). *Person-centred counselling in action*. London, England: Sage.

Meier, S. T., & Davis, S. R. (2005). *The elements of counseling* (5th ed.). Belmont, CA: Thomson/Brooks/Cole.

Meier, S. T., & Davis, S. R. (2011). *The elements of counseling* (7th ed.). Belmont, CA: Thomson/Brooks/Cole.

Nelson-Jones, R. (2009). *Introduction to counseling skills: Text and activities* (3rd ed.). Thousand Oaks, CA: Sage Publications.

Neuliep, J. W. (2015). *Intercultural communication: A contextual approach* (6th ed.). Thousand Oaks, CA: Sage Publications.

Okun, B. F. (2002). *Effective helping: Interviewing and counseling techniques.* Pacific Grove, CA: Brooks/Cole.

Okun, B. F., Fried, J., & Okun, M. (1999). *Understanding diversity: A learning-as-practice primer.* Pacific Grove, CA: Brooks/Cole.

Okun, B. F., & Kantrowitz, R. E. (2015). *Effective helping: Interviewing and counseling techniques* (8th ed.). Stamford, CT: Cengage.

Parsons, R. D. (2011). *Fundamentals of the helping process* (2nd ed.). Long Grove, IL: Waveland Press, Inc. Retrieved from http://www.amazon.com/Fundamentals-Helping-Process-Richard-Parsons/dp/1577667166

Parsons, R. D., & Meyers, J. (1984). *Developing consultation skills.* San Francisco, CA: Jossey-Bass.

Pope, R. L., Reynolds, A. L., & Mueller, J. A. (2004). *Multicultural competence in student affairs.* San Francisco, CA: Jossey-Bass.

Richmond, V., & McCroskey, J. (2000). *Nonverbal behavior in interpersonal relationships.* Boston: Allyn and Bacon.

Rogers, C. R. (1956). A counseling approach to human problems. *The American Journal of Nursing, 56*(8), 994–997.

Routh, T. (2011). The importance of body language in counseling. *Vocational Guidance Quarterly, 6*(3), 134–137.

Sharpley, C. F., & Sagris, A. (1995). Does eye contact increase counsellor-client rapport? *Counselling Psychology Quarterly, 8*(2), 145–155.

Shaw, D. E. (2004). Genuineness: An overlooked element of inviting behavior. *Journal of Invitational Theory & Practice, 10*, 1047–1051.

Silverman, J., Kurtz, S., & Draper, J. (2013). *Skills for communicating with patients* (3rd ed.). New York, NY: Radcliffe Publishing.

Sommer, R. (1969). *Personal space: The behavioral basis of design.* Englewood Cliffs, NJ: Prentice-Hall.

Sue, D. W., & Sue, D. (2013). *Counseling the culturally diverse: Theory and practice* (6th ed.). Hoboken, NJ: John Wiley & Sons.

Weaver, C. H. (1972). *Human listening: Processes and behaviors.* Indianapolis, IN: Bobbs-Merrill Educational Publishing.

Wicks, R. J., Parson, R. D., & Capps, D. (Eds.). (1993). *Clinical handbook of pastoral counseling.* Mahwah, NJ: Paulist Press.

Wilkins, P. (2000). Unconditional positive regard reconsidered. *British Journal of Guidance & Counselling, 28*(1), 23–36.

Winokuer, H. R., & Harris, D. L. (2016). *Principles and practice of grief counseling* (2nd ed.). New York, NY: Springer Publishing.

Wolfgang, A. (1985). The function and importance of nonverbal behavior in intercultural counseling. In P. Pedersen (Ed.), *Handbook of cross-cultural counseling and therapy* (pp. 99–105). Westport, CT: Greenwood Press.

79

Chapter 4

Moving Toward Action

Student affairs professionals can use helping skills, discussed in Chapter 3, to assist students in exploring their emotions, gaining self-understanding, choosing positive coping strategies, and moving toward goal setting. In the helping process, students have an opportunity to explore their feelings, their situation, and their concerns. In addition, they have an opportunity to make a plan and take action and, ultimately, action is about moving toward goals.

The goal-setting process "involves narrowing the focus of the helping dialogue to a smaller range of manageable units" (Young & Chromy, 2005, p. 89). In the helping process, it requires collaboration between the helper and the helpee to develop constructive goals. For college students, setting goals and working toward them may be particularly difficult. This process requires clarity of thinking and often a great deal of self-reflection for the student and the maintenance of an affirming environment by the student affairs professional.

THINKING ABOUT MY PRACTICE

Do you believe a person can change? If so, what do you believe will motivate a person to change?

How can you involve students more in deciding upon their goals?

What skills and approaches can you use to encourage students to engage in self-reflection and self-exploration?

Are you willing to assist students in goal setting and not take it upon yourself to set the goals or tell them what to do since you have more life experience?

GOAL SETTING

One of the most important activities college students can engage in involves goal setting (Wiggins, 2015). It is important to realize that awareness does not always lead to action, even with someone who is motivated to implement changes he or she realizes are necessary and desirable. It is not enough just to be aware that change would be advantageous, it is important that students act upon this knowledge to realize the benefits that accompany the vision of how they would like things to be in the future. Before they jump in, however, and start making changes, it is very important that students develop a plan for accomplishing what they have identified as being beneficial and any serious plan must include goal setting (Dobson & Wilson, 2008).

Goals and Objectives

First, it is important to distinguish between goals and objectives when it comes to formulating an appropriate course of action (Meurisse, 2015). A goal is something an individual hopes to achieve; it does not specify how the achievement will be realized. For example, a person may have a goal of adopting a healthier lifestyle in order to better cope with the stress in his or her life. The goal is to modify his or her personal habits (e.g., eating, exercising, sleeping) in order to attain what he or she sees as being beneficial to several aspects of his or her life. Once he or she has identified this as a goal, specific actions have to be developed in order to reach that goal. These are objectives; that is the specific action steps a person will take in order to accomplish a stated goal. Again, goals are *what* a person hopes to achieve; objectives describe *how* the person is going to achieve the goal. In other words, goals are the strategic component of the planning process and objectives constitute the tactical component (Dobson & Wilson, 2008).

Once a goal has been established, an action plan usually consisting of several objectives must be developed (Dobson & Wilson, 2008). Using the previous example, if the goal is to develop a healthier lifestyle, then several objectives naturally extend from that overarching ambition. Objectives that contribute to achieving the goal might include engaging in a regular exercise schedule, developing a better diet, and establishing parameters regarding the amount of sleep needed; all of these tactical objectives work together to help realize the strategic goal. When developing goals and objectives, it is important to analyze them to make sure everything fits together logically and appropriately so that they are not ambiguous or contradictory. A legitimate goal is one that does not clash or conflict with other goals; similarly, a valid objective is one that does not interfere with, or distract from, the other objectives identified as part of the overall action plan (Wiggins, 2015). Finally, short-term goals and objectives should support and reinforce long-term goals and objectives; it is going to be challenging if they are not in perfect alignment.

"SMART" Objectives

In order for objectives to be effective in accomplishing the desired result, five conditions must be met. These requirements are often referred to as "SMART" objectives (Scott, 2014). First, the objective should be Specific—it should address, in detail, exactly what criteria will be used to determine its success. As such, it is not enough to state that one of my objectives is to lose weight. A specific objective would be to consume no more than 2,000 calories a day in order to precipitate a weight loss of one pound per week over the next eight weeks. Second, the objective must be **M**easurable. Simply stating that "I am going to engage in more exercise" is not enough. I need to know how I am going to measure the amount of exercise to engage in during each 24-hour period in order for the objective to be measurable. Third, the objective must be **A**chievable. One of the reasons many objectives fail to help meet an overall goal is because they are developed more for motivational purposes than for actual implementation. When developing objectives, it is essential they be kept within the realm of probability. An achievable objective might be to run a mile a day at a 12-minute pace for the first two weeks of an exercise plan. An unrealistic objective might be to run five miles a day at a 7-minute pace for the first two weeks.

Fourth, the objective must be **R**ealistic, which is an added dimension to the achievable consideration. Not only must it be attainable under ideal conditions, it must be achievable under more practical circumstances. When a person is surrounded by family and friends who can provide the support needed to complete an objective, it may indeed be realistic to accomplish an objective of running one mile each day. But in the absence of that support system, is it still realistic to assume that a person has the intrinsic motivation to engage in the same behavior consistently?

Finally, the objective must be **T**ime bound. All objectives must be set within a specific timeframe. For instance, instead of setting an objective to run one mile per day, a more appropriate objective might be to run five miles over the course of each week. This gives a window in which to accomplish the objective and some flexibility if unforeseen and unfavorable conditions arise during the course of the week. When establishing objectives designed to meet a goal, it is always prudent to keep the "SMART" factors in mind as they help to ensure accountability and ultimate success (Scott, 2014).

Donohue's Six-Step Process

In assisting a student with identifying desired goals and evaluating coping resources, various techniques can be used. Donohue (2011) identified six steps that student affairs professionals can use as a framework when working with college students. First, it is important to help students understand that they should be working to achieve something of genuine value to them—not just something that sounds good or could be used for ulterior purposes, such as pursuing acceptance within a particular group. The true motivation behind any goal should always be identified and analyzed. Second, a goal should not contradict any of the other goals set by the student. One of the goals of most college students is to perform academically at a level commensurate with their ability in order to eventually graduate. All other goals should be evaluated in terms of their ability to contribute to, or distract from, this primary goal. Third, goals should always take into account the integrated nature of life and thus be developed in a holistic manner. Donohue (2011) pinpointed these areas as family and home, financial and career, spiritual and ethical, physical and health, social and cultural, and mental and educational. When working with college students to develop a reasonable and balanced plan, all of these crucial areas need to be represented in the resulting set of goals and objectives.

Fourth, remind students that it is always best to state goals in affirmative terminology as opposed to more pessimistic language. As such, a desirable goal might be to engage in a healthier lifestyle instead of avoiding a lethargic and hedonistic lifestyle. How something is conceptualized and framed almost always is related to the degree of dedication and enthusiasm with which it is pursued. Fifth, students need to be encouraged to develop somewhat challenging goals as goals that are too easily achieved tend to be less apt to bring about the preferred benefits. All goals should precipitate at least a moderate degree of effort on the part of the student; nothing meaningful is ever achieved without some degree of exertion (Wiggins, 2015). At the same time, and as alluded to previously, students should never be encouraged to develop goals that require a disproportionate amount of commitment that could negatively impact other critical areas of their lives. Finally, and this is especially relevant given the technology-permeated culture that characterizes most campuses, it is important that goals be put in writing in complete detail. Not only does this process provide the student with a tangible record of what he or she has identified as significant desired outcomes, the act of committing goals to written form can be motivating in and of itself.

In sum, success is often directly related to careful and thoughtful planning and this process usually begins with identifying the desired outcomes and converting those into a manageable and realistic game plan consisting of appropriate goals and objectives (Meurisse, 2015). Student affairs professionals are in a unique position to facilitate this with the students they serve and since we all tend to learn best by example, it is important that those working with students practice good goal setting themselves. The only way to have credibility with others is to personally utilize what you expect them to implement and pursue (Wiggins, 2015).

Furthermore, in discussing and developing goals with students, the collaborative nature of the helping process in a warm environment can create a closeness between the student affairs professional and the student he or she is helping. Due to this closeness, there could be an inclination on the part of the student affairs professional to attempt developing a connection with a student by relating to his or her experience through self-disclosure and advice giving.

RELATING YOUR EXPERIENCES: SELF-DISCLOSURE AND ADVICE GIVING

In moving toward action and goal setting, there may well be times you wish to offer advice in an effort to help or reassure a student. It feels natural because with our friends and loved ones, we give advice as a way to help. Often, we share a personal experience with someone to show understanding. "For most, being helpful suggests giving advice" (Parsons, 2011, p. 4), although helping is more than advice giving.

Clark (2009, p. 158) asserted that "giving advice poses several threats to effective helping" and generally, should be avoided. Instead of giving advice, your goal as a student affairs professional is to act as a facilitator as the student finds his or her own answers, chooses solutions, and reflects on his or her choices. Furthermore, if you give advice, be cautious that students will not always listen, but might blame you if you give them advice and it fails.

Self-disclosure, sharing of your own personal experience, can provide insight and reassurance and encourage the student to talk; however, boundaries can also get blurred if you self-disclose and shift the focus of the conversation to you (Nelson-Jones, 2009) instead of on the student. Nonetheless, if self-disclosure is used, it must be used appropriately and should be limited in its use. For example, it is inappropriate to share, "When my partner cheated on me, I was so angry that I threw a brick through his car window and keyed the car." It is more appropriate to say, "A partner has cheated on me and I was very upset."

To share your wisdom effectively as a student affairs professional, thus giving the students the benefit of your experience vicariously, the following suggestions may be helpful. When sharing advice, it is important to first make sure the student wants to hear it. Not everyone wants advice, even if he or she could potentially benefit immensely from it. The student affairs professional may indeed have something valuable and relevant to offer, but if a student has not explicitly asked for advice, he or she may not be in a place to hear it at all. If a student has not asked for advice directly, the professional may be more helpful by just listening to what he or she has to say and serving more as a sounding board for the student and his or her ideas. This will give the student an opportunity to work things out on his or her own.

If, however, after actively listening to a student, the professional still feels inclined to share his or her advice, it is usually best to begin by asking if the student would be open to hearing it. If he or she is not receptive to being given advice, the most prudent course of action is always to appreciate the student's wishes and simply let it go. People who are not open to the advice of others generally do not pay much attention when provided with this information.

When a student does seem amenable to the advice being offered, the student affairs professional needs to share insights in a nonthreatening manner and in a way that is easiest for the student to hear and reflect upon. If a student seems to value frankness, for instance, the best course of action may be to state the advice directly but always in a supportive and empathetic manner. For a student who is trying to remain independent in his or her decision process, a different approach may be more beneficial. Not everyone values a straightforward communication style and may even interpret this kind of forthrightness as blunt and insensitive. With these individuals, advice has to be distributed much more tentatively, such as via a suggestion or even a question they can accept or answer more indirectly. For many students, how they respond to advice is often a reflection of the way it was parsed out to them in the past by authority figures or significant others in their lives (e.g., parents, guardians, teachers, etc.).

The student affairs professional should also be aware that a student's ego can play a significant role in determining how receptive he or she is to receiving advice from others. Some students, just like many individuals with more life experience, respond best when they perceive they are ultimately in control about what path they wish to pursue. Sometimes, the best strategy for giving advice entails simply planting a seed in the mind of someone who may not be seeing all the available options. There are many times when student affairs professionals may feel that a student is making a bad decision because of youth and inexperience and although there is usually an element of truth to this assessment, it is important to keep in mind that college is a time when most students are learning to make better decisions on their own.

VOICES FROM THE FIELD

Self-Disclosure and Advice Giving

Dr. Cheryl Wolf

Working with students can be rewarding and fun. However, at times it can feel challenging when they need guidance. You might feel tempted to give advice or share an event from your past when you encountered a similar situation. Sometimes that can help a student understand possible options and outcomes. At other times, it can hinder your ultimate goal of supporting the student. When advice is directive and not meaningful to a student, it may serve to unintentionally create distance, especially if the student has rebelled against his or her parents, teachers, or other authority figures. When self-disclosure turns the spotlight on the details of your story rather than the student's concern, it will likely create a disconnect even when that was not your purpose.

In order to share your wisdom most effectively as a student affairs professional, the following tips may help guide you. When sharing your advice, first make sure that the student wants to hear it. Not everyone wants advice, even if you feel they need it. You may have some gems to offer but if a student has not asked for your advice, he or she may not be in a place to hear it at all. If students haven't directly asked for your advice, it may be helpful to just listen and provide a sounding board for their ideas. That will give them the opportunity to work things out on their own. If after you have actively listened to them and you still feel inclined to share your advice, start by asking if they would be open to hearing it. If they do not want to hear it, take their cue and let it go. They will probably not hear what you have to say anyway. If they are open to hearing it, share it in a way that is easiest for them to hear. For someone who values frankness, you may wish to state your advice directly but in a supportive manner. For a student who is trying to remain independent in his or her decision process, it will help to deliver the advice more tentatively, as a suggestion or question that he or she can accept more easily, ultimately making his or her own choice on what path to pursue.

There are many times when you may feel that a student is young and/or making a bad decision. You may be right but college is a time where students need to learn to make better decisions on their own. Directive, parental-sounding advice can limit a student's growth. Whereas, using advice to expand their options and offer alternative ones can be more effective. For example, if Sarah, a 19-year-old female student, came to you because she has been struggling with roommate challenges, you might be tempted to give her advice, especially if you knew the roommate. If the roommate was headstrong and liked her music loud, you may be tempted to tell Sarah to study somewhere else to avoid the conflict or offer to help her confront her roommate. If Sarah has already considered these options and neither sounded helpful to her, she may dismiss them as bad advice and go talk with someone else.

However, if you asked Sarah to tell you more about her concerns and the things that she has tried, Sarah would tell you that she tried studying in the library but found it difficult because so many of the things she needed for studying were back in her room. She would also tell you that she asked her roommate to turn down the music on several occasions but the roommate just laughed at her and ignored the request. She feels that neither one of these options worked for her, which is why she came to you for help. She is open to new suggestions so offering them as questions might work easier to let her work through her additional options. You would want to validate her actions and then ask a question that helps her identify alternative options such as "You asked her to turn down the music and she dismissed you. Is there a time when you were able to ask for something when she did respond positively?" If so, "What was the difference in the way you asked or in the way she heard it?" If not, "Does she dismiss you in other ways as well?" Helping Sarah understand what has worked and what has not can help her identify potential solutions that she would be willing to try.

When talking with students, part of the advice you wish to give may be based on your own experiences. Therefore, at times you may feel like sharing a past event, how you handled things, the positive or negative consequences, and the lessons you learned from it. When used to benefit the student, self-disclosure is ethically appropriate (Remley & Herlihy, 2016) and involves sharing information about yourself and/or your experiences in order to improve rapport and maintain a positive connection with the student. However, to keep self-disclosure meaningful, the focus must remain on the student and quickly relate back to his or her issue. To keep it ethical, it must not be used to meet your own personal needs for understanding or intimacy (Remley & Herlihy, 2016).

Effective helping skills include good communication and valuable self-disclosure to develop trust (Kline, 2003) and make the discussions meaningful to a student. Self-disclosure should only be used briefly to help illustrate a point; it should not redirect the conversation to where the focus is on you. The student will likely get frustrated that the conversation turned to your story rather than his or her problem and then will often disconnect from you because the student cannot see how your story is relevant to his or her issue. The student may assume that you are not really listening to him or her. Therefore, keep the self-disclosure relevant and brief, and then bridge it back to the student's issue before you lose his or her interest. For example, in Sarah's roommate issue, if you had a similar issue with a friend or roommate during your college years, you might be tempted to share that. After listening to Sarah's concern and helping her identify the potential problem, you may realize that her roommate dismissed her because Sarah was too soft spoken and not heard over the music or Sarah joked so much about the music that her roommate didn't take the request seriously, which is why she laughed and ignored the request.

If you had an experience in college where you were joking and sarcasm made people dismiss your serious requests, that could be helpful to share because it is relevant to her situation. After you listened to her, you might share your story, relate it to her, and then help her identify actionable steps to solve her dilemma. An example could be "I remember I was very sarcastic and liked to joke in college. Consequently, I had friends that never knew if I was joking or serious with them. One time I really needed them to take me seriously and they would not; it was very frustrating. It was a time when my mom went into the hospital and I needed a ride to the bus station. I was upset and concerned but they thought it was a prank so I ended up getting mad, yelling at them, and showed them my texts to let them know I was serious. It was not the best way to handle it because they got mad at my conflicting signals and I felt bad about the entire incident. After that, we talked and decided that I would cut back on my sarcasm and be more direct when I wanted to make a serious request. It solved most of the communication problems we had so I was grateful I learned from that experience. I wonder if your roommate doesn't take your requests seriously because you joke a lot. Do you think it would help if you were more direct and serious with her about this issue, letting her know when it is ok to listen to her loud music and when you need her to turn it down so you can study? How do you think she might react to your serious request?"

In this example, using self-disclosure to explain your problem, solution, and how it relates to her concern is an effective way to share a personal story but not turn the attention to you for more than a brief moment. It may also be more effective than not sharing your story at all; by hearing that you successfully navigated a similar situation, she may be more open to hearing how you overcame your challenges and be willing to try to overcome her own through using some of your ideas. However, Remley and Herlihy (2016) caution that not all topics are considered appropriate for disclosure; they warn against sharing your "current stressors, personal fantasies or dreams, and . . . social or financial circumstances" (p. 233).

Hearing how analogous challenges have been successfully navigated by others can be instructional and even motivating; moreover, these exchanges—if handled with genuine care and concern—can also serve to strengthen the trust of the relationships student affairs professionals have with students.

Applications to Student Affairs

Using advice to serve as a mechanism to expand a student's options and provide him or her with more suitable alternatives can be valuable and effective. Remember, the student affairs professional and the student are at two different places in life with respect to how they conceptualize and respond to the troublesome situations life inevitably presents to them. What is obvious to the professional may make very little sense to the student. Moreover, most students have a natural inclination to take whatever advice given them by older individuals with a healthy dose of skepticism (Jones & Abes, 2013). This is the essence of the learning process and allows students to expand their understanding of the problem-solving process while retaining personal responsibility and a sense of ownership when the ultimate solution is identified and implemented. Most interpersonal conflicts do have a win-win resolution, but to find it often requires significant effort and a willingness to think outside limitations that tend to be inherently linked to where one is developmentally (Brams & Taylor, 1999).

In the goal-setting process, the student should engage in self-exploration, a process that usually leads to new insights. Self-exploration strategies can be utilized to encourage students to be self-aware, contemplating what is occurring internally without judgment or questioning, and to engage in introspection as they set their goals. A discussion follows about two techniques that can be used by student affairs professionals to facilitate the self-exploration process for students, mindfulness and therapeutic photography.

SELF-EXPLORATION STRATEGY: THE PRACTICE OF MINDFULNESS

Mindfulness is a process of being fully present in the moment, suspended from judgment or correction and starting with a simple awareness of one's body and thoughts (Kabat-Zinn, 2003), without attachment to a particular point of view, resulting in freedom from automatic, habitual views of the self and others (Martin, 1997). The potential benefits of engaging in the practice of mindfulness for college students are enormous, specifically in working with students to objectively explore their emotions, find meaning, and formulate potential actions.

Mindfulness is the awareness that emerges through paying attention on purpose in the present moment while nonjudgmental observation is increased and automatic responding is reduced (Kabat-Zinn, 2003). Mindfulness practice gently counters the mind's inherent need to evaluate experiences as positive or negative. Instead, the mind begins to observe experiences with an attitude of curiosity, suspends judgment without worry of the future or regret of the past, and this improves mental clarity. Mindfulness is also associated with a range of psychological and physical health benefits (Mehranfar, Younesi, & Banihashem, 2012). It can be cultivated through formal (e.g., yoga and sitting meditation) or informal practice (e.g., noticing the sounds of water and the scent of the soap during a shower). Skills associated with mindfulness have been shown to be effective in increasing relaxation and coping skills when faced with stressful situations (McKay, Wood, & Brantley, 2007). Cashwell, Bentley, and Bigbee (2007) suggested that mindfulness practice may be beneficial for enhancing an individual's capacity for attention and concentration, strengthening ability to accept the present moment, possessing a greater self-awareness and compassion, and increasing one's capacity for self-regulation.

VOICES FROM THE FIELD

Using Mindfulness to Help College Students

Lacretia Dye

As a licensed psychologist, Yoga Calm Instructor and Trainer, and Adult Yoga Instructor, I often use an integrative approach to wellness, combining counseling and yoga/meditation techniques that encourage an integrative health, which includes mindfulness. I sincerely believe in the heart, mind, and body connection that allows you to come back into your body, your breath, and your immediate sensate reality. In helping others, individuals can be taught how to "be still and still moving." When I work with students and present to student affairs professionals, I stress the benefits of mindfulness practice as a means to help them manage the normal stresses of life effectively and explore their mind and body in the present moment.

Mindfulness practice with college students can be adapted to fit the unique experiences of college life. Coaching students to use mindfulness techniques can be life giving and life changing. It can help a student embrace reality and the present moment, instead of referring to the past or to the future. Although there are a multitude of techniques that may be implemented when learning to experience mindfulness, I suggest that student affairs professionals include the following activities to engage students in self-exploration when working with students.

Applying Your Skills: Breath Work

Breath work is the heart of mindfulness practice. Breathing patterns have such a profound effect on a student's general health as well as mental well-being. Gillen and Gillen (2007) report that "breathing interacts with and affects the cardiovascular, neurological, gastrointestinal and muscular systems" (p. 47). Often symptoms of stress, disease, fear, and anxiety can lead to unhealthy breathing habits. Irregular breathing patterns such as breathing very rapidly, jerky, or high in the chest can activate the fight-or-flight response, resulting in anxiety and chronic overstimulation of the sympathetic nervous system.

By contrast, the intentional act of slowing one's breathing and relaxing muscles can calm the nervous system, lower heart rate and blood pressure, and change the body's stress response (NurrieStearns & NurrieStearns, 2010). Through breath work, students can learn to slow their nervous system, develop self-control, and connect with their bodies and feelings.

Skill Building

In the world of higher education, it is common to come across a student that feels prepared for an exam but leaves the scene feeling anxious, worried, and stressed. As a university professor, at the close of each course exam, I communicate the following to students, "Now that you have completed the exam, the most obvious and immediate way to feel less anxious is to change the way you are breathing." I demonstrate the following technique and then do it with the students.

1. Become aware of your breathing pattern.
2. Breathe in through your nose (mouth closed).
3. Relax. Make sure the abdominal muscles are not overly tense, which can interfere with the action of the primary breathing muscle, the diaphragm.
4. Now blow the air out through your mouth, as if you were blowing out a candle.
5. Again, breathe in through your nose and slow the breath cycle, particularly the exhalation.
6. Pause at the end of each inhalation and exhalation.

Guided Mental Relaxations

Guided mental relaxations are a form of mindfulness. These activities can be described as paying attention on purpose with an affectionate awareness and a lack of judgment. Listening with their eyes closed, students practice receiving information in an unprejudiced, nonjudgmental manner. These experiences contribute to the development of focused concentration and creative thinking abilities as well as enable clarity of perception and more balanced emotional responses to situations. In guided relaxations coupled with low lighting and soft, soothing music, I have seen the hearts, minds, and bodies of students relax.

Skill Building

- Scripted Relaxations: One of my favorite activities to use when working with anxious or nervous college-age students is scripted relaxations. Many times students have forgotten how to connect with their playful, imaginative self. Through the use of stories, books (often children's fantasy books), or poems, I invite students to imagine or visualize peaceful, restful, or joyful places or situations. When using scripted imagery, an item that has plenty of visual imagery should be used. During the script reading, it is important to go slowly to give students time to process the images and situations. Taking the time to pause after the imagery and tuning into student breathing allows me to become more aware of the "body time" needed by students. One excellent resource is the book *Yoga Nidra for Complete Relaxation and Stress Relief* by Julie Lusk (2004). A simple "relaxation script" search on the Internet can produce a variety of relaxation journeys as well.
- Personalized Relaxations: There are times where I have created short journeys that include relevant content from the student's life or short impromptu stories. When working with a small group of students from Housing and Residence Life, I invited students to identify locations, animals, people, and objects to incorporate within the short journeys. Sample images to weave into guided journeys could include:
    - riding a dolphin through the ocean;
    - enjoying a quiet walk in a dense field of magical flowers; or
    - entering a campus building where all the people are kings and queens.
- One-minute explorations can enable students an easy transition from one stressful situation to a more relaxed state of mind (i.e., confrontation with a roommate, right before a difficult conversation with an instructor). Students are able to focus their minds on positive thoughts and emotions as well as experience a brief minute of stillness. Student affairs professionals can help spark students' imaginations by offering ideas of where they might mentally go:
    - go to your favorite spot in your house and take three deep belly breaths;
    - remember a favorite time with a friend or family member;
    - imagine the kind of day you would like to have today; and
    - think of three compliments you can give your professors or classmates.

Application to Student Affairs

The pressures facing today's college students are substantively different from those of previous generations for a variety of factors, including financial, technological, and social considerations (Iarovici, 2014). Incorporating mindfulness activities, whether in small or large ways, can contribute to mental, emotional, and physical self-care, which has been growing as a need on the contemporary college campus for the past several decades (Amanda, 2015). The practice of mindfulness has the potential of giving students an opportunity to use a framework to engage in self-exploration. Student affairs professionals can use the mindfulness techniques to foster self-exploration and help students guide themselves to finding out more about themselves, their decisions, and actions at that moment. These techniques can be used in discussing issues ranging from anxiety and stress to academic and relationship problems.

SELF-EXPLORATION STRATEGY: EXPRESSIVE ARTS

Expressive therapies are defined as "action therapies" (Weiner, 1999) because they are action-oriented methods that promote the exploration of issues and their thoughts and feelings. Self-expression, such as painting or movement, can recapitulate past experiences and even be cathartic for some (Malchiodi, 2005). Expressive arts are the use of techniques that employ a variety of mediums to enhance one's well-being. For example, the American Art Therapy Association (as cited in Malchiodi, 2005) contends that art therapy uses art media, images, and the creative process, and respects responses to the created products as reflections of development, abilities, personality, interests, concerns, and conflicts; a means of reconciling emotional conflicts, fostering self-awareness, developing social skills, managing behavior, solving problems, reducing anxiety, aiding reality orientation, and increasing self-esteem.

Knill, Barba, and Fuchs (1995) reported that while all of the expressive therapies involve action, each form of expressive therapy has its unique properties and roles depending on its application and objectives. An emerging area of expressive arts is the use of photography to facilitate therapeutic intervention and facilitate healthy development. This trend has been augmented by the proliferation of smartphones with built-in cameras; virtually all college students are tethered to their mobile devices continually these days, as such no special equipment is needed to utilize the technique.

VOICES FROM THE FIELD

Using Expressive Arts for Self-Expressing and Self-Reflection

Imelda N. Bratton

As a Professional Clinical Counselor and Play Therapist, I often integrate expressive arts into the counseling process. An expressive arts project can facilitate student empowerment through self-expression and if used in a group setting, a shared art experience can promote community building. There is a broad choice of media that can be used in expressive arts activities. One activity that I use, therapeutic photography, is a constructive avenue for self-exploration and self-change through the use of images or pictures. Images can provide context and also a way for the student to reflect on specific moments of time that were meaningful.

Therapeutic Photography

The experience of sharing and discussing images can provide context and also a way for the student to reflect on specific moments of time that were meaningful. A student can use therapeutic photography for self-exploration, self-change, or for personal pleasure. The intent is to have students reflect on the personal thoughts and feelings as well as increase their self-knowledge, awareness, and well-being. Students are given an opportunity to reflect on the pictures as well as discuss current feelings or thoughts. The emphasis is on the memories or feelings of the students rather than the image itself. Furthermore, there is no interpretation placed on the images. The intent is to have the student reflect on the personal thoughts and feelings instead of being analyzed by the helper.

When I use a therapeutic photography activity with adults in a college setting, either with an individual student or with a group, the focus is on the student learning more about himself or herself and how the student sees the world. Although a therapeutic photography experience can be facilitated by another person, it is not required. You can ask a student to engage in an expressive art activity independently and meet with you at a later date to process and discuss.

Processing questions help provide a focused conversation to help the student reflect and learn a positive coping strategy to utilize when he or she is experiencing stress or self-reflecting. Furthermore, I allow time for students to share additional thoughts or feelings. Some processing questions that I use when talking with the student include the following:

- What does this picture mean to you?
- What do you like about this image?
- What did you feel when the picture was taken?
- What do you feel now as you look back and reflect on this moment?
- What would you like to change about this moment?
- What would you like to remain the same?

Therapeutic Selfies Activity

Selfies are less threatening as this is a common act used in social media or messaging. I ask each student to spend about 10 minutes taking a selfie and invite the students to take selfies that represent how they feel. I allow them to take as many pictures as necessary, representing different emotions. Students choose how they want to represent their emotions as well as what they want to include in the selfie. After students have completed the selfies, I have them select a few images to share and allow time for the

93

students to discuss the image, what feelings they were representing, and what it means to them. Students are asked what they would like to change and what they would need to do for the change to happen. Goals and potential plans could be explored.

In a group setting, some students may be embarrassed, so I always encourage them to take photos in a place that is comfortable, such as the hallway or away from others. Afterward, students may pair up and take pictures of each other. I have encouraged students to pose the person or direct the person to do different movements while taking pictures. This can allow the student taking the image to show a different image than what a selfie might capture. Students seem to enjoy comparing their selfies to the images that the other person captured. Many times the selfie is different than the other images, which can lead to insightful discussions. There have been times where students have taken up to 30 minutes creating their selfies and taking images of each other. It really seems to be a valuable activity as students seem to be surprised how they view themselves versus how others see them.

One person in particular that I worked with in the past did not have much self-confidence, and her selfie only included a small portion of her face. As she looked at the other images captured by the other student, she saw how the other student viewed her; not as lacking self-confidence, but a strong person. They had a chance to talk about the differences and it was a valuable experience that she was able to visually see and hear how she was perceived.

Reflecting on Images Activity

With this activity, I ask the students to view images or pictures stored in their camera, smartphone, or social media accounts, select several images that stand out to them, and allow time for the students to discuss the image, what it means to them, and to share any additional thoughts or feelings of when the image was taken and how they feel about it in the present moment. Even though the students may not fully disclose their emotions or thoughts during the conversation, they may continue to reflect internally on their own after the conversation. I consider the fact that some students may not be comfortable showing an image or picture they selected.

It is not necessary for me to view the image as the benefit of the activity is gained through the process the student experiences. What is important is that I listen to the story or description that the student shares before making any assumptions. In teaching others about using expressive arts activities, I always suggest that if you have a concern regarding what the student shares, then refer the student to a clinical mental health counselor for follow-up.

While also encouraging students to share additional thoughts or feelings, some processing questions that I use when talking with a student after the selfie activity include:

- What was it like to take a selfie to show your emotions?
- What was difficult about the activity?
- What was easy for you?

- As you look at your selfie, what stands out to you?
- How do you think this selfie compares to how you see yourself or how you think others see you?
- What would you like to change about this selfie?
- What would you like to stay the same?
- What would you like to say to your selfie? Consider what you think would help the person in the selfie.
- What would you tell the person in the selfie to do to help things get better?
- What would you tell the person in the selfie to help keep things going well?

By allowing students to tell their story with photos, I am providing an opportunity for them to be their best and most authentic selves. It is important that each student feels validated, listened to, and taken seriously.

Application to Student Affairs

Working with college students can provide opportunities to discuss emotional issues and provide helpful interventions. Interventions using expressive art techniques can promote positive coping strategies such as emotional regulation and reflection (Malchiodi, 2005). Using a creative approach, such as expressive arts, student affairs professionals can help students work through immediate feelings as well as identify a positive coping strategy. Furthermore, being able to do a simple expressive arts intervention may help the student gain insight and be a starting point to considering and exploring counseling, as even the thought of needing counseling can be stressful for students.

Selfies and taking pictures have become increasingly common in today's society. With the increased use of social media and smartphones, using selfies with students is a way to connect and provide a nonthreatening intervention. Student affairs professionals can easily perform expressive arts interventions to assist in self-awareness and promote positive coping strategies.

What's more is that minimal words are required as it is the act of the creation that has restorative value as opposed to the final product in expressive art. It is important that the focus of the activity be maintained on the process and not the outcome. Moreover, students that have limited English or verbal ability may benefit from this type of intervention as the expectation to describe their thoughts or feelings in detail is not necessary.

CONCLUSION

College life can be filled with excitement, confusion, social opportunities, autonomy, and emotions ranging from happiness to loneliness and fear (Hunt & Eisenberg, 2010). The appropriate and purposeful use of self-disclosure and

95

advice giving, goal setting, together with interventions that promote self-reflection, such as the practice of mindfulness and employing expressive arts in the form of therapeutic photography, can all help students objectively analyze their lives and situations as well as develop more effective coping strategies that can help them have a more productive and satisfactory collegiate experience.

REFERENCES

Amanda, G. (2015). *Mental health and student conduct issues on the college campus: A reading.* Prospect, CT: Biographical Publishing Company.

Brams, S., & Taylor, D. (1999). *The win-win solution: Guaranteeing fair shares to everybody.* New York, NY: W. W. Norton and Company.

Cashwell, C. S., Bentley, D. P., & Bigbee, A. (2007). Spirituality and counselor wellness. *The Journal of Humanistic Counseling, Education and Development, 46*(1), 66–81.

Clark, M. R. (2009). Microcounseling skills. In A. Reynolds (Ed.), *Helping college students: Developing essential support skills for student affairs practice* (pp. 131–167). San Francisco, CA: Jossey-Bass.

Dobson, M., & Wilson, S. (2008). *Goal setting: How to create an action plan and achieve your goals.* New York, NY: AMACOM (American Management Association).

Donohue, G. (2011). *Goal setting: Powerful written goals in seven easy steps.* Top Achievement. Retrieved from http://topachievement.com/goalsetting.html

Gillen, L., & Gillen, J. (2007). *Yoga calm for children: Educating heart, mind, and body.* Portland, OR: Three Pebbles Press.

Hunt, J., & Eisenberg, D. (2010). Mental health problems and help-seeking behavior among college students. *Journal of Adolescent Health, 46*, 3–10.

Iarovici, D. (2014). *Mental health issues and the university student.* Baltimore, MD: Johns Hopkins University Press.

Jones, S., & Abes, E. (2013). *Identity development of college students: Advancing frameworks for multiple dimensions of identity.* San Francisco, CA: John Wiley & Sons.

Kabat-Zinn, J. (2003). Mindfulness-based interventions in context: Past, present, and future. *Clinical Psychology: Science and Practice, 10*(2), 144–156.

Kline, W. B. (2003). *Interactive group counseling and therapy.* Upper Saddle River, NJ: Merrill Prentice Hall.

Knill, P., Barba, H. N., & Fuchs, M. N. (1995). *Minstrels of soul: Intermodal expressive therapy.* Toronto, Canada: Palmerston Press.

Lusk, J. (2004). *Yoga nidra for complete relaxation and stress relief.* Oakland, CA: Harbinger Publications.

Malchiodi, C. A. (2005). Expressive therapies: History, theory, and practices. In C. A. Malchiodi (Ed.), *Expressive therapies* (pp. 1–15). New York, NY: The Guilford Press.

Martin, J. R. (1997). Mindfulness: A proposed common factor. *Journal of Psychotherapy Integration, 7*(4), 291–312.

McKay, M., Wood, J. C., & Brantley, J. (2007). *Dialectical behavior therapy skills workbook: Practical DBT exercises for learning mindfulness, interpersonal effectiveness, emotion regulation, & distress tolerance.* Oakland, CA: New Harbinger Publications, Inc.

Mehranfar, M., Younesi, J., & Banihashem, A. (2012). Effectiveness of mindfulness-based cognitive therapy on reduction of depression and anxiety symptoms in mothers of children with cancer. *Iranian Journal of Cancer Prevention, 5*(1), 1–9.

Meurisse, T. (2015). *Goal setting: The ultimate guide to achieving goals that truly excite you.* Seattle, WA: Amazon Digital Services.

Nelson-Jones, R. (2009). *Introduction to counseling skills: Text and activities* (3rd ed.). Thousand Oaks, CA: Sage Publications.

NurrieStearns, M., & NurrieStearns, R. (2010). *Yoga for anxiety: Meditation and practices for calming the body and mind.* Oakland, CA: New Harbinger Publications, Inc.

Parsons, R. D. (2011). *Fundamentals of the helping process* (2nd ed.). Long Grove, IL: Waveland Press, Inc.

Remley, T. P., & Herlihy, B. (2016). *Ethical, legal, and professional issues in counseling* (5th ed.). Upper Saddle River, NJ: Pearson.

Scott, S. (2014). *S.M.A.R.T. goals made simple: 10 steps to master your personal and career goals.* San Bernardino, CA: CreateSpace Independent Publishing Platform.

Weiner, D. (1999). *Beyond talk therapy: Using movement and expressive techniques in clinical practice.* Washington, DC: American Psychological Association.

Wiggins, D. (2015). *Goal setting: 21 days to achieving life changing goals and being happy happy happy.* San Bernardino, CA: CreateSpace Independent Publishing Platform.

Young, M. E., & Chromy, S. (2005). *Exercises in the art of helping* (3rd ed.). Upper Saddle River, NJ: Pearson.

Chapter 5

Conflict Resolution

If two people always agree, one of them is unnecessary.

Robert Frost

Dealing with conflict was an almost constant part of my (third author) daily existence when I was a residence hall director. There were conflicts between roommates, conflicts between staff members, and conflicts between students trying to maintain relationships. There were also conflicts between supervisors and staff members and as well as conflicts between groups of students. There were conflicts with the administration, conflicts with the community, and conflicts on the intramural fields. In short, the typical college campus is a hotbed for conflict—not unlike the greater society in which it is situated.

It did not take long to figure out that one of my primary responsibilities as a student affairs professional was to help resolve all kinds of conflicts in all kinds of situations. Like the Geico commercial says, "It's what you do!" One of the more enlightening things discovered along the way was that life experience really is the best teacher. As a young professional just starting out in the field, I was not very proficient at conflict resolution. I made a lot of mistakes. I sometimes caused more conflict than I resolved. But I learned from my mistakes and eventually, I got better at diagnosing the root cause of the conflicts I encountered.

Like most everything else in life, conflict resolution is both an art and a science (Lechman, 2007). You have to develop your own style of intervening in conflict situations to achieve the best possible result for everyone involved. Your style is a combination of many factors, including your personality, your background, and your preferences. Those who are proficient at dealing with conflict tend to be able to adapt their approach based on the circumstances surrounding each individual situation. There is no one best way to resolve conflict; each episode must be treated as unique and your strategy must be tailored to the characteristics of the situation at hand.

In conflict resolution, you also need to facilitate effective communication using attending skills and microskills (discussed in Chapter 3). Active listening skills are particularly important for building positive relationships with the students in the conflict (Barsky, 2014). Think about how often you hear "you are not listening to me" when people are in a debate or argument. Understanding comes through listening, therefore, attending skills and microskills are important for facilitating the interaction between the students in conflict since they can be encouraged to use listening skills to build trust and comprehend each other's perspective. Active listening and attending skills can also encourage the students to open up, demonstrate understanding, and clarify any misunderstandings. However, not all listening promotes effective communication since a connection is almost always related to a genuine desire to understand what others are trying to communicate. You should note that "Listening, even if focused and energetic, that is mostly motivated by desire to debate, argue, convince, or discount, is likely to lead to further conflict and distance" (Mayer, 2000, p. 125). In addition, you can use attending and microskills to assist the students in the conflict to get to the root of the issue.

It is important to remember that dealing with people is different from dealing with things (Harper, 2004). When working with a technical problem, it is often beneficial to focus on its source. If you know why your car will not start, then you have a pretty good idea of what needs to be fixed. When dealing with people, however, experience has shown that the focus must be on solutions. In many instances, knowing why a conflict exists brings you no closer to resolving it. Still, a realistic understanding of the underlying dynamics of a conflict situation helps you to choose the best course of action.

CONFLICT RESOLUTION AND MATURITY LEVEL

Any serious discussion of conflict resolution must take into account developmental considerations. How an individual goes about trying to resolve the conflicts that inevitably arise in life, as well as how the individual responds to the efforts by others to assist in resolving these disagreements, is inherently linked to his or her level of maturity. Most college students, as well as many of your staff members and colleagues, tend to be at one of three developmental stages:

- Adolescence—late teens to early 20s.
- Early adulthood—early 20s to early 30s.
- Middle adulthood—early 30s to mid-40s.

As cognitive neuroscience has demonstrated, the prefrontal cortex continues to develop in most individuals until around the ages of 25 to 27 (Jensen & Nutt, 2015), which has profound implications for how complex interactions, such as those involved in resolving either interpersonal or professional conflicts, are conceptualized and acted upon. The way someone in his or her teens or 20s deals with the differences the person encounters with others is often substantively different from how an older person tends to respond in a similar situation.

Most scientists agree that adolescence is divided into three stages: early adolescence, which lasts from ages 12 to 14, middle adolescence, which encompasses ages 15 to 17, and late adolescence, which extends from age 18 to the mid- or later 20s (Siegel, 2015). Since human development is inevitably linked to a variety of factors, these categorical distinctions are somewhat generic and do not necessarily correspond to the indicated age groupings in a rigid manner. As anyone familiar with developmental theories knows, every individual should be seen as unique and, as such, the maturity level may or may not conform to the norms for his or her chronological age.

For instance, it is interesting to note that research has found most of the accidents caused by younger drivers are due to poor judgment, bad decision making, and a lack of maturity—not just a lack of experience behind the wheel (Kahn & Lacorte, 2013). Expertise at driving increases not only as a function of experience; it also increases as the person becomes more capable of exercising sound judgment and more cogent decision making. Conflict resolution, in a fundamental sense, is all about action and reaction based on the perceived motives of all those involved in the equation. If the part of the brain responsible for helping an individual see the world in a more comprehensive and integrated way is not fully developed, it is unrealistic to expect the person to respond in a manner characteristic of someone who is more mature and, as such, more in tune with how the actions of one person tend to affect the actions of others.

The important consideration here is that an individual's understanding of the nature of relationships, and the behavior that is manifest as a result of that understanding, is connected to the development of the individual's brain in general and the prefrontal cortex in particular. The prefrontal cortex is responsible for a person's emotional maturity, self-image, and judgment, as is the hormonal activity which accompanies those characteristics (Jensen & Nutt, 2015). The approach to conflict resolution taken must take into account where someone is on the spectrum of emotional and rational development. What may appear to be an entirely logical strategy for resolving differences to someone in his or her 30s and beyond may not be so clear-cut to someone in his or her teens or 20s. The concepts and applications that follow should, therefore, be considered and implemented judiciously within the context of these basic assumptions about where someone may be in his or her developmental evolution.

THINKING ABOUT MY PRACTICE

What has been your experience when trying to resolve the conflicts that inevitably arise between incoming students and their older, more experienced counterparts?

How might knowing about differences in maturity level between students affect your approach to dealing with them?

Do you sometimes have expectations of students, staff members, or colleagues that might be unrealistic given their level of maturity?

TODAY'S COLLEGE STUDENTS AND CONFLICT

As we will see, conflict resolution has many facets, especially on the contemporary college campus. In order to effectively resolve disagreements that involve college students, it is important to understand the characteristics that define this particular generation, especially the so-called traditional age students. As the median age of those attending college continues to rise, and as we noted in the last section, it is important to be aware that these characteristics are also evolving in conjunction with the changes that can be anticipated as the population becomes more mature. Successful attempts at conflict resolution tend to always take into account the attributes of those involved in the process, so it is important to examine some of the more defining qualities of today's students. Compared to previous generations, contemporary college students as well as many of your staff members and colleagues tend to be digital natives with an expectation of immediate gratification; have different expectations regarding confidentiality and privacy; be more comfortable multitasking than single tasking; and have a different conceptualization of adulthood.

- **They tend to be digital natives with an expectation of immediate gratification.** The current generation of college students comprises "digital natives" who have come to expect that their needs will be met in an almost immediate timeframe. Indeed, instant gratification has been their collective mantra for most of their lives, fueled by parents and guardians who catered to their every need with an unprecedented sense of urgency. As a group, contemporary college students are used to having their needs met almost instantaneously, including the need to have any conflicts they experience resolved immediately and often without too much investment on their part (Levine & Dean, 2012). As such, they are often ill equipped to engage in the problem-solving and decision-making processes that characterize successful conflict resolution.
- **They tend to have different expectations regarding confidentiality and privacy.** Today's college students do not tend to value confidentiality to the same degree as their counterparts from years

past; they are used to having every detail of their lives documented and on display through various social media platforms (Strayhorn, 2012). They define privacy differently than members of other generations and this can cause difficulties when it comes to the resolution of differences between their peers, coworkers, and supervisors. Many conflicts, especially those that are interpersonal nature, are best handled in a sensitive manner, where the discourse is limited to those directly involved in, or affected by, the disagreement. This is challenging when opinions, feelings, and perceptions are routinely broadcast through Facebook, Twitter, Instagram, and a whole host of still-emerging social media outlets.

- **They tend to be more comfortable multitasking than single tasking.** Modern-day college students are much more adept at multitasking than was the case with their predecessors, which often further complicates the conflict resolution process (Bercovitch & Jackson, 2009; Fletcher, Najarro, & Yelland, 2015). They grew up in a world that required them to focus on many different inputs simultaneously in a way that would have been overwhelming to previous generations simply because most of those inputs did not exist until the advent of the digital communications revolution. In order to effectively resolve differences in perceptions, observations, and positions, however, the individuals experiencing these differences must be able to isolate and prioritize the issues and other considerations related to the conflict in a focused manner. It is not unusual to find students engaging in several activities at the same time they are also trying to resolve a significant conflict with either their peers or their supervisors. The inability to deal with the issues related to a conflict in a sequential and attentive fashion can be frustrating for those attempting to assist them with its resolution and this can often generate even more conflict.

- **They tend to have a different conceptualization of adulthood.** As society has become more sophisticated and consumer-driven, definitions of what it means to be an adult have also experienced a metamorphosis (Strayhorn, 2012). In previous generations, expectations regarding where a person should be at certain milestones in his or her life were often unspoken but generally recognized as being somewhat universal. In many quarters, young adults were expected to graduate high school, move straight into the workforce or go to college, get married, start a family, and be on their way to a successful career by their mid-20s. These expectations have changed dramatically, driven in part by changing societal norms and less-than-ideal economic realities. It is not unusual these days for students to move back in with their parents after graduation and even defer marriage and/or starting a family for several years, which has the net effect of extending their adolescence. As a student recently put it, "Growing older is mandatory, growing up is optional."

The shift in what it means to assume what in the past would have been considered adult responsibilities has profound implications for how younger individuals approach conflict resolution (Levine & Dean, 2012). Those who are older tend to attach more significance to developing good conflict resolution skills as they see the innate connection between those skills and their ability to successfully attain important life goals. However, in the absence of similar life goals, the importance of this skill set becomes somewhat marginalized. If you have not had a great deal of personal experience resolving conflicts, or if you have always had your conflicts taken care of by others, then you likely do not see the ability to deal effectively with disagreements as a particularly useful competency and, as such, you are probably not very good at it. The important point here is that today's college students tend to have a decidedly different life orientation than members of other generations; this manifests itself in a variety of tangible ways that can be perplexing to those who do not understand, or cannot relate to, the value system of these individuals. It is not that college students do not care about conflict resolution; rather it is that they often see it in a completely different light than their supervisors, who have not shared their backgrounds and formative experiences. If you are working with college students, it is your responsibility to do everything you can to appreciate where they are developmentally, how they got there, and what modifications you need to make to your own worldview in order to accommodate their needs with respect to dealing with conflict.

THE CAUSES OF CONFLICT

There are many causes of conflict affecting college students, new professionals, and your colleagues; these include:

- Practical considerations/preferences; situational factors.
- A lack of trust; more fundamental considerations.

You do not have to look very far to see why conflict is a defining characteristic of most college campuses. Conflict is a necessary prerequisite for growth and development and a key ingredient in the educational process. Personality differences can often produce conflict—even between people who are genuinely focused on getting along with each other (Mayer, 2012). We all have distinct personalities that either make it easier for us to associate with other individuals or make it more challenging. This is why most professional development and staff training activities often include some type of personality assessment. Understanding your own personality is a key factor in understanding the personalities of others and, as such, one of the necessary prerequisites for most successful relationships.

Other causes of conflicts include schedules, differing priorities, competition for resources, technical opinions, performance trade-offs, and administrative procedures (Furlong, 2005). Think about the last time you were involved in a serious disagreement with someone. Chances are good the conflict was either initiated or augmented by one (or a combination) of these factors. Conflicts related to scheduling, for instance, are commonplace on a college campus where staffing is a perpetual headache. How many times have you found yourself in a heated debate because your priorities were different from those of students, coworkers, or your supervisor? Administrative procedures, in and of themselves, are conflict-producing. The more hoops you have to jump through to get something accomplished, the more conflict you can expect to encounter.

Finally, a lack of trust can be a huge cause of conflicts as disagreements cannot be successfully managed in an atmosphere of distrust (Sande & Johnson, 2011). Distrust causes people not to share information or ideas. Relationships, regardless of whether we are talking about romantic relationships or supervisor–supervisee relationships, are difficult to maintain without an underlying foundation of trust. For example, success in group decision making, which is essential to effective teamwork, depends on utilizing the creativity of each member to solve problems and overcome obstacles. Additionally, unlocking creativity is contingent on providing a climate of trust where individuals do not fear the consequences that may result from sharing information or ideas.

In order to deal with a lack of trust, its causes must be understood and minimized. Distrust results from the fears we all experience from time to time and includes fears related to reprisal (better watch your back), failure (I think I'm being set up), providing information (why do you want to know?), not knowing (everybody else seems to understand), giving up control (I hate committees), and change in general (things are fine just the way they are). The first thing you need to realize is that these fears are completely normal and universal. Part of your job as a student affairs professional is to help those around you recognize and deal more effectively with these fears.

THE TWO TYPES OF CONFLICT

Fundamentally, the conflicts you will encounter on a college campus can be categorized as either:

- Healthy—the conflict remains focused on resolving the issue at hand.
- Unhealthy—the conflict digresses into other issues such as personalities and other factors unrelated to the issue at hand.

The first question you should always ask before attempting to resolve a disagreement relates to whether the conflict is healthy or unhealthy (Dana, 2001). Healthy conflict occurs when there are differences of opinion about an issue or concern, but the focus stays on the particular issue or concern under consideration. For instance, if you are part of a task force charged with developing a new retention policy, you will no doubt experience conflict as individuals representing different segments of the campus population will invariably have different ideas about what contributes to student attrition. The conflict that results from these discussions is considered healthy as long as the focus stays on the issue at hand. You genuinely think your approach is better and I genuinely think mine is more appropriate. You present your case and I present mine and then we hash it out between ourselves. It's not personal.

Often, however, healthy conflict can digress into unhealthy conflict when the focus slowly shifts away from the issue or concern at hand and toward personalities, ulterior motives, hidden agendas, and other considerations that have very little to do with what generated the disagreement in the first place. Unhealthy conflict is detrimental to individuals, departments, organizations, and ultimately entire institutions. If two people have a disagreement, the question to ask is whether the conflict is related to differences of opinion about the way a decision should be made or a problem should be solved, or is it based more on the personalities and/or the special interests of those involved in the discussion? In other words, is a person disagreeing with you because he or she legitimately thinks his or her way is better or is the person disagreeing because he or she does not like you?

THINKING ABOUT MY PRACTICE

- We all have students and staff members we tend to "like" more than others. How do you make sure when you disagree with a student or a staff member that you do not particularly like that the focus stays on the issue at hand and not on the personality and attributes of the individual you are dealing with?
- How difficult is it for you to separate a divisive issue from those who are involved in a conflict about the issue?

THE THREE LEVELS OF CONFLICT

The strategy used to resolve a conflict should also be related to the degree to which the individuals who are engaged in the conflict are invested in the potential resolution (Fisher, Ury, & Patton, 2011). There are basically three levels of conflict; these are especially relevant to the contemporary college campus, whether we are talking about the student union or the classroom:

Level I: Neither person really cares about the issue. In a Level I conflict, nobody is intensely interested in seeing the conflict resolved in a particular way (i.e., they really do not care about the eventual resolution of the conflict). These kinds of disagreements are at the low end of the spectrum and are generally easy to negotiate as long as the conflict is healthy. A typical Level I conflict might be: We can't decide on where to eat dinner tonight but neither of us really cares all that much about where we go. If, on the other hand, I draw a line in the sand just to make the point to you that I should have more power or control than you do about where we go eat, then that's crossing the line to unhealthy conflict. By the way, this type of interaction is usually symptomatic of deeper issues in the relationship.

Level II: One person cares about the issue but the other person does not. Level II conflicts occur when one individual feels strongly about an issue, but the other person does not. For instance, a practitioner may feel that a key check-in procedure needs to be set up in a very particular way because he or she is the one who is going to be responsible for the check-in process and wants it to proceed smoothly. His or her colleagues may have a passing interest in the check-in procedure, but if they are not responsible for the process, then they would typically defer to the practitioner when it is time to make a decision about the proper protocol. These kinds of conflicts can lead to more conflict; especially if the person who feels strongly about the issue senses that others are condescending or express that the issue really is not all that important (Sande & Johnson, 2011). The resolution to a Level II conflict can be more complex than the initial assessment might indicate and can potentially move in an unhealthy direction if not handled appropriately.

Level III: Both people genuinely care about the issue. Level III conflicts are typically the most powerful and, as such, they have the greatest potential to precipitate the most damage to the effectiveness and efficiency of both individuals and organizations. In a Level III conflict, everyone involved in the dispute is very invested in how the conflict is resolved (i.e., everyone advocates passionately for his or her proposed resolution). Level III conflicts can precipitate a high degree of emotion and can lead to some very heated exchanges, which is fine and even desirable as long as the conflict continues to be healthy. These kinds of conflicts also have the potential to bring about very positive changes as long as they are handled respectfully and there is a concerted effort by everyone not to allow them to become unhealthy (Coleman, Deutsch, & Marcus, 2014).

COMMONALITIES OF BEHAVIOR

The behavior of most college students, staff members, and colleagues tends to be related to three principles:

1. People choose to act the way they do.
2. Rules, by themselves, do not change behavior.
3. The ultimate goal of most behavior is to belong and to feel worthwhile.

In order to be better equipped to deal with conflict, it is important to understand some basics about human behavior. First is the truism that most people consciously choose to act the way they do (i.e., they do not "stumble into" the situations they find themselves in without sharing some responsibility for how their circumstances evolved) (Hamilton, 2013). As such, one of the inaugural steps in attempting to resolve any conflict is to recognize or help the other person recognize his or her role in creating or perpetuating the conflict. Obviously, the accountability in most situations is not equally distributed; it is often the case that some individuals are more responsible than their counterparts for the development and maintenance of a disagreement, and this needs to be factored into how the conflict is eventually resolved.

Second, everyone involved in the resolution of a conflict needs to recognize and appreciate that rules, in and of themselves, do not precipitate lasting changes in behavior (Ramsbotham, Woodhouse, & Miall, 2011). Staff members sometimes attempt to resolve conflicts by developing and implementing rules that were designed to effectively put an end to potential conflicts by imposing a set of guidelines everyone is expected to adhere to in the performance of their job responsibilities or when engaged in personal interactions. This approach seldom works except on a superficial level, and when it does, it often creates a myriad of new problems and conflict scenarios. In order for a conflict to be resolved successfully and permanently, those involved in, and affected by, the conflict must truly understand why the conflict has occurred, along with the underlying factors that contributed to it. When people do not understand the underlying reasons for a rule or a guideline designed to resolve a conflict, they are not sufficiently motivated to conform their behavior to it; in fact, they may expend a lot of time and energy trying to defeat or work around the original intent of the regulation.

Finally, and this is especially true for student affairs professionals, it is important to be cognizant and accepting of the fact that the ultimate goal of most human behavior entails the need to belong and to feel worthwhile (Hamilton, 2013). For many students, this is the primary reason they are attending college and it is the strongest motivational force that keeps them moving forward in their attempt to reach graduation. Social integration is at least as important as academic achievement to most college students. As such, we can never rely on an appeal to rationality alone to serve as the only criterion for resolving conflicts. A potential resolution to a conflict that makes sense but does not take into account how it affects the self-esteem and feeling of connectedness of those experiencing the conflict will only generate superficial agreement and set the stage for more complicated and paralyzing conflicts in the future.

THE TELLTALE SIGNS OF CONFLICT

When interacting with college students, staff members, and colleagues, it is important to be tuned into the "symptoms" of an impending conflict, which often include:

- Verbal indicators—pay close attention to the language a person uses.
- Nonverbal indicators—pay even more attention to his or her gestures and body language.

- Emotional signs—changes in temperament often signify conflict.
- Behavioral cues—certain actions usually accompany the manifestation of conflict.

Student affairs professionals need to be able to instantly recognize the key indicators that tell them when a potential conflict may be brewing. This can be especially challenging for those who lack the innate ability to read other peoples' feelings and dispositions at a deeper level. Some individuals are simply better at recognizing the signs that a conflict is developing; they seem to be more empathetic than other people when it comes to sensing when a disagreement may be mounting. Whereas this is a skill that can be somewhat difficult to develop later in life, it is important that everyone be acutely aware of his or her own innate limitations in this area and take them into account when handling conflict situations.

There are a few relatively universal (and somewhat obvious) indicators that should tell you a potential conflict is developing. These include too much strong feeling attached to seemingly trivial topics; rapidly shifting eyes or glaring; name-calling and personal attacks; implied or expressed threats; expressions of panic, desperation, or despair; needless harping on the same point; an effort to gather allies and set up opposed camps on an issue; and inappropriate use of biting humor and sarcasm (Anderson, 2015). Always keep in mind the possibility that some of these signs may simply be personality characteristics. Further, as more of these signs are expressed, the likelihood increases that a major conflict may be emerging.

When dealing with staff members, there are also a few signs that the prudent supervisor should recognize as symptomatic of potential discord in the ranks. These include an unwillingness to discuss anything except safe topics, always letting others carry the ball, silence from usually talkative people, or a lot of talking from people who are usually more reserved, failure to move on to the next logical steps, an unwillingness to share information, knowing glances and nonverbal cues, recycling of old ideas, and premature agreement just to keep the peace (Anderson, 2015). Some inexperienced supervisors may incorrectly interpret these signs as part of the normal group process, but rest assured when these characteristics are manifest among several individuals, trouble is most likely just around the corner. In conflict-prone environments, attitudes are almost always poor, and behaviors tend to be unreliable and inconsistent. The earlier you recognize the warning signs that there may be trouble in paradise, the better prepared you will be to intervene appropriately and effectively.

THE THREE BASIC CONFLICT RESOLUTION STRATEGIES

As mentioned previously, the typical college environment is often riddled with conflict and, given the intrinsic nature of higher education, this should not be a very surprising or unexpected revelation. Most campuses are, by design, dynamic cauldrons of opposing viewpoints and perspectives; the search for truth can be a very messy and convoluted endeavor. In addition, institutions of higher learning are notoriously political in nature, which only intensifies the frequency and passion with which conflicts are generated, processed, and, it is hoped, resolved. It is as important for student affairs professionals to understand who they are dealing with, and the context in which their interactions occur, as it is for them to understand their own approach to dealing with conflict. In general, there are three ways most individuals attempt to resolve conflicts, regardless of whether the disagreement is interpersonal or organizational in nature—the power-play approach, the bargaining approach, and the collaborative approach. College students, staff members, and colleagues, as is the case with most people, tend to deal with conflict using one of these three basic strategies.

The Power-Play Approach: Attempting to Dominate or Control the Other Person

Some individuals employ the "power-play" strategy for dealing with conflict situations (Rain, 2014). In this particular approach, the person seeks a win/lose solution to most disagreements. The person tends to assume that people act primarily in ways that further their own self-interests and are skeptical of anyone who claims to aspire to more altruistic motives. The power-play approach is often characterized by secrecy and distortion, and unilateral manipulation is considered a normal part of the process. Moreover, power inequities are accepted as being natural and even desirable and anything that furthers the interests of the person employing the approach is considered justified. In personal relationships, those who espouse this style of conflict resolution tend to be calculating and controlling and can be seen as bullies by their friends, peers, and associates. Unfortunately, this characterization often bleeds over into their professional relationships and can be extremely detrimental to staff morale.

The Bargaining Approach: Coming Together for the "Common Good"

Other individuals utilize a bargaining approach to resolving conflicts, where the goal is either a compromise or a win/lose outcome (Bercovitch & Jackson, 2009). With this strategy, the individual assumes that people are often united for a common good and, as such, any sharing of information and resources is engaged in for strictly strategic reasons. Every interaction is viewed as a potential trade-off; if I help you, then I will expect you to help me when I need you. The expectation of reciprocity is a key characteristic of this style of dealing with conflict and there is always a struggle for power parity. In personal relationships, those who exercise the bargaining approach tend to come across as competitive and comparison-based. In their career pursuits, these are the professionals who always expect something in return for their assistance and like it when you owe them something. The idea of doing something to help others simply because it is *the right thing to do* is a foreign concept to those who see conflict resolution as nothing more than a continual bargaining process.

The Collaborative Approach: Seeking a "Win-Win" Resolution to the Conflict

The collaborative approach to conflict resolution is the style student affairs professionals should aspire to with some important caveats. With the collaborative strategy, the assumption is made that only a win/win resolution to conflict should be considered acceptable by everyone involved in, and affected by, a disagreement scenario (Arbinger Institute, 2015). Further, those who utilize this strategy truly believe that people are, or have the inherent capacity to be, open and honest in their dealings with others. The collaborative approach is characterized by an open sharing of information, with the expectation that others should also be open with what they contribute. The problem-solving and decision-making orientations associated with the collaborative style are seen as part of a larger mutually beneficial process. Power parity is accepted as the norm rather than the exception; the objective is never to put the other person in his or her place or one up anyone. Consensus building, which will be discussed a little later, is considered the gold standard when attempting to resolve conflicts with the collaborative approach.

Keep in mind that how individuals attempt to resolve conflicts in their personal relationships is often mirrored in the strategies they impose in professional settings. Most of us are remarkably consistent when it comes to the different dimensions of our personal and professional lives. In work situations, though, how a supervisor approaches conflict is a key component of his or her overall supervisory style and contributes significantly to how effective he or she is as a leader. Moreover, each of the three strategies outlined below has a set of underlying assumptions that add coherence to the techniques that stem from them, and this needs to be understood when dealing with individuals who utilize them.

It is very important to recognize that the collaborative approach only works efficiently if there is a preliminary discussion and an agreement among everyone engaged in the conflict resolution process that this is the strategy that will be employed. In other words, everyone has to agree to play by the same rules. Again, this will only be possible if the trust level between the individuals involved in the disagreement is sufficiently high and if the conflict falls into the healthy category (Arbinger Institute, 2015). If one person is attempting to be collaborative in his or her efforts to resolve a conflict, and another person is coming from a power-play or a bargaining perspective, then the stage is set for failure. In this scenario, the person who is using the collaborative approach can be taken advantage of by the other individual, and this will only lead to more entrenched and protracted conflicts in the future. On the other hand, if you know which strategy the other person is attempting to pursue, you can be better prepared to thwart his or her advances and advocate for the collaborative approach. Conflict resolution works best when the playing field is as level as possible.

THINKING ABOUT MY PRACTICE

When a staff member challenges your judgment regarding how you have dealt with a conflict, do you ever resort to the "power-play" approach in addressing his or her concerns? What type of response has this approach elicited from the staff member?

Why is it so difficult for many student affairs professionals to think "win-win" when resolving conflicts with staff members or their colleagues?

USING CONSENSUS TO RESOLVE CONFLICTS

The collaborative approach to conflict resolution, as mentioned previously, is built on the consensus-building process. Consensus building is one of those unique concepts that can be explained in a relatively straightforward manner, but it can be extraordinarily difficult to conscientiously implement on a consistent basis (Ramsbotham et al., 2011). Consensus building requires a specific mindset, the collaborative attitude, and an unwavering dedication to the method combined with a great deal of patience. The more serious the disagreement, the more dedicated and patient the individuals involved in resolving the conflict will have to be in order to see it through to conclusion; it is not a quick fix.

Serving on committees, task forces, and other working groups is a basic expectation of those working in higher education, especially for those on the student services side of the aisle. Some of the most effective leaders tend to be collaborative problem-solvers who employ the consensus-building process to achieve desired outcomes—outcomes to which everyone is ultimately able to pledge loyalty and allegiance. The process also seems to be as useful for resolving the interpersonal conflicts that invariably accompany the professional disagreements that are commonplace in any meaningful endeavor. In short, consensus building should be used as the primary conflict resolution technique in virtually any situation. It works just as effectively for resident assistants as it does for vice presidents.

Consensus building involves five steps which follow a logical progression; the steps are sequential and cannot be circumvented or employed in random order. When attempting to reach consensus, regardless of whether the decision making involves college students, staff members, colleagues, or some combination of these individuals and groups, it is helpful to keep the following five steps in mind.

1. **Know your position: Cognitively decide how you would like the issue resolved.** The first step in reaching consensus is knowing what your position is regarding how a conflict should be resolved before you propose it to others (Coleman et al., 2014). Regardless of whether we are talking about what restaurant we want to go to for dinner tonight or what items need to be fiercely defended at the next budget reduction meeting, the concept is the same: Always know what your position is as well as the underlying rationale and supportive evidence for that position before you try to advocate it to others. We all know people who start talking before they know precisely what they are trying to say. So-called thinking out loud may be a great way for you to collect and organize your thoughts, but it can be very painful for the listener. You should have a clear and unambiguous picture in your own mind before trying to describe it to others.

2. **State your position: Verbally present your case to the others involved in the conflict.** The second step entails taking the time to state your position to others in an explicit and transparent manner (Caspersen, 2015). It is not enough to have a lucid understanding in your head of how you think the conflict should be resolved, you have an obligation to explain it to the others who are involved in, or affected by, the disagreement. Again, this is as important in your interpersonal relationships as it is in a more professional context. This is also where good verbal skills are important, so if you need to work on those, please find an appropriate venue for enhancing this vitally important skill set. Then, once you have effectively articulated what your position is, you have an obligation to answer questions about it. Some people have difficulty with this part of the process, typically due to insecurity or an inflated ego; they only want to give press releases or sound bites, leaving those with whom they are attempting to resolve the conflict with a take-it-or-leave-it option. This is counterproductive to the consensus-building process; you must always be willing to provide additional information about your proposed solution. It is not enough just to tell your associates how you think the situation should be resolved and why, you have to be able to sell them on your ideas.

3. **Listen to others. Actively try to understand the other individuals' positions.** The third step involves the responsibility to actually listen to the other person (or persons) when they state their position(s) regarding how they think the conflict should be resolved (Miller, 2015). Yes, most of us have been hearing about the importance

of active listening since we were in kindergarten, but the reality is that many of us are simply not good listeners. When the other person is talking, we are often showing all the outward signs of listening, but internally we are trying to figure out a better way to re-state our position when the person pauses to catch his or her breath or finish making his or her case. In order to employ the consensus-building process to effectively resolve conflicts, it is imperative that we actively listen to what others are saying and earnestly try to and accurately decipher their position and the reasons behind it. This is the point at which well-developed critical thinking skills can be extremely useful to the consensus-building process. Remember, the objective is to honestly appraise the efficacy of alternative approaches to resolving the conflict; it is not just to win the argument. Subjective bias enters the equation when you only listen in order to be able to criticize those who disagree with you and this is counterproductive to consensus building.

4. **Avoid counterproductive behaviors such as voting or giving in "just to keep the peace."** The fourth step involves the need to avoid certain behaviors that distract from, instead of contributing to, the consensus-building process. These include the tendency to give in just to keep the peace, or to keep the discussion on a superficial level so that the underlying issues and concerns are never truly addressed when attempting to resolve the conflict (Furlong, 2005). The primary inclination that should be avoided at all costs in group problem-solving situations is the human inclination to resort to some form of voting when a win-win solution is not forthcoming within a relatively short timeframe. Voting may work well for elections or policy decisions that affect large numbers of people, but it is not a good way to resolve interpersonal conflicts or those that characterize many student affairs departments. Voting creates animosity and lays the groundwork for future conflicts. In a nutshell, anything done because it is the safe alternative is almost always symptomatic of a low level of trust and serves as an indicator that the root cause of the conflict is not being addressed, and until the conflict is explored at that level, there is very little chance a lasting outcome will be achieved.

5. **Recognizing that conflict is an inherent part of all progress.** Finally, it is important that everyone recognize that conflict is normal in all relationships (personal or professional) and that experiencing disagreement does not indicate an inherent failure on the part of those involved in the conflict nor does it necessarily reflect deep-seated dysfunction in the organization (Fisher et al., 2011). A true failure is an event in which everyone typically agrees that something went wrong and that whatever it was should be avoided in the future. Moreover,

those responsible for the failure should play an integral role in rectifying the damage inflicted by the event. Holding people accountable for . their actions is essential to effective conflict resolution at all levels. Remember, conflict is essential to progress and is a necessary ingredient in the ultimate success of interpersonal relationships and departmental efficacy as long as it is the healthy variety. Conflict is not inherently good or bad, nor is it something to fear. A good leader uses conflict to enhance quality; a bad leader uses the same conflict to manipulate others.

APPLYING YOUR SKILLS: SELECTING YOUR TEAM

This exercise demonstrates how the consensus-building process typically works. It can be used with students or staff members to help them understand their differences in perceptions and priorities and how they can negotiate and resolve the conflict that inevitably arises when people value different things.

Each participant in the exercise is to select a team of five members (from the 11 potential team members listed) he or she feels would be best able to accomplish the stated goal. Then, using the consensus-building process outlined above, all of the participants are to reach consensus regarding the five team members everyone can support.

You recently accepted responsibility as the Senior Programming Coordinator in the Craig Boyden Health and Activities Center at Burchfield University. Your primary responsibility involves facilitating the implementation of a new program designed to foster closer ties between the faculty, staff, and students who use the Boyden Center on a regular basis. You have been given two months to develop and implement this program. Your first task is to select a team of five individuals to help you implement your program. Who do you choose?

Adam Tice has been a student staff member at the Boyden Center for the past three years. He will be graduating at the end of the current year.

Patrick Gillon was recently hired as a student staff member at the Boyden Center. He was selected as an "alternate" during the regular hiring process and then was contacted when one of the other students selected did not meet the grade requirements to be a student worker. Prefers a "laid back" approach.

James Graham, a graduate student majoring in Recreation who lives on a graduate floor at Burchfield University. Wants "to make a difference."

Rita Morris, the president of the Boyden Center Student Association at Burchfield University. Is interested in making the Boyden Center the best in the state; is also interested in being governor someday.

Ricardo Peay, a student "shift supervisor" at the Boyden Center. Is universally liked by everyone; likes to use his own judgment rather than referring to the handbook when situations arise.

Becky Sircy, an instructor in the Psychology Department. Worked at the Boyden Center when she was an undergraduate student at Burchfield University 10 years ago. Knows psychology backward and forward; is known as a "hard" teacher; can come across as insensitive sometimes.

Mandy Taylor, a first-semester freshman at Burchfield University.

Shannon Toomey, an instructor in the History Department. Not the best teacher, but gets along with just about everyone. Was told she might want to "volunteer" for this assignment as she needs some "community service" activities for her resume.

Karen Upchurch, a second-year student at Burchfield University majoring in Communications. Knows all the rules and regulations inside and out and is knowledgeable about virtually everything. Helped to create a similar program at another university that was very successful. Is seen as arrogant and intolerant of others' viewpoints; is disliked by almost everyone.

Scott Dinwiddie, administrative assistant in the Boyden Center. Knows "the system," but has no actual programming experience.

Melinda Ehresman, a sophomore resident who wants to be a student employee at the Boyden Center next year. She is a pre-med major who is very motivated and competent. She is currently taking 18 hours.

Your Team (in order of preference):

1. _____
2. _____
3. _____
4. _____
5. _____

RESOLVING CONFLICT FOR PRODUCTIVE RESULTS

One of the desired outcomes in any conflict situation is a better relationship than existed before the disagreement occurred (Mayer, 2012). Again, the objective should not be to win the argument or impose your will on others, but to develop a resolution that strengthens mutual respect and promotes a heightened sense of trust among everyone. The idea is to learn from our experiences in order to become better and better at managing conflict, as there is very little chance that it will ever become extinct. In order to accomplish this in more than a transitory sense, there are certain guidelines that need to be followed when attempting to resolve conflict in a productive manner. As you read and reflect upon the following recommendations, keep in mind they are purposefully designed to be both integrated and developmental; they support and reinforce each other so that the whole is greater than the sum of its parts. In order to use conflict to improve relationships between college students, staff members, or with your colleagues, the following suggestions are essential.

Establish a Positive Atmosphere That Encourages Students to Be Open and Honest

First and foremost, you should always try to establish a positive atmosphere that encourages people to discuss conflict, and their feelings about it, it an open and honest manner. It is going to be exceptionally difficult to move forward if people feel they cannot express their perspectives and feelings in a candid and straightforward way. Obviously, it is important to be tactful, diplomatic, and civil in all of our interactions, both personal and professional. But we do not want to diffuse or downplay the significance of our differences by trying to be overly polite with our communication. Many conflicts drag on way too long and cause much more harm to everyone than they should because those involved in the disagreement are not being as direct with their communication as they should.

Stress the Importance of Keeping the Focus on the Desired Outcomes

Everything we say and do when dealing with conflict should be focused on the desired outcomes (Bercovitch & Jackson, 2009). At the end of the day, what would we like to see as the tangible manifestation of our deliberations? If the intent of our consensus building is to develop a solution that takes everyone's interests and feelings into account, then it should not be too challenging to keep our conversations centered on the ultimate goal. This tends to be especially true with conflicts involving work–life balance issues such as scheduling. Most staff members are protective of their time and how it is spent; certainly, they want to feel that the division of labor is equitably distributed. In this case, a desired outcome may be to make sure the desk is covered at all times and that all staff have enough free time to take care of their personal and other needs.

Emphasize a Collaborative "Win-Win" Process

When dealing with conflict, it is important to make sure a "win-win" attitude is driving the entire process (Fisher et al., 2011). If those involved in a dispute know that everyone is willing to keep working on resolving the matter until everyone is reasonably satisfied with the outcome, then the entire process will tend to be seen in a more positive light. In other words, you should always proceed from a collaborative strategy, even when it is necessary to confront others about their positions or especially their behaviors. People generally respond in a more favorable manner if they know your primary concern is their behavior and that you are not making a judgment about their worth as human beings by confronting them about their decisions. It is imperative to always separate the behavior from the person being confronted about the behavior. There is a huge difference between calling someone a screw-up and saying that person screwed up. In the first instance, you are using a power-play approach; in the second, you are emphasizing a win-win attitude. How you communicate is usually at least as important as what you communicate.

Consider Bringing in Someone From the "Outside" Only as a Last Resort

Keep in mind that resorting to external assistance to help resolve a conflict should generally be avoided if at all possible; certainly it should only be considered after all other options have been exhausted (Furlong, 2005). Anytime you have to bring someone from the outside in to help resolve a disagreement, it is an admission that you do not have the ability to deal effectively with conflict, and this can significantly impact your credibility as a student affairs professional. At the same time, you should also realize that in the real world there will be occasions when you will have to refer a difficult conflict—one that has potentially serious repercussions for you and the department—to someone who has more experience, skill, and authority. Most disputes, however, are better dealt with directly by the individuals involved in, or affected by, the conflict situation under consideration.

Use "Constructive Confrontation" When Appropriate

Finally, it is essential that everyone be comfortable using constructive confrontation when appropriate (Stone, Patton, & Heen, 2010). As the old adage goes, it is as important to give as it is to receive. For some, the term *confrontation* tends to have a negative connotation; it can sound aggressive and even punitive. But within the context of conflict resolution, all a confrontation really entails is providing someone with information you feel the person needs to be aware of for his or her own benefit. It is a vital component of collaborative conflict resolution. If a staff member reveals personal information about a student he or she is working with after assuring the student that the information would remain confidential (and the information is within the limits that always accompany this kind of assurance), then the staff member needs to be confronted about his or her actions. This has to be done for both the benefit of the staff member as well as the long-term efficacy of the department in which he or she works.

THE FIVE TENETS OF CONSTRUCTIVE CONFRONTATION

There are five things you should keep in mind when constructively confronting someone.

1. Being honest—keeping the focus on what is actually causing the conflict.
2. Taking the initiative—not waiting for the other person to "make a move."
3. Being aware of timing—not rushing in without knowing the complete story, but not waiting too long before addressing the conflict.
4. Being specific—always be ready to give examples and details if requested.
5. Meaning it—never say anything you are not willing to follow through with or implement.

Using constructive confrontation, especially with college students, staff members, or colleagues, entails:

- **Being honest—keeping the focus on what is actually causing the conflict.** First, you should always be honest with the person you are confronting (Fisher et al., 2011). What you tell an individual you are upset with him or her about, for example, should really be what you are upset with him or her about. We have all been on the receiving end of hidden agendas, situations in which what is happening on the surface is not really what's occurring at a deeper level. You have a staff member whom you suspect has been behind several lapses in judgment that have been embarrassing to you and your department, but you have never been able to catch the person in the act, so to speak. Eventually, you do catch the person in a lie that actually does minimal harm to the credibility of your staff, but you decide to throw the book at the person anyway, even though the offense was relatively minor. In this case, you are not being honest with the staff member, and he or she picks up on this, especially when a coworker who did the same thing recently was only given a slap on the wrist. Being truthful with those you are confronting sets the stage for a more positive outcome and helps to establish a culture that promotes more effective conflict resolution.
- **Taking the initiative—not waiting for the other person to "make a move."** Second, you have to take the initiative when it comes to facilitating the confrontation; this is especially critical if you are in a leadership role (Dana, 2001). Sometimes, student affairs professionals wait for the person who needs to be confronted to approach them on

an unrelated matter, and then they take the opportunity to confront the person while he or she is there, almost as a matter of convenience. Unfortunately, what staff members learn is to avoid you when they think there is a chance you might need to bring something to their attention. By initiating contact in order to confront someone who needs to be confronted, you demonstrate that the issue is important enough for you to be proactive about it. This sends a very powerful signal regarding the necessity of the confrontation and helps to reinforce the seriousness of the issue you are attempting to address.

- **Being aware of timing—not rushing in without knowing the complete story, but not waiting too long before addressing the conflict.** Third, always be cognizant of the fact that timing is very crucial when it comes to engaging in a confrontation (Caspersen, 2015). When someone engages in a behavior that is inappropriate, it is essential that he or she be confronted about that behavior in a timely manner. If you wait too long, the message is sent that the matter must not have been too significant, otherwise the confrontation would already have taken place. At the same time, you do not want to stop in the midst of a crisis to confront someone when it can wait until the urgency of the present moment has subsided. When the flames are up around your waist, you should probably defer the confrontation until the fire has been extinguished. Choosing the right moment to confront someone is directly related to how effective the encounter will be in resolving the conflict that necessitated the confrontation in the first place. In any event, always make sure you have all the relevant facts before initiating a confrontation, regardless of how long it takes to ascertain those details.

- **Being specific—always be ready to give examples and details if requested.** Fourth, you should be as specific as possible when confronting someone about inappropriate or counterproductive behavior as substandard performance always tends to generate unhealthy conflict (Anderson, 2015). People have a right to be given examples of the kinds of activities that have precipitated the need for a confrontation. Telling a staff member, for instance, that he or she has a bad attitude is relatively meaningless without also giving examples of the behaviors that have led you to conclude that the person has such an attitude. If you have a staff member who does not fill out his or her paperwork correctly, when you confront him or her about the inattention to detail, you should be able to provide specific examples of what was actually submitted as well as examples of what should have been submitted. Not only does this help your credibility as a good supervisor, it also helps the staff member to understand exactly what you are talking about during the confrontation. By the way, the same principle applies to peer-to-peer confrontations.

■ **Meaning it—never say anything you are not willing to follow through with or implement.** Finally, when you state something in a confrontation, you should always mean it (Stone et al., 2010). You should never say anything during the course of a confrontation that you do not have the legitimate authority to back up if necessary nor should you use inappropriate humor or figurative language. If you tell a staff member that if he or she does something one more time, he or she will be terminated, then you should be prepared to terminate the person if he or she engages in the indicated behavior again. If you do not follow through as you indicated you would, then you lose all credibility with the staff member, his or her peers, and (eventually) your peers and supervisors. Moreover, you should never say anything even remotely along the lines of "I just need to take you out behind the residence hall and teach you a lesson." When you are tempted to use this kind of language, remind yourself that the way things sound on campus may not be the way they sound coming from the witness stand in a courtroom. With respect to the use of humor, keep in mind that what is funny today might be detrimental to your career tomorrow.

AN ACTION PLAN FOR DEALING WITH CONFLICT

You probably know colleagues who are convinced that they are good at thinking on their feet and shooting from the hip, so to speak. Unfortunately, they are oftentimes the only ones who rate themselves highly on this attribute. The reality is that most of us need a plan when it comes to dealing with conflict situations. Although the particulars of any plan will have to be adapted to the circumstances unique to each conflict, there are some general recommendations you should follow when attempting to resolve disagreements.

Although some student affairs professionals prefer to "play it by ear" when resolving conflicts between college students, staff members, and colleagues, it is always advisable to have a structured outline from which to proceed. A solid action plan for effectively dealing with conflict typically includes addressing the conflict to the right person; dealing with one conflict situation at a time; staying in the present moment; and avoiding the use of comparisons.

Addressing the Conflict to the Right Person

First, it is always prudent to address the conflict to the appropriate individual or individuals (Furlong, 2005). If a staff member is not performing his or her duties and responsibilities in a satisfactory manner, the only person you need to involve in the discussion of his or her performance is that particular staff member. You do not need to discuss his or her performance with other staff members, students, their parents, or colleagues across campus, the only exception being when you are consulting in an official capacity with a more knowledgeable colleague about how to handle the situation. Many conflicts snowball into a lot more than they should simply because people who have no real connection to the conflict were brought into the conversation.

THINKING ABOUT MY PRACTICE

Why is it so important to "follow through" when you have identified the consequences that will be applied if a student or staff member does not live up to his or her responsibilities with respect to a mutually agreed-upon action plan?

Under what circumstances is it acceptable to modify the predetermined consequences when a student or staff member does not adhere to his or her designated role in resolving a conflict?

Dealing With One Conflict Situation at a Time

You should limit yourself to addressing one conflict situation at a time (Coleman et al., 2014). Multitasking is a great skill to have under most circumstances, but when resolving disagreements, it is best to deal with them one at a time. Ideally, you should start with the most pressing conflicts and work your way down to those with lesser potential to be disruptive to organizational efficacy. Also, try to identify the root cause of a conflict before attempting to deal with it. If you only address the symptoms and not the root cause, often you will simply transform the conflict into a different form, and one that might be harder to resolve.

Staying in the Present Moment

It is best to stay in the present when dealing with most conflicts (Dana, 2001). Having a historical perspective will sometimes help you understand why a conflict is occurring or how it originated, and this information may help you determine if you are dealing with a systemic problem, but these considerations are not typically all that relevant to determining what needs to be done in the present tense. Along these same lines, do not spend a great deal of time trying to determine reasons and motives. In most cases, you are looking for the solution that will allow everyone to move forward instead of staying mired in the present circumstances. When dealing with machines, it is obviously instructive to know why something is broken because it gives you a good indication of what needs to be fixed. When dealing with people, the focus always needs to be on solutions, not causes.

Avoiding the Use of Comparisons

Finally, avoid the use of comparisons when attempting to resolve conflicts (Lechman, 2007). Pointing out how well one staff member performs his or her job responsibilities seldom motivates a less proficient staff to do better. Supervisors who do not understand this can mistakenly think they are engaging in good practice when they say things at a staff meeting like "We all need to be more like Brad." This type of well-intentioned praise often served to create resentment toward Brad, which meant that after a while Brad was not particularly fond of being singled out as an example of someone to emulate. The truth is that the only person most of us will allow to compare ourselves to others is ourselves—and we tend to do it only in private.

RESOLVING CONFLICTS WITH DIFFICULT INDIVIDUALS

There will be times when you will face conflicts that are especially daunting. This could be due to the complexity of the situation or the unwillingness of staff members to play by the rules and do their part to contribute to a positive work environment. In these special cases, it is exceptionally important that the situation and/or the individuals responsible be constructively confronted in a more direct manner. Occasionally student affairs professionals will encounter conflicts with college students, staff members, and colleagues who are particularly challenging. When dealing with these more demanding circumstances, the following guidelines may be helpful.

- **Gaining agreement that a conflict exists.** First, you should work to gain agreement that a problem exists and that it must be addressed (Harper, 2004). Disruptive staff members sometimes continue to engage in counterproductive behaviors because they do not personally feel their behavior is a problem and others should just get over it. Often, those who have this attitude are unaware of the overwhelming conflicts they are generating on a continual basis. These individuals will not be seriously motivated to work on changing their behavior if they legitimately do not see the problem or if they do not care about the problems they are creating. You may have to work diligently to get these staff members to see how their behavior affects others and that they must change what they are doing for the benefit of the department.
- **Discussing viable and realistic alternatives.** Second, you need to discuss alternatives (Mayer, 2012). As a supervisor, one of your favorite

phrases should probably be "How do you think the situation should be handled?" Coming up with more positive alternatives should not be the responsibility of only one of the people involved in a conflict; it needs to be a mutual quest. It is important that the uncooperative or egocentric staff member understand how his or her actions affect those around him or her and create serious conflicts that ultimately kill morale and impede effectiveness. As such, the person needs to play a key role in determining what changes need to be made in order to diminish the frequency and severity of conflicts in the future while helping to resolve conflicts when they do occur.

■ **Mutually agreeing on an action plan (and associated consequences).** Third, you and the person with whom you are engaged in a conflict need to agree upon an action plan, which should include what the consequences will be for lack of adherence to the plan (Rain, 2014). Ideally, the motivation for improving performance is most effective if it is intrinsic (i.e., the staff member should want to decrease conflict-inducing behavior because it will help him or her to function more competently as a viable member of the team). When this does not occur, however, you should be prepared to apply more extrinsic motivation, not in the form of threats, but as logical consequences for lack of compliance. Everyone needs to know that he or she will be held accountable for his or her actions.

■ **Following up and rewarding adherence to the plan (or applying the previously determined consequences if warranted).** Finally, you should be prepared to follow up and measure progress and any achievement should be recognized and rewarded (Anderson, 2015). If a staff member makes a conscientious effort to do a better job but he or she perceives that no one ever notices the effort, then it should not come as a surprise when he or she backslides into the previous counterproductive conduct. If an action plan has been agreed upon, it is essential that the plan is monitored to make sure that it is being followed. Remember, the overarching objective is to resolve conflicts effectively and efficiently, for everyone concerned. Those who seem to have a special penchant for causing conflicts must be dealt with in a timely and conscientious manner.

The following case study will provide you with an opportunity to engage in a more thorough analysis of a situation related to conflict resolution. After reading the case, take time to honestly reflect on the discussion questions that follow.

CASE STUDY

Josh and Carlos Have a Blow-Up

Josh is a pre-med major who is very serious about his studies. He spends 2–3 hours every evening doing his homework and completing his reading assignments for the 18 hours he is taking this semester. He usually goes to bed by 11 p.m. each night and is usually up by 6 a.m. every morning. Carlos, his roommate, is a sports recreation major who is paying for college with an athletic scholarship. He is a very sociable student who has many friends; they like to hang out in the room until late at night.

Josh and Carlos like each other even though their interests vary greatly. They met during orientation and are generally respectful of each other's lifestyles. Lately, however, as the semester has progressed, their relationship has become more strained. Josh has a couple of mid-term exams coming up in the next few days and he feels he needs to do well on both of them in order to enhance his chances of getting into medical school.

Josh planned to spend Thursday night studying for his upcoming mid-term exams. About 8 p.m. that night, Carlos comes to the room with a couple of friends. He had done a great job at the track meet earlier that afternoon and he was planning to celebrate by having a few beers with his friends and listening to some music. Whereas Josh is usually pretty easy-going when it comes to Carlos having his friends over, tonight he is fairly agitated by his roommate's guests.

After about 15 minutes, Josh asks Carlos if he and his friends could "take their party somewhere else" as he really needs to study for his mid-terms. Whereas Carlos is usually receptive to this kind of request, on this particular occasion, he is not feeling so obliging. He has already had a couple of beers. He basically ignores Josh and keeps talking with his friends. A little later, Josh jumps up, shakes his fist in the air, and yells, "I said I need to study! Take the party somewhere else!"

At this point, Carlos also jumps to his feet and gets in Josh's face. "Look, I'm always the one who has to leave so you can study. I'm tired of you acting like this is your room. It's my room, too. If you want to study, why don't you go to the library or something?" Upon hearing this, Josh throws the textbook he is reading at Carlos and screams that he and his buddies need to get "the hell out of my room right now!" Carlos responds by throwing his beer at Josh, barely missing his head.

Josh then takes a swing at Carlos and his friends respond by grabbing Josh and pushing him to the floor. The shouting continues until a loud knock is heard at the door. It's Dalton, the resident assistant, who wants to know what's going on "in there." One of the other residents on the floor has alerted him to what sounded like "a fight" going on in Carlos and Josh's room. After a few tense moments, Carlos opens the door and invites Dalton into the room.

What Do You Do Next?

You are Dalton, the resident assistant. Using the information and insights discussed in this chapter, decide how you would go about dealing with this situation.

Questions you might want to consider:

1. What is the most important consideration in the short-term?
2. What are the relevant factors in addressing this situation?
3. What are some potential options that might resolve this conflict?
4. What are the potential long-term consequences of this incident?
5. How can this situation be used to enhance Carlos and Josh's friendship?
6. How could you minimize the negative consequences of this incident for these roommates as well as the rest of the residents on the floor?

People who tend to be proficient at resolving their own conflicts, as well as the ones experienced by those around them, seem to have mastered three fundamental skills (Miller, 2015).

1. They understand themselves very well, that is, they are acutely aware of their competencies and deficiencies, as well as the unique attributes and imperfections that make them who they are. They tend to accentuate their strengths and compensate for their weaknesses.
2. They have an accurate and realistic sense of how they are seen by others, which is extremely important in resolving conflicts. After all, when you approach me about a situation, I am not reacting to how you see yourself, I am responding to how I see you. In the most successful professionals, there is very little discrepancy between the two.
3. They are good at reading other people, which is the most difficult of the three skills to master. To some extent, the degree to which you are empathetic is determined by your background and upbringing, but we can all improve on our ability to see inside others if we are observant, ask questions, and work to enhance the connection we all have to each other as members of the human race.

Consequently, if your intention is to move into progressively higher levels within the organizational hierarchy in student affairs, the art and science of resolving conflicts is a skill you will have to master (Bercovitch & Jackson, 2009). Throughout your career, you will be given ample opportunity to hone your individual conflict resolution style and you should take full advantage of this opportunity. Even if you plan to stay in your current position for the rest of your career, the ability to deal with conflict appropriately will increase your value to the department, the institution, and especially to the students you serve; it is a competency that will help you become a more capable student affairs professional. Practice the principles of conflict resolution explained throughout this chapter. Learn from your mistakes. Ask for feedback and insight into how you can refine your ability to effectively, efficiently, and humanistically manage disagreements for the good of everyone involved in, and affected by, these challenging and complex situations.

CONCLUSION

One of the most important skills any student affairs professional can possess is the ability to recognize, accurately diagnose, and resolve conflicts (Bercovitch & Jackson, 2009). The more successful approaches for dealing with disagreements in both the interpersonal arena as well as the professional environment are based on the same underlying principles outlined in this chapter. If one is good in one realm, he or she certainly has the potential to be good in both areas. People who handle conflict in their personal lives appropriately tend to be better at dealing with disagreements at work, and often the two worlds, as most student affairs professionals know, are inexorably intertwined. As the human development specialists have tried to impress upon us for the last few decades, compartmentalization does not work very well as an adaptive strategy.

REFERENCES

Anderson, A. (2015). *Management: Take charge of your team: Communication, leadership, coaching and conflict resolution* (2nd ed.). San Bernardino, CA: CreateSpace Independent Publishing Platform.

Arbinger Institute. (2015). *The Anatomy of peace: Resolving the heart of conflict* (2nd ed.). Oakland, CA: Berrett-Koehler Publishers.

Barsky, A. (2014). *Conflict resolution for the helping professions* (2nd ed.). New York, NY: Oxford University Press.

Bercovitch, J., & Jackson, R. (2009). *Conflict resolution in the twenty-first century: Principles, methods, and approaches.* Ann Arbor, MI: University of Michigan Press.

Caspersen, D. (2015). *Changing the conversation: The 17 principles of conflict resolution.* New York, NY: Penguin Books.

Coleman, P., Deutsch, M., & Marcus, E. (2014). *The handbook of conflict resolution: Theory and practice* (3rd ed.). San Francisco, CA: Jossey-Bass.

Dana, D. (2001). *Conflict resolution: Mediation tools for everyday worklife.* New York, NY: McGraw-Hill.

Fisher, R., Ury, W., & Patton, B. (2011). *Getting to yes: Negotiating agreement without giving in.* New York, NY: Penguin Books.

Fletcher, J., Najarro, A., & Yelland, H. (2015). *Fostering habits of mind in today's students: A new approach to developmental education.* Sterling, VA: Stylus Publishing.

Furlong, G. (2005). *The conflict resolution toolbox: Models and maps for analyzing, diagnosing, and resolving conflict.* Mississauga, Ontario: John Wiley & Sons.

Hamilton, D. (2013). *Everything is workable: A Zen approach to conflict resolution.* Boston, MA: Shambhala Publications.

Harper, G. (2004). *The joy of conflict resolution: Transforming victims, villains and heroes in the workplace and at home.* Gabriola Island, BC: New Society Publishers.

Jensen, F., & Nutt, A. (2015). *The teenage brain: A neuroscientist's survival guide to raising adolescents and young adults.* New York, NY: HarperCollins.

Kahn, M., & Lacorte, R. (2013). *Don't die in a car: Simple tips for staying out of automobile accidents.* San Bernardino, CA: CreateSpace Independent Publishing Platform.

Lechman, B. (2007). *Conflict and resolution* (2nd ed.). New York, NY: Aspen Publishers.

Levine, A., & Dean, D. (2012). *Generation on a tightrope: A portrait of today's college student.* San Francisco, CA; Jossey-Bass.

Mayer, B. (2000). *The dynamics of conflict resolution: A practitioner's guide.* San Francisco, CA: Jossey-Bass.

Mayer, B. (2012). *The dynamics of conflict: A guide to engagement and intervention.* San Francisco, CA: Jossey-Bass.

Miller, R. (2015). *Conflict communication (ConCom): A new paradigm in conscious communication.* Wolfeboro, NH: YMAA Publication Center.

Rain, A. (2014). *Dealing with difficult people: Coping with conflict, angry people, abusive behavior and rage.* Seattle, WA: Amazon Digital Services.

Ramsbotham, O., Woodhouse, T., & Miall, H. (2011). *Contemporary conflict resolution* (3rd ed.). Malden, MA: Polity Press.

Sande, K., & Johnson, K. (2011). *Resolving everyday conflict.* Grand Rapids, MI: Baker Books.

Siegel, D. (2015). *Brainstorm: The power and purpose of the teenage brain.* New York, NY: The Penguin Group.

Stone, D., Patton, B., & Heen, S. (2010). *Difficult conversations: How to discuss what matters most.* New York, NY: Penguin Books.

Strayhorn, T. (2012). *College students' sense of belonging: A key to educational success for all students.* New York, NY: Routledge.

127

Chapter 6

Helping Students in Distress

The motto "College should be challenging, not overwhelming" will serve as an introduction to this chapter on providing assistance to students with psychological disorders. The college experience has unique stressors and protective factors for students; I (fourth author) don't think it makes sense at all to say that being in college is more stressful than any other education or career path. Life is hard at times. College life is hard at times and honestly, I would not change that about college even if I could; but student affairs professionals can prepare themselves to help students as they face the usual and sometimes unusual challenges of life while in college.

This chapter will focus on, generally, the idea of stress and how some stress can lead to the development of psychological disorders. There is also a brief description of the broad areas of psychological disorders, specifically anxiety and depression, and a focus on working with students who become at risk for suicide. Eating disorders and substance abuse are also discussed, including the impact of these disorders on students. Although there are various disorders that impact college students, this chapter will only discuss those previously mentioned; however, you are encouraged to read and research others to increase your understanding. In addition, there is a discussion on the cultural considerations for helping diverse students in distress.

ARE COLLEGE STUDENTS TODAY MORE TROUBLED, LESS ABLE TO COPE WITH LIFE?

Students come to college with higher amounts of pathology and experience greater stress than previous generations of college students (Twenge et al., 2010a). While many disagree with this statement in part, there is no doubt that today's college students do continue to suffer at least as much as previous generations and there is a lot that student affairs professionals can do to address this issue. Twenge et al. (2010b) compared cohorts of clients on their MMPI and MMPI-2 profiles. They reported increases in narcissism, impulsivity, and anxiety. Whether these differences are the result of increasing pathology or decreasing resilience remains to be investigated. In other words, universities are now admitting many more students that would not have been admitted 20 to 30 years ago. While today's entering college students may in fact contain more students who are less able to function as self-assured and autonomous individuals, one should not conclude that students in general are worse off today. In much the same way, colleges and universities are admitting more students today with lower academic ability but it does not mean that all college students today are less prepared to handle the academic challenges of college.

Gallagher (2014) reported that 94% of counseling center directors indicated a continued increase in students with severe psychological problems on their campuses and that 86% of directors believed that more students are entering college on psychiatric medications. While this is clearly concerning information and no one would just assume that the directors are pulling numbers out of thin air, the annual survey that Gallagher is using is just that, an annual survey of directors. It is self-reported data and essentially opinions. Singal (2015) observed that counselors always think things are getting worse. In 2004, 85.8% of counselors surveyed indicated that they thought students were presenting with worse pathology. In 2012, the percentage was in fact higher, but only 87.9%. While this is a statistically significant increase, it hardly speaks to an overwhelming epidemic. Certainly useful information but hardly evidence-based. There is an old saying that every minister needs a congregation of sinners; without sinners, ministers don't have jobs. Those of us who care about students' mental health have to be careful we do not let our own needs and biases distort our data.

So let us agree that colleges should provide some level of service for psychological disorders regardless of how pressing the numbers of distressed students. If we are going to bring large numbers of people to a college campus and create an experience that favors those who live on campus, we have to provide services that would normally be obtained within the city or county. Sanford (1969) provided a perspective to student affairs work in which he argued that if we are going to challenge students, which is a common intention in higher education, then we must also support students; we must provide support to help students face and grow through their challenges.

HOW DOES A PSYCHOLOGICAL DISORDER DEVELOP?

Generally speaking, stress is a state of demand; a temporal state in which a person must use additional energy to respond to an environmental challenge or demand. Stress is really a neutral term; it is neither "good" nor "bad"; it is simply a state of being. Stress that leads to growth and happiness is called eustress (Lazarus, 1974), "a positive psychological response to a stressor, as indicated by the presence of positive psychological states" (Nelson & Simmons, 2011, p. 59). Stress that leads to physiological or psychological damage and suffering is called distress, defined as a negative reaction to a stressor which is manifested through negative psychological states (Nelson & Simmons, 2011). Distress usually occurs when the demand we are experiencing is perceived as threatening, harmful, or unwanted. In a state of distress our bodies first respond with autonomic arousal to meet the demand, the flight-or-fight response. Over time this elevated level of arousal can cause physiological and psychological damage.

The amount of distress that a college student might experience at any given time can be described by the following equation. The source/author of this equation is regretfully unknown, although it is something I was taught early in my (fourth author) career.

Distress equals the sum of exposure and vulnerability divided by the sum of psychological resources and social support or

$$D = (E + V)/(PR + SS).$$

Exposure refers to the stressors a student is experiencing; the real, or perceived, or expected demands the student is facing. Stressors are broadly categorized as catastrophic events, major life events, and hassles (Selye, 1974). Catastrophic events are stressors that are beyond the usual or normal life experience. They would include most events we associate with psychological trauma (e.g., natural disasters, interpersonal violence, and war). Major life events are stressors that may also be quite threatening but would be within the range of normal human existence (e.g., job loss, divorce, death of close friends or family, chronic illnesses). Hassles are the daily stressors we routinely face. By themselves, they do not have much effect on our well-being but they can create additional demand or stress as we deal with other major life events or catastrophes.

Vulnerabilities are the "cards life deals us." They are the result of genetics and development; they inhibit our ability to respond in an assertive or healthy manner to stressors. Vulnerabilities include chronic health issues, growing up in poverty, growing up in neglect, or being raised with particular values and beliefs that leave us feeling inadequate or unimportant.

Psychological resources are, so to speak, the opposite of vulnerabilities. They are skills, beliefs, and attitudes that we can learn along the way through life. Faith, hardiness, approach strategies to problem solving, and self-care are examples of psychological resources. A great deal of the educational programming done through student affairs is, essentially, an effort to provide psychological resources to students who come to campus without these competencies.

Social support is, quite simply, the presence of friends, peers, and family that provide a sense of connection, purpose, and information. It refers to general support and/or specific supportive behaviors from others that enhance a person's functioning and/or buffer him or her from adverse circumstances (Malecki & Demaray, 2002). We assume when talking about social support that the other people providing the support are in fact healthy individuals.

As the numerator of this equation (exposure plus vulnerabilities) increases, the level of distress increases. As the denominator increases (psychological resources and social support), the level of distress decreases.

So this model helps us understand why one student quickly becomes depressed following a break-up while another student shows little distress despite the death of a parent. The stressor alone will not predict level of distress; we must know the student's vulnerabilities, psychological resources, and amount of social support.

TAKE A TIME OUT

What do you think?

Imagine two students, one who has few vulnerabilities and many psychological resources and another who has many vulnerabilities and few psychological resources; both are entering into finals week. Finals week by definition is a hassle; it is a very usual, expected, and necessary part of college life.

Which student do you think will experience more distress during finals week?

Kobasa's (1982) discussion of hardiness would appear to be a major effort in the literature to address the individual qualities that mediate risk for depression and suicide. Today's literature is experiencing a renewed interest in the quality of hardiness, though most contemporary publications use the term *resilience*. Whatever term we use, we can see that distress and the resultant psychological disorders have both environmental causes (stressors) as well as personal or personality causes.

WHAT ARE THE BASIC OR COMMON CATEGORIES OF DISORDERS?

Depression and anxiety are the two most significant and threatening disorders among college students. Substance and alcohol abuse, eating disorders, and aggressive/violent behavior, while very costly and demanding, are less common among college students. The fifth edition of the *Diagnostic and Statistical Manual of Mental Disorders (DSM-5)* (APA, 2013), a book that contains the names, distinguishing characteristics, and prevalence of psychological disorders, is an excellent source if you want to know more about psychological disorders. In short, when distress levels reach a significant level and maintain this level, a psychological disorder may appear.

131

Disorders are organized or categorized around the dominant symptom or symptoms; the *DSM-5* provides criteria to make a diagnosis for anxiety disorders, mood disorders, thought disorders, impulsive/conduct disorders, personality disorders, sexual disorders, developmental disorders, and adjustment disorders, though this is not an exhaustive list of disorders. However, most all disorders include or contain symptoms of anxiety and depression. For example, there are several known eating disorders in which eating behavior is the identifying symptom but most models and theories of eating disorders conceptualize the disordered eating as an expression of high anxiety and/or depression. Substance abuse disorders are considered by many to begin with anxiety or depression and the person stumbles into a habit of abuse to self-medicate and alleviate the pain of anxiety and/or depression.

Anxiety Disorders

People usually first experience anxiety in response to significant distress. Anxiety disorders are significant patterns of behavior in which the person is experiencing debilitating anxiety. Anxiety disorders are broken down into smaller categories like panic disorder, post-traumatic stress disorder, phobias, social anxiety, and anxiety disorders in which the person becomes preoccupied with bodily concerns (somataform disorders) or loses parts of his or her identity (dissociative disorders). High levels of anxiety can be very unpleasant; many people who experience their first panic attack think they are having a heart attack. People with anxiety disorders probably have a genetically determined predisposition to experience stronger anxiety to normal anxiety-causing stressors, but they also seem to have a greater preoccupation about avoiding the anxiety. This avoidance tendency is what maintains an anxiety disorder for many people. In the case of a simple phobia, like fear of the water, the first time someone gets a mouthful of water, he or she has a stronger-than-average panic sensation, and then seeks to avoid going back in the water. The avoidance of water protects the person from anxiety in the short run but also prevents the person from learning how to manage getting a mouthful of water. So the person enters into an ongoing avoidance of water, which can limit one socially and recreationally but the person also spends a lot of time worrying about staying away from water.

Again, the majority of college students experience anxiety first which may become an anxiety disorder or their anxiety eventually overwhelms and exhausts them at which point a depression may begin. There is a great deal of overlap between anxiety and depression. For example, anxiety often co-occurs in college students who report experiencing depression (Krumrei, Newton, & Kim, 2010).

Anxiety disorders and other disorders that are grounded in anxiety, like eating disorders, are best treated by professionals. Treatment can and should include medical assistance (medication), relaxation and recreation coaching, personal and/or group therapy, and increased social interaction. While most counseling centers can and do provide therapy for anxiety disorders, medication may not be available on campus if no health services exist. Fortunately, most family physicians are willing to provide prescriptions and monitoring.

Depression

Depression is usually experienced in college students when they are no longer able to respond to the demands in their life. Depression is often thought of as a breach of defense; the student has been struggling to cope but reaches a point of exhaustion and surrender. For example, Hysenbegasi, Hass, and Rowland (2005) determined that depression and academic performance were interrelated and Eisenberg, Golberstein, and Hunt (2009) found that depression is predictive of lower grade point average and a higher probability of dropping out.

Depression, like anxiety, can have genetic causes; both disorders seem to run in families. But childhood development and threatening life events can also lead to depression. A number of observations have been made over the years regarding depression. Children that lose parents early in life are more likely to experience depression later on. Young women are more likely to experience depression in the first year of college; we assume this has something to do with the young women feeling anxious and guilty about being away from family. People that come from families that have substance abuse and anti-social behavior are more likely to experience depression. Again, we assume that a genetic predisposition to experience stronger negative mood is involved, but there are also many life experiences that make people vulnerable to depression. A therapist might at times share with some clients that depression is even helpful. People may become depressed when they are not living by their own values and goals. College students that feel a duty or burden to come to college to make their parents proud could be more likely to experience depression as it is exhausting to live by someone else's expectations. For example, consider college athletes that are depressed because they really don't want to play their sport but feel they are obliged to continue playing for the pride and financial contributions to family.

Not only do both anxiety disorders and depression cause tremendous suffering and impairment, they also, if untreated, can lead to suicide. Student affairs professionals can help students with anxiety disorders and depression by being good listeners and developing trust and credibility with students so that referrals to physicians and counselors will be perceived as genuine, sensitive, and nonjudgmental. It is when students become suicidal that we must be prepared to do more than just advising a student to make an appointment with the counseling center.

SUICIDE

If you don't like seeing animals in pain, don't become a veterinarian.

Unknown

The statement above seems a bit harsh and counter-intuitive. I (fourth author) heard this statement somewhere over the years being raised by and growing up with veterinarians in my family. If you dislike seeing animals in pain, one would think you might choose to become a veterinarian to end animals' pain. The point is that as a veterinarian, you must be with the animal while it is in pain, you have to do work that might cause more pain, and you also have to accept that you may not be able to ease some animals' pain. The same can be said for those of us that choose to work with students. If you don't like to see students struggling, suffering, and losing hope, then you might want to avoid student affairs as a career.

Anxiety, fear, worry, disappointment, sadness, and anger are as much a part of life as joy, passion, curiosity, delight, and contentment. Growing and learning often involve unpleasant emotions. To take in "new" knowledge we must first let go of "old" knowledge; we must let go of familiar rituals and patterns. Learning is both exciting and a bit scary at times. If you want to work with students, you need to be ready to be with them while they struggle. While we seek to help students learn from struggles, avoid unnecessary struggles, and tolerate necessary struggles, we cannot do this by preventing their struggles or rescuing them. Often the work we do requires us to simply be with students while they struggle. To ignore a student while he or she struggles is much like being a neglectful parent. Rescuing a struggling student is much like being a spoiling parent.

THINKING ABOUT MY PRACTICE

What personal/philosophical/theological beliefs do you have that might influence how you respond to a person that is suicidal?

How would you describe/explain the origin of suicidal thoughts from your personal theory of counseling or knowledge of human behavior?

What is the liability and/or duty of your profession to identify people who are at risk for suicide versus provide referral to treatment when someone who is at risk asks you for help?

What follows is an introduction to a variety of concepts and findings related to suicide among college students. Steps one can take when interacting with a college student or colleague who is suicidal will be described. This part of the chapter is *not* a substitute for suicide prevention/intervention training. Reading this chapter may prepare you to be more effective when encountering suicidal people, but student affairs professionals should consider completing a certified/ accredited training program in suicide intervention.

There are many suicide prevention and intervention training programs available today (www.sprc.org/sites/sprc.org/files/library/SPRC_Gatekeeper_ matrix_Jul2013update.pdf). QPR (www.qpr.com) and ASIST (www.sprc.org/ bpr/section-III/applied-suicide-intervention-skills-training-asist) are two of the more heavily used training programs and will be referenced throughout this chapter. More information about these programs can be found at the end of the chapter. *Again*, to work with a suicidal person you really need to complete a training program in which you practice the conversational skills with a qualified professional. But there is certainly a great deal of information that can be presented here for those who are interested in working with people who are depressed and/or suicidal.

Before choosing suicide, first do the thing that you fear the most.

Unknown

Perhaps it is best to begin this section with the above quote. If we chose to think of suicide as something people think about or do for understandable reasons, we have a better chance at preventing it (Quinnett, 2000). In other words, our society tends to be better at preventing things when it is willing to be open, honest, transparent, and logical. When we began to talk openly about sex, we were able to prevent or reduce the number of unwanted pregnancies and the spread of some diseases. When we began to talk openly about breast cancer or prostate cancer, we saw a decrease in death from these types of cancer and an increase in early detection. Part of being able to talk about something previously considered to be taboo is a willingness to no longer mystify or vilify the thing.

We come from cultures that have very strong moral opinions about suicide. Suicide is one of the most profoundly personal actions and socially disturbing events (Stauffer, 2004). To some faiths, suicide is a sin. In some cultures, suicide is a forbidden topic. But if we choose to see suicide as nothing more than a choice made by people who, at the time, are facing something very frightening, then suicide becomes more understandable. Furthermore, as it becomes more understandable, it becomes safer to talk about, and the more we talk about it, the less often it happens.

A number of references describing how well-developed programs are associated with a reduction in suicide behavior can be found here: www.sprc.org/bpr/ section-ii-expertconsensus-statements. In short, the literature strongly suggests that if we address suicide with an attitude of openness and frankness, we can expect to see a reduction in suicide attempts and completions. This finding should also hold true for the university campus.

The balance of this section will address the prevalence and mythology of suicide, the warning signs of suicide, and the progression of steps one can take with a person who is suicidal. Again, this section is written to provide the nonmental health professional an overview of what is included in suicide prevention and intervention training. While this would be helpful to a nonmental health professional who will encounter peers and students that are suicidal, it should not and cannot substitute for supervised in-person training in suicide prevention and intervention.

Prevalence and Mythology

Most suicide prevention and intervention programs incorporate discussion/ presentation of suicide facts and myths to familiarize the participant with a current view of the impact of suicide in our society and to identify misperceptions about suicide that complicate delivering assistance to people who are suicidal.

Examples of suicide facts include:

- About two thirds of those who attempt suicide in a given year do not wish to die.
- Talking about suicide does not increase its occurrence.
- The highest rates of suicide are among the elderly, but suicide continues to be the second or third leading cause of death for teens and young adults, and the 11th leading cause of death overall.
- More people die from suicide than homicide in America.
- Around 40,000 deaths per year due to suicide.
                    (www.afsp.org/understanding-suicide/facts-and-figures)

Examples of suicide myths include:

- People that talk openly about suicide will not actually attempt suicide.
- There is nothing you can do to stop someone from killing himself or herself.
- Suicide rates are higher during the holidays.
                    (www.afsp.org/understanding-suicide/facts-and-figures)

These facts and myths represent a small percentage of what is known to be true about suicide but the taboo nature of suicide continues to permeate our culture and complicates efforts to educate the public about the reality of suicide. Pre-Christian society glorified some types of suicide (Stauffer, 2004), and this theme continues today in literature and film. How many of us have not read or watched Juliet end her life when convinced that her first true love, Romeo, is dead? Socrates was said to have chosen his own death over silencing his opinions, yet Judas was so vilified that he was reported to have committed suicide out of shame or guilt. The first step in addressing suicide and in reaching out to students that are suicidal begins with dispelling myth from fact about suicide. We must also understand the biased impact culture has on how we perceive or define suicide.

TAKE A TIME OUT

How would you respond to the following statements?

I would date/marry someone who had made a suicide attempt.
I would be okay if my child had a friend that had been or was suicidal.
I wouldn't mind working for a boss or supervisor that had a history of suicide.

Suicide continues to be something of a taboo topic for our society. It can help to be fully aware of your own beliefs and attitudes about suicide before working with students that are suicidal.

Terms of Suicide

Most intervention and prevention programs will also take time to clarify suicide-specific terms. Here are some examples of terms that are defined to enable participants to have more productive discussions:

- Suicide ideation: thoughts of suicide, thinking about suicide.
- Suicide intention: plans of suicide, the choice to commit to a plan to attempt suicide.
- Lethality of method: how likely it is that a particular method will cause death; highly lethal methods include the use of guns, methods of low lethality include ingestion of less harmless pills.
- Attempt versus Completion: an attempt describes action taken that could end one's life. A completion is an attempt that results in death. This distinction is made because many people attempt suicide but do not die.

Types of Suicide

Suicide attempts can be roughly placed into one of three categories. These categories vary by ideation/intention, lethality, warning signs, and outcomes. The chart below summarizes these differences.

	To Be	Not to Be	To Be or Not to Be
Ideation/Intention	Person wants life to change, doesn't want to be dead, but is willing to risk death.	Person wants to be dead, is comfortable with being dead.	Person goes through phases of suicidal intention and ideation.
Lethality	Tends to use less lethal, easier to reverse or undo methods.	Tends to use very lethal, immediate, irreversible methods.	Lethality varies with depth of ideation.
Warning Signs	Doesn't want to be dead, usually gives clues, signals, warning signs. Wants to be stopped, interrupted, prevented.	Wants to be dead, doesn't want to be stopped, may take great effort to appear to be "okay," will avoid clues, warning signs.	Maybe give clues or warning signs in phases of lesser ideation and intention.
Outcomes	More likely to be able to return to campus life with assessment and treatment.	Given high mortality of this category, return to campus life is rare.	Probably the more challenging student; if cycles or phases are not controlled, this student may have numerous attempts, hospitalizations.

Awareness of Risk for Suicide

If we can accept that most (about two thirds) of those who attempt suicide do not want to be dead and will give warning signs, then we can take some comfort in knowing that we can prevent suicide if we know the more common risk factors, precipitating stressors, and warning signs. Most suicide prevention and intervention training programs will address these variables.

Risk Factors

1. A history of suicide in the family and/or one's own past. Families that speak French are more likely to have children that speak French. Families that smoke are more likely to have children that smoke. Families with a history of suicide are more likely to have children who know suicide to have been an option. We suspect that suicide might seem less taboo or prohibited if it has already occurred in the family. Regarding one's own past, anything we have done once is more likely to be done again. People that survive a suicide attempt might carry unresolved guilt or shame if they don't seek supportive therapy.

2. Drug/alcohol abuse. Severe depression is a result of psychological phenomena as well as neurobiological phenomena. Drug and alcohol abuse can further impair a depressed person's mental capacity and function. Also, with heavy drug/alcohol use we see again the role of shame and guilt feeding depression.

Precipitating Stressors

Most any event that is perceived by a person as threatening, a stressor, can precipitate anxiety and/or frustration, which in time can build into a depression, and then thoughts of suicide. Stressors more often associated with depression and suicide are:

1. Relationship problems;
2. Legal problems;
3. Substance abuse;
4. Death/suicide in family/friends;
5. Bullying/stalking;
6. Coming out; and
7. The loss of hope, a dream, or bodily function.

The number one cause of suicide for college students is untreated depression (www.suicide.org/college-student-suicide.html). College students that are experiencing untreated depression tend to be quiet, reserved, and socially isolated. They often feel lost, lonely, anxious, inadequate, and have more difficultly moving through the typical challenges of the college experience.

Signs or Signals

As depression worsens and the idea of suicide becomes more prominent in a person's mind, certain signs or signals might appear. Here are some of the more common indications that a person is becoming more comfortable with the idea and intention of suicide.

1. Isolating, withdrawing, spending little or no time with others, avoiding friends and family. This goes beyond typical shyness or introversion; the person seeks to be alone, often in quiet and less visible places.
2. Becoming fascinated with death, dying, and the philosophy of life and death. The person may seem interested in how others view death, the meaning of life, etc.
3. Putting affairs in order, making a will, giving away prized possessions.
4. Using social media to say goodbye to large numbers of people.

139

5. Relapsing into substance abuse or engaging in legally risky behavior as well as physically dangerous behavior.

It is important to remember that while not one of these risk factors, stressors, or signs or signals will predict that a person attempts suicide, we do know that people who have attempted suicide are much more likely to have these risk factors, experience these stressors, and give these signs or signals.

Verbal Warnings

Many people who are suicidal will make some kind of verbal statement that expresses their intent to harm themselves. The intent of these statements is to communicate to whoever is listening that the person is suffering. Sadly, verbal warnings that are vague often go undetected.

Vague verbal warnings

"It would be better if I wasn't here."

"I don't want to be a burden."

"I wish I could just go to sleep and not wake up."

Specific verbal warnings

"If things don't change soon, I am going to give up and kill myself."

"I would rather die than have to go through that again."

"I want to die, I want to die now."

Taking Action

Most suicide prevention and intervention programs will address when and how to take action with someone you suspect to be suicidal. These programs, generally speaking, lay out the response to a suicidal person in three broad steps or stages:

- Awareness: Recognizing that a person is at risk for suicide and sharing one's concern for that person immediately and verbally.
- Interaction: Engaging the person in a conversation about his or her ideation and intention of suicide. Encouraging the person to share his or her history, level of distress, and plans for suicide so that steps may be taken to both support the person's experience and to interfere with the plan if a plan exists.

- Connecting to Treatment: Ensuring an agreement with the person that he or she will seek professional help and/or connect with appropriate authorities to provide safety and begin treatment for being suicidal.

In QPR training (www.qpr.com) the three broad stages are described as Question, Persuade, and Refer. In ASIST training (www.sprc.org/bpr/section-III/applied-suicide-intervention-skills-training-asist), the three broad stages are described as Connecting, Understanding, and Assisting. In these two programs, as it is in most suicide intervention programs, the first step begins with Awareness.

The Awareness Stage

In the Awareness Stage our knowledge of suicide risk factors, stressors, and signs/signals lead us to an awareness that a person may be at risk for suicide. There is no set rule for making this determination; there are no specific criteria of how many risk factors, how many stressors, or how many signs/signals must be present before we ask a person if he or she is suicidal. Generally speaking, if we are aware of the risk factors and stressors in a person's life, and we are noticing signs/signals, that should be enough to raise our awareness of the risk for suicide and warrant making contact with the person. With some students we may not be aware of the risk factors or stressors, but if there are signs/signals, we would make contact.

In the Awareness Stage we want the person to confirm if he or she is suicidal. We want an answer to the question "Are you going to commit suicide; are you going to kill yourself?" Recall our earlier discussion that suicidal people are relieved when someone asks this question; they tend to see the person asking the question as someone who is empathetic and in touch with the suicidal person. When we ask the question, we ask with genuine concern and interest. We ask as if suicide is something that could be on anyone's mind given certain circumstances.

A TIME OUT VISUAL

Imagine you are sitting in a bar and the person next to you bursts into flames. How does that person feel if you think to yourself "Oh my, I imagine he/she is very embarrassed, this is so personal, I will help by acting like nothing is happening so he/she can have some privacy." How does that person feel if you think to yourself that it might be best to beat around the bush instead of coming right out so you say "Is it me or is it hot in here?" The person probably feels that you can't be trusted even if you mean well; if you can't talk about what is happening, then maybe you are too anxious, afraid, or judgmental. If you say to the person "It looks like you are on fire; let me help," then the person knows you are safe, you can understand the situation.

The same is true for someone who is suicidal. If we come straight out and ask if he or she is suicidal, then the person knows we can be trusted, we have an idea of what is going on, and we don't seem to be disgusted or afraid. We finish the awareness step by asking the question "are you suicidal?," what Quinnett (2004) called the forever decision.

The Interaction Stage

Asking the question begins a conversation of hope; the taboo topic is now open for discussion. The Interaction Stage may now begin in which we engage the person to talk at will about his or her suicidal thoughts and plans. Remember, this is NOT therapy. You are not trying to talk the person out of his or her suicidal ideation. You are simply wanting to get the person to talk about all his or her thoughts and feelings so that they seem more concrete, less abstract, and therefore more real and subject to change/treatment. Talking reduces the mystery, as well as the shame, of suicidal thought. The ASIST program is particularly helpful in recommending that the interaction begin with why the person is thinking about suicide. Most people would assume that the conversation should start with why the person should not think about suicide, or, what the person will lose by being dead. But ASIST, and other programs, understand that we build an alliance and we gather useful information by asking the person questions like:

- How does ending your life now make sense to you; what do you see coming from it?
- How do you think you will kill yourself; do you have a plan?
- Is the pain unbearable—how long before you kill yourself?
- Who else knows about your desire to die, your plan to die, the pain?

Once you have answers to these questions you will then have solutions; if the person is allowed to talk about why he or she is considering suicide, he or she is then more likely to talk about why he or she wants to live. Once the person has described the plan, you can then see if he or she will undo the plan or put up barriers to the plan. For example, if the plan is to take a large amount of pills, then you and the person can talk about how to get rid of the pills or have someone else hold the pills. Knowing about the level of pain gives you an idea of how much distraction, comfort, or even sedation might be needed.

Connecting to Treatment Stage

In the Interaction Stage we gather information about the person's risk for suicide; that is, we get an idea of how soon the person intends to act on his or her thoughts of suicide. Obviously, people with no plans, bearable pain, lots of social support, and a desire to not be dead are at less risk of attempting suicide. People with specific plans and methods, unbearable pain, a lack of social support, and a strong desire to end their pain are at high risk.

Joiner (2009) provided a very clear, yet easy-to-understand, model of risk for suicide. He proposes that people who hold two specific states in their minds, perceived burdensomeness and social alienation, long enough will become more comfortable with the idea of death as a solution. As this comfort grows the person may engage in behaviors that increase the person's comfort with death and reduces the person's natural desire for self-preservation. So we know that even people at low risk still need to make contact with mental health professionals. In the *Connecting to Treatment Stage*, we put our energy into inviting the person to make contact with a professional mental health service provider. We can offer to assist with this process. We can offer to make phone calls or provide transportation. You may have students that will feel better about going to a counselor if you accompany them on their first visit. All of these options are appropriate. Remember the goal in this stage is to get the suicidal person to someone who can provide treatment or someone who has the authority to keep the student safe.

In the *Interaction Stage*, we discovered if the person had a plan and, if so, did the person dismantle the plan. This was only to keep the person safe until he or she can make contact with a professional. But what can we do if the person does not want to dismantle the suicide plan and/or refuses to make contact with a professional? As uncomfortable as this may be for us, we need to commit to the idea that we will not tolerate suicide as a solution and we will then use any available authority to step in and see to the safety of the person. This means we might call local law enforcement and report the person has a plan to commit suicide. Law enforcement will intervene and if they believe the person is a risk for suicide they can initiate involuntary hospitalization. While this may leave us feeling angry or guilty, it is okay to insist that suicidal people get help. If you come upon a person with a compound fracture of the leg, you are going to call an ambulance even if the person says "No, don't, I don't want to go, leave me alone, I can get home okay." Right?

So in the Connecting to Treatment Stage we might take the person to an emergency room, we might call the person's therapist, we might just call the person's spouse or family. The point is we help the person get to treatment or the safety of someone who has authority. We don't leave the person alone until we can make this connection. If desired, you can ask the person to contact you once he or she has received help.

TAKE A TIME OUT

Practice Makes Perfect

This may sound silly, but it can help to practice saying the words before you find yourself with someone who is suicidal. Take some time, right now, to practice saying the

143

sentences below out loud. Make a recording if you can and listen to it. Do you notice your voice changing at certain words? Do you pause or rush at certain parts of the sentence? Keep saying these sentences out loud until you sound "normal," like the way you sound when you are reading from a menu or telling a classmate the reading assignment from last night's class. Repeat these practice sentences:

- "Sounds like you have been hurting a long time. Are you having thoughts of suicide?"
- "With that much pain going on, I wonder if you find yourself ever thinking about killing yourself?"
- "I think something like that would make me wonder if I want to go on living . . . what about you, do you think about being dead? Do you think about ending your life?"

KEY POINTS WHEN INTERACTING WITH SOMEONE WHO IS SUICIDAL

Some key points to remember when interacting with someone who is suicidal include the following.

1. Suicide is scary, no doubt. It is okay to be anxious when talking with someone who is suicidal; accept the anxiety, appreciate the anxiety. Being anxious does not mean you are incompetent; it means you are concerned about a fellow human who is suffering. Think of it this way— firefighters probably don't enjoy running into burning buildings, but they do it. They accept the anxiety, don't fear the anxiety, and use the anxiety for energy.
2. Because suicide is scary, and serious, you really do not have to handle someone that is suicidal by yourself. Always consult with your supervisors and do not be reluctant to bring other people in on the conversation with the suicidal person. You do not want to overwhelm the person by bringing 10 peers, but it is okay to have one or two other people with you.
3. The bottom line is that we are keeping someone alive long enough to get professional help. See the Golden Gate Bridge discussion below (Take a Time Out). Put your faith in the idea that most people want help and most people can change their minds.
4. Keep your skills sharp. Practice "asking the question," seek out professionally conducted training, and take time with your staff to talk about the challenges of encountering suicidal students. Experience of working with suicidal students for over 20 years (fourth author) has shown me that while it gets "easier," there is always an anxious feeling.

TAKE A TIME OUT

The Lesson of the Golden Gate Bridge

Freedenthal (2013) provides a useful summary of an investigation conducted on people who were interrupted in their suicide attempts at the Golden Gate Bridge or who did in fact jump from the bridge but survived the fall. In sum, an overwhelming number of these people who were interrupted have not made another suicide attempt and several who did jump have shared their immediate regret of jumping as they were falling.

Imagine being so sure that you wanted to attempt suicide that you actually stepped off the bridge and then immediately wanted to be back on the bridge. Does this help you believe in the hope of keeping people alive long enough for them to change their minds?

PRACTICE SCENARIO

Read the following scenario and respond to the discussion items that follow.

You get a call from a coworker who expresses concern about a student that has been sitting in the lobby of your building for several hours. The student appears distressed; he or she is sullen, quiet, and occasionally tearful. You sit down next to the student and ask if you can help. The student is a bit reluctant to speak, but offers that he or she hasn't made friends since coming to college, doesn't feel like his or her major is a good choice, and worries that his or her family is going to be disappointed with his or her grades. The student then shares that he or she is supposed to go home the next day for a short holiday vacation but then begins crying. The student mumbles "Maybe it would be better for everyone if I just didn't show up at home, ever."

1. Do a free association thing here; write down the thoughts and feelings you are having; try to not edit or judge, just make a list.
2. Okay, now that your head is clear or clearer, thinking of the Awareness Stage, what risk factors, stressors, and signs/signals do you see in the scenario?
3. How do you "ask the question" with this student?
4. How might you get the student to share more about what he or she is experiencing?
5. Thinking about the Interaction Stage, how would you get the student to discuss his or her pain, plan, and possible support?
6. Thinking of where you work and/or take classes, how would you approach the Connecting to Treatment Stage? What service providers or authorities would you recommend or contact?

145

FINAL THOUGHTS, MAKING BETTER REFERRALS, AND UNDERSTANDING COUNSELING CENTERS

Given the code of conduct (state law) and code of ethics (professional organizations) that most counselors, psychologists, and other professional helpers follow, communicating with a counseling center can at times seem confusing. Generally speaking, counseling centers can take in information with fewer restrictions or limitations than letting information out. Client information is confidential information. It cannot be shared without the client's permission.

Consider the following scenarios.

A hall director encourages a student to make an appointment at the counseling center. The hall director gives the student a number to call and asks permission from the student to call the center to make sure the student was able to get an appointment. The hall director calls the center and asks if the student was able to get an appointment. The staff person on the phone says that the center can neither confirm nor deny that an appointment was set.

1. The ethical issue is that the center must have permission to release information; it does not matter what arrangements were made between the hall director and the student.
2. Another ethical issue would be why does the hall director need to know if the appointment was made? Additionally, could the student not share that information with the hall director or does the hall director not trust the student to give an honest answer?

The Office of Judicial Affairs is concerned about a student that is making odd and potentially threatening comments on campus. The Director of Judicial Affairs calls the counseling center to see if the student is also a client. The director says that if the student is a client, then he or she will not treat this as a conduct issue.

1. Again, the ethical issue is that the center must have permission to release information from the student; permission cannot come from another person in authority. The center could release information if there was an immediate threat to self or others, but no such threat exists in this scenario.
2. Another issue would be why would the director not treat this as a conduct issue? Even if the student has a psychological disorder, he or she should not be excused or dismissed from the code of conduct. Psychological disorders are rarely the cause of anti-social or criminal behavior.

Another misunderstanding about counseling centers is that they keep all their information to themselves. Many people are not aware that if a client tells a counselor that he or she intends to hurt someone, the counselor not only can disclose that information to other staff and authorities, he or she must disclose the information to prevent harm to others. So counseling center staff can and will take action when students are a threat to self or others, but counseling center staff may not be able to share with others what action is being taken due to confidentiality.

One very important action that student affairs professionals can take is to build their relationships with the counseling center. Take time at the first of the academic year to introduce your staff to the counseling center, and vice versa. Hold a joint staff meeting or potluck lunch and become familiar with one another. Just because counseling is private work does not mean counselors have to be private people. Share what you do on campus as well; counselors need to know more about student affairs work in general.

In the next sections, eating disorders and substance abuse among college students as well as multicultural considerations are discussed. Eating disorders, serious disturbances in eating behavior and weight regulation, present a wide range of adverse psychological, physical, and social consequences for college students (National Institute of Mental Health, 2014). In addition, substance use disorders, a cluster of cognitive, behavioral, and physiological symptoms associated with recurrent use of alcohol and/or drugs that cause clinically and functionally significant impairment (American Psychiatric Association, 2013), produces harmful consequences for college students such as repeated failure to fulfill roles for which they are responsible, legal difficulties, or social and interpersonal problems. Furthermore, since environmental factors on college campuses can influence co-occurring disorders, college students with eating disorders often suffer from depression, anxiety, and substance abuse (Zaider, Johnson, & Cockell, 2000). Considering the effects of these prevalent issues, it is important for student affairs professionals to be aware and knowledgeable of the symptomology and effects of these disorders. The more student affairs professionals know about eating disorders and substance abuse, the better they will be able to determine whether students are exhibiting symptoms related to eating disorders or substance abuse, engage in conversations about these disorders, and support students who display symptoms of these disorders. In addition, since culture plays a relevant role in a person's life and influences the helping relationship, multicultural considerations are discussed. To effectively support all students in distress, student affairs professionals should be aware of multicultural considerations and how to be aware of culturally learned assumptions as well as comprehend the culturally relevant elements and knowledge about a student's culture.

EATING DISORDERS

Eating disorders are serious mental health issues that cause substantial emotional distress for individuals and their friends and families, that can have lasting physical implications, or that can even result in death. Given that eating disorders are considered a prevalent health problem on the college campus (Hoyt & Ross, 2003), it is prudent that student affairs professionals are aware of the types and symptoms related to eating disorders so they will be better equipped to determine whether a student is exhibiting signs of having an eating disorder. According to the *Diagnostic and Statistical Manual of Mental Disorders*, fifth edition (*DSM-5*) (APA, 2013), late adolescence/early adulthood is the typical age of onset for people most diagnosed with an eating disorder such as anorexia nervosa, bulimia nervosa, and binge eating disorder. Since traditional college students fall into this age group, student affairs professionals need knowledge and understanding of the diagnostic criteria and warning signs so that they are able to assess, identify, approach, and refer.

VOICES FROM THE FIELD

College Students and Eating Disorders: What College Professionals Need to Know

Susan E. Belangee

The commonly known eating disorder diagnoses are Anorexia Nervosa (AN), Bulimia Nervosa (BN), and, with the publication of the *DSM-5* (American Psychiatric Association, 2013), Binge Eating Disorder (BED). The typical symptom people think of with AN is restricting food intake because of an extreme fear of becoming fat, whereas the most known symptom of BN is the consumption of large amounts of food in short periods of time and then the compensatory behavior of purging (vomiting, usually). With BED the same binge behavior as BN is present but the difference is there is no compensatory behavior to rid the body of the food consumed. (Readers are encouraged to pursue more comprehensive resources for a deeper understanding of eating disorder symptoms and behaviors.)

In addition to the common disorders, there are other diagnoses comprising symptoms and behaviors that while not meeting full criteria can still cause significant distress and impairment for individuals. Previous versions of the *DSM* system labeled these as Eating Disorder—Not Otherwise Specified, and in the current *DSM-5*, there are two classifications: Other Specified Feeding or Eating Disorder and Unspecified Feeding or Eating Disorder (APA, 2013). In "Other Specified Feeding or Eating Disorder," the symptoms present for a person may be similar to the main diagnoses of AN, BN, or BED, but not all criteria are met. For instance, an individual could be exhibiting all of the criteria for AN but the individual's weight is within or above the normal range for the person's age and height. The "Unspecified Feeding or Eating Disorder" applies to persons who present with symptoms characteristic of an eating disorder that causes significant impairment or distress, but there is not enough information to make a clear diagnosis.

These disorders are the most lethal psychological illnesses with which one can be diagnosed, mainly because of the physiological side effects (heart arrhythmias, electrolyte imbalances, high cholesterol, and heart attacks) stemming from the various symptoms and behaviors or suicide resulting from the tremendous emotional and mental distress associated with these disorders. The mortality rate for individuals with a history of eating disorders (i.e., complete diagnosis and also those with a subclinical form) has been reported in some study samples to be 13% or more (Crow et al., 2009; Suokas et al., 2013). Thus, college counseling and student affairs professionals need to be prepared to recognize and offer support to those individuals who may be struggling with full-blown eating disorders as well as those seemingly "less serious" cases of eating disorder symptoms and behaviors (those that may not meet all criteria).

Who Is Dealing With Eating Disorder Symptoms and Behaviors?

Eating disorders were believed at one time to be an issue only for affluent Caucasian women (Gordon, 2000); that picture has definitely changed with more ethnically and socioeconomically diverse populations as well as more males being identified. It is estimated that 20 million women and 10 million men suffer with a clinically significant eating disorder during their lifetime (Wade, Keski-Rahkonen, & Hudson, 2011). By age six, girls especially start to express concerns about their own weight or shape (Smolak, 2011). Males are not immune either as Lowes & Tiggemann (2003) found that 35% of boys (aged 5 to 8 years old) in their study wanted to be thinner and were aware that dieting was a means of achieving the ideal body shape. According to Neumark-Sztainer (2005), over one-half of teenage girls and nearly one-third of teenage boys reported using unhealthy weight control behaviors, such as skipping meals, fasting, smoking cigarettes, vomiting, and taking laxatives, as a means of reaching an ideal body size or shape.

Given these findings, it may be safe to assume that college students are also struggling with eating disorders. In fact, much of the research in the field has utilized college populations as sample participants. In a survey of 185 female students on a college campus, 58% felt pressure to be a certain weight, and of the 83% that dieted for weight loss, 44% were of normal weight (Malinauskas, Raedeke, Aeby, Smith, & Dallas, 2006). Wade et al. (2011) also reported that 25% of college-aged women engage in bingeing and purging as a weight-management technique. For college-aged males, it appears that the reason to engage in the same types of eating disorder symptoms and behaviors is to achieve the ideal, lean body type. In Ousley, Cordero, and White (2008) "a greater percentage of eating-disordered men (compared with no-diagnosis men) reported that they always, often, or frequently felt fat and were very or moderately fearful of becoming flabby or untoned" (p. 618). It is clear from this research that eating disorders are a serious issue across the first few decades of life regardless of gender or other characteristics. The typical age of onset for a diagnosis of an eating disorder is mid- to late teens and early 20s, so it is quite common for these disorders to be present and/or develop during an individual's time at college (Swanson, Crow, LeGrange, Swendsen, & Merikangas, 2011).

149

Why Do Eating Disorders Develop?

Many studies that have addressed the etiology, or development, of eating disorders have found a number of related factors. These factors range from early childhood experiences as viewed through the psychodynamic theories (e.g., Dare & Crowther, 1995), to faulty or distorted ideas about body weight, body shape, and eating as proposed by the cognitive approaches (e.g., De Silva, 1995; Fairburn, 1981; Fairburn & Garner, 1986), to negative family environments as developed by the family systems models (e.g., Eisler, 1995; Minuchin, Rosman, & Baker, 1978; Wisotsky et al., 2003). Likely, a complex interplay of social, familial, personal, and biological variables best explains how eating disorders develop and persist; Adlerian, or Individual Psychology, theory combines all of these variables into a single model (for a comprehensive review of this model and eating disorders, see Belangee, 2006).

For college counseling professionals, one or more of the above theoretical frameworks may prove useful when assisting students with these issues in a counseling setting. However, the sociocultural model, especially in light of the influence social media has on today's college students, offers an essential framework for *all* student affairs professionals. This approach examines the influence of factors such as the media, societal context, beauty industry, etc., on the drive to achieve the "thin ideal" and the resulting link to eating disorders. Thin-ideal internalization refers to the extent to which an individual cognitively "buys into" socially defined ideals of attractiveness and engages in behaviors designed to produce an approximation of these ideals (Thompson, Heinberg, Altabe, & Tantleff-Dunn, 1999). The degree to which the societal values are internalized predicts eating-disorder-related pathology (Stice, 2001), such that the stronger the internalization, the worse the eating disorder symptoms. Many studies have shown that exposure to thin media images leads to body dissatisfaction, lowered self-esteem, and negative emotions in young women and men (e.g., Agliata & Tantleff-Dunn, 2004; Groesz, Levine, & Murnen, 2002; Stice, 2001; Vartanian, Giant, & Passino, 2001). Thus, the link is quite strong between the amount a person "buys into" the cultural value of the thin ideal and higher levels of body dissatisfaction and eating disorder symptoms and behaviors.

Another issue to consider is the impact of social media sites, such as Tumblr, Vine, and Secret, and websites specifically designed to promote the thin ideal internalization. New terms were developed—pro-mia, pro-ana, thinspiration, and pro-ED—as abbreviations for websites promoting bulimia, anorexia, and general eating-disorder behaviors as well as images of the thin ideal. There has been an explosion of research over the last 10 years targeting the impact that these websites and social media platforms have and the connections to eating pathology (e.g., Bair, Kelly, Serdar, & Mazzeo, 2012; Borzekowski, Schenk, Wilson, & Peebles, 2010). In other words, for those participants who had internalized the thin ideal, there was a significant connection between viewing image-focused websites and Internet sources and higher levels of body dissatisfaction. For those who had not internalized the thin ideal, that connection was not present or at

150

least not in a statistically significant way. Today's college students are the most technologically savvy generation, pursuing the latest advances in smartphones and personal electronic devices with exuberance and passion, and with it comes significant media exposure and instant access to information that may negatively impact mental health.

How Are Eating Disorders Treated on College Campuses?

Back in 2000, Richard Gordon published his updated book *Eating Disorders: Anatomy of a Social Epidemic,* and in his revised edition he stated that over 700 studies on eating disorders are published annually in professional journals. It may be safe to assume that this number would have increased over the last 15 years. Even with the significant numbers of studies conducted each year, there is still no treatment available that is 100% successful in alleviating eating disorders in clinical/counseling settings, let alone the college environment outside of the counseling center. Recidivism rates are still significant with some studies reporting 10% (Bergh et al., 2013) to as much as 33% (Stice, Marti, & Rohde, 2012) in other studies. Eating disorders fall in the category of severe psychological problems and even for highly skilled counselors, they present a challenge. In most cases, students who meet criteria for AN, BN, or BED will likely be referred out for specialized treatment from a dedicated eating disorder treatment facility, and in order to return to campus students would probably be required to continue ongoing counseling from an experienced outpatient therapist or counselor in the on-campus center knowledgeable enough to manage the recovery process.

How can a student affairs professional identify when a student's situation reaches a critical point where counseling of some kind is warranted? This author believes that the best place to start is to ask these questions: How much impact on daily functioning are the symptoms having? Is the student able to attend classes and turn in assignments? Is the student negatively impacting the living environment (e.g., eating all the food in the room and/or food that does not belong to him or her, purging after eating, etc.)? Are roommates reporting significant changes in the student's mood and/or behavior patterns? Can the student maintain the usual activities such as sports practices or other extracurricular pursuits? Based on the answers to these questions an evaluation of symptoms at the counseling center on campus would be a good start. Involving the staff members, or supportive friends/roommates, most closely associated with the student (the Resident Assistant or Residence Hall Director) may help ease the stress caused by such an evaluation. Strong relationships among student affairs offices (e.g., Residence Life, Student Services, Counseling Center, Health Center) will allow for seamless transitions and thorough follow-through so students do not get lost "in the shuffle."

If it is determined that the student's needs can be addressed on campus, then the assigned counseling center professional can make contact with professors to discuss the situation and how to address the coursework for any and all classes. If, however, it is decided that the student's needs cannot be met by professionals on campus, then it is the responsibility of the school to establish connections with outside referrals and

151

ensure that the student attends the initial appointment. It may make sense to involve the student's family at this point as another support for the student and especially if there are no appropriate referrals in the area. Parents may decide to take the student home and pursue treatment in the home area. In either instance, a single point of contact within the student affairs offices (e.g., Residence Hall Director, Dean of Students, etc.) should be chosen to help maintain the connection between the student and the school and to help ensure the successful completion of treatment as well as courses.

When a student leaves school for treatment and is ready to return, student affairs professionals should follow an established protocol that confirms the student's readiness to return to the environment and academic rigors of college. This protocol should include strategies for managing stress, including continuing counseling either on or off campus, as well as steps to take if the student needs additional support with coursework.

Can Eating Disorders Be Prevented on Campus?

For many years, professionals in the field of eating disorders thought that educating people about the dangers of AN and BN would be enough to stop people from developing these disorders. Various programs and curricula were developed outlining specific symptoms and behaviors and detailed accounts of how people would engage in the symptoms. Yet none of these programs seemed to decrease the prevalence rate or lessen the impact.

Stice and his colleagues approached this issue from a new perspective in the late 1990s and early 2000s, employing the concept of cognitive dissonance in an educational program about eating disorders and the internalization of the thin ideal. This program asked participants to voluntarily argue against the thin ideal in magazine ads and other advertising images during a three-session intervention program. The results showed a reduction in bulimia behaviors, less "buy in" to the thin ideal, lower body dissatisfaction, reduced dieting behaviors, and less negative affective symptoms (Stice, Mazotti, Weibel, & Agras, 2000). Several studies since this initial exploration have yielded the same results, most notably Rodriguez, Marchand, Ng, and Stice (2008) because they found this intervention to be successful across White, Asian American, and Hispanic participants.

Carolyn Becker and her colleagues extended this line of research by examining the efficacy of peer leaders in delivering the same cognitive dissonance–based program. Results yielded significant results for these peer-led prevention groups with reductions in thin ideal internalization, dieting behaviors, eating disorder behaviors, and body dissatisfaction (Becker, Bull, Schaumberg, Cauble, & Franco, 2008). Stice and colleagues then explored whether the same program could be delivered via the Internet with the same results. They found that the results were solid enough, and consistent with previous findings, to warrant a full trial of this Internet version of the program (Stice, Rohde, Durant, & Shaw, 2012).

Therefore, the most promising development in the prevention of eating disorders is the cognitive dissonance–based programs. Stice and Presnell (2007) published a manual, titled *The Body Project: Promoting Body Acceptance and Preventing Eating*

Disorders Facilitator Guide, which outlines the structure and delivery of the program. The manual is available through major book retailers. Student affairs professionals would be wise to take advantage of this program that has 16 years of research supporting it, with more innovative studies in progress, regardless of whether there is a known issue with eating disorders on campus.

Conclusion

Eating disorders are complex and serious mental health issues that disrupt the daily functioning of individuals usually in young adulthood. The college environment can be a breeding ground for the development of these disorders and the sociocultural model offers explanations as to why college students might be highly impacted. Thin ideal internalization seems to play a significant role in how these issues are perpetuated. Student affairs professionals are wise to assume that there are students struggling with these disorders on campus on any given day. Protocols for handling when to refer and managing students as they seek treatment should be established and adhered to in these situations. Finally, cognitive dissonance–based prevention programs appear to be efficacious in reducing many of the serious eating disorder symptoms and behaviors, and student affairs professionals should pursue the implementation of these programs immediately.

SUBSTANCE ABUSE

Unfortunately, the number of college students with addictions has increased dramatically over the last few decades (Kuhn & Swartzwelder, 2014). Substance abuse continues to be a persistent problem on college campuses (Jordan, 2009). Although statistics differ on the extent of the problem, there is general agreement among health care and related professionals that many college students abuse alcohol and illicit drugs, especially prescription medications, on a regular basis (www.drugstatistics.org/College_Drug_Use_Statistics.htm; Ruiz & Strain, 2011). It is important that student affairs professionals know how to recognize the basic symptomology associated with substance abuse and what to do when they suspect that a student may be in the throes of addiction. In many cases, the student affairs professional may be the student's initial point of contact regarding his or her situation and, as such, the professional is in a unique position to influence the trajectory of the institutional response to the student's challenging circumstances.

Some of the telltale signs that a student may have a substance abuse problem include failure to follow through on school-related responsibilities, poor class attendance, falling grades, increased disciplinary problems, mood changes, and physical or mental challenges such as memory lapses, poor concentration, lack of coordination, or slurred speech (Duke Student Wellness Center, 2016; Fisher & Harrison, 2012). Additional indicators of a potential addiction include experiencing withdrawal symptoms (i.e., nausea, insomnia, sweating, tremors, and anxiety), abandoning activities that were previously considered enjoyable, and mounting legal issues (Cazar, 2015; Duke Student Wellness Center, 2016). The relevance of these symptoms is especially significant if the student exhibiting them previously did not demonstrate these characteristics in a tangible manner or did not exhibit them to the present degree. Moreover, as the number of symptoms displayed increases, the likelihood that an addiction may be the underlying cause is enhanced. Whereas most human beings experience one or more of these characteristics from time to time, they tend to be more pronounced and systematic in individuals who have a substance abuse problem (Cazar, 2015).

Before proceeding with a discussion of the best course of action when attempting to intervene with a student who may be addicted to drugs or alcohol, it is useful to mention some of the myths that are often associated with addiction (Robinson, Smith, & Saisan, 2015). First, overcoming addiction is not simply a matter of willpower; that is, the idea that the student can stop using if he or she really wants to. Addiction is a disease, not a choice, and it has to be dealt with as such (Hogan & Gabrielsen, 2002). Second, some people make the erroneous assumption that students have to reach rock bottom before they will get serious about overcoming their addiction. This is patently false and even dangerous as it may create the illusion that the need for an appropriate intervention is not acute. The reality is that recovery can begin at any point in the addiction process (Cleveland & Harris, 2010).

Third, many individuals, and even some professionals, believe that it is not possible to force someone into treatment if they do not want to be helped. Contrary to this often self-serving rationalization, however, treatment does not have to be voluntary in order to be successful (Robinson et al., 2015). Many addicts have recovered from their dependence on alcohol or drugs after being forced into treatment programs either by concerned relatives or the courts (Connors, DiClemente, Velasquez, & Donovan, 2013). Finally, some espouse the idea that if treatment was not effective in the past, it will most likely not be effective in the current circumstances. It is important to remember that relapse is very common in the treatment process and should be seen as a natural part of the healing process (Miller & Carroll, 2010). Some addicts go through several cycles of relapse and recovery before finally learning how to manage their condition (Robinson et al., 2015).

Although student affairs professionals are not counselors or therapists, there are a few strategies they can employ in helping students with addictive disorders, especially in the identification and referral stages (University of Central Florida Counseling and Psychological Services, 2015). First, everyone who interacts with students should be aware of the signs that indicate a student may be experiencing an alcohol or substance abuse problem. Moreover, training in recognizing these indicators should be provided for anyone who interacts with students as a daily part of their job responsibilities. Second, the situation should always be treated as serious; it is not within the prevue of the educator to question the validity or severity of a student who is experiencing addictive behaviors (Robinson et al., 2015). There will obviously be times when the authenticity or the degree of the student's disorder will be questioned and there will also be instances when a response may be judged to be an overreaction, especially in hindsight. At the same time, it is always better to be safe than sorry as the old adage goes.

Third, it is imperative that the professionals interacting with a student who is suspected of having an addiction not blame the student for his or her circumstances (Kuhn & Swartzwelder, 2014).

Students can be held accountable for the consequences of their actions without being made to feel that they are totally responsible for their circumstances (Jordan, 2009). Most addicts will readily admit that this is not the kind of life they would choose if left to their own devices. Fourth, the professional should share legitimate and heartfelt concern with the student and encourage him or her to seek help (White & Rabiner, 2011). Referrals are rarely successful when the student perceives that the person making the referral is judgmental or condescending toward him or her. Expressing genuine concern, which human beings instinctively pick up on, is always the best way to approach a student suspected of having an addictive disorder (University of Central Florida Counseling and Psychological Services, 2015). Finally, the student affairs professional should always be cognizant of the fact that denial is a very powerful coping mechanism; it is how many addicts manage to get through the day without losing their self-respect and may entail conscious or even unconscious lying and distorting of the truth (Miller & Carroll, 2010). The challenge is to respond to the student in a manner which gains his or her confidence, keeping in mind that what the student is telling you may not be objective reality, but he or she may not be aware of the deceit being perpetuated (Miller & Carroll, 2010). Confrontations, such as those seen in many "reality" shows, rarely achieve the desired results and can even be harmful to the student (Cleveland & Harris, 2010).

Although most recommendations are best stated in the affirmative, when dealing with students who may be experiencing an addiction, it is equally important to know what not to do. Inappropriate interventions include threatening to punish the student or preaching to him or her, acting like a martyr with emotional appeals that only increase the student's guilt and therefore his or her inclination to use drugs, covering up or making excuses with the intent of shielding the abuser from the negative consequences of his or her behaviors, completely taking over his or her responsibilities, which only leaves the student without a sense of dignity or self-worth, or arguing with the person when he or she is obviously under the influence of drugs or alcohol addiction (Robinson et al., 2015; Ruiz & Strain, 2011). The primary responsibility of student affairs professionals when they encounter students who may be dealing with an addiction is to refer them to those who can provide the treatment they need to overcome their disorder

(University of Central Florida Counseling and Psychological Services, 2015). As such, knowing how to make an effective referral is a skill that should be mastered by anyone who works with these students. Although every situation will be different, there are some general guidelines that will help to increase the probability that a referral will be successful and that the student will actually follow through and seek the help he or she needs.

First, it is important that the student knows the professional is sincere in his or her desire to assist him or her with the struggle. This goes a long way toward winning the confidence of the student. Second, mutual decisions usually precipitate the best outcome (Jordan, 2009). The student needs to feel he or she has a key role in the decision-making process and that he or she is not simply being told what to do (Connors et al., 2013). People like to feel that they have some control over their own destiny. Third, the purpose of the referral needs to be made clear to the student; it is in the best interest of the student to see the counselor or therapist to whom he or she is being referred. Fourth, timing is extremely critical when making a referral for substance abuse; in general, sooner is always better than later (Fisher & Harrison, 2012). If the student is receptive to the idea of seeing a counselor or therapist, that is the time to pick up the phone and tell the helping professional that you are bringing the student to his or her office or clinic (University of Central Florida Counseling and Psychological Services, 2015). Fifth, if possible, it is always prudent if the student affairs professional accompanies the student to the referral agency and then stays with him or her until the counselor or therapist can see the student (eDrug Rehab, 2015). It is also beneficial if the student affairs professional introduces the student to the counselor or therapist to whom the student is being referred as this reinforces the importance of the therapeutic relationship by letting the student know that those who care about him or her and are trying to help are coordinated in their efforts to provide the help he or she needs (Cazar, 2015; White & Rabiner, 2011). Finally, the student affairs professional should always be mindful that it is not his or her responsibility to make a diagnosis or otherwise judge the student's state of mind (University of Central Florida Counseling and Psychological Services, 2015). Those considerations should be left to the clinician to whom the student is being referred; the clinicians have the necessary qualifications to make these determinations. Additionally, if a student does not follow through with the mental health clinician to whom he or she was referred, do not take it as disrespect toward you or as a personal failure on your part. Unless mandated by a student conduct office, a student affairs professional cannot make a student go to his or her appointment with a clinician. Moreover, it is not appropriate for you to criticize or chastise a student who did not follow through. Unfortunately, setbacks are a reality in working with students. Review the case of Wilson and reflect on your thoughts about the role of the student affairs professional in this situation. Particularly, think about what you would do in this situation.

VOICES FROM THE FIELD

Wilson's Calmed Nerves

Fred E. Stickle

Wilson is a 20-year-old sophomore track runner at a university in Kansas. His major is Business Marketing. His hometown is about 1½ hours away; he lives in a residence hall at the university. One of the student affairs staff individuals has talked with Wilson on several occasions about college life, career goals, football, and girls. It was a week before Thanksgiving and the two were talking when the staff member asked if he was going home for the holiday break. Wilson hesitated and finally answered that he was driving to Colorado for a few days. When asked if he had relations in Colorado, Wilson answered no and stated that there were things he could buy in Colorado cheaper than in Kansas.

The staff member believed he knew Wilson well enough to ask the question, "Do you mean marijuana?" Wilson's response was yes, and they continued the conversation. Wilson explained that even at the age of 20, in Colorado, the substance was easy to get and it was cheaper there as well. After 10 to 15 minutes of conversation on the topic, an all-important question was asked, "How much are you using each week?" Wilson responded, "Well, I used to just use it on the weekends, but it helps me with feeling anxious so I use it when I feel that way." The staff member recalled a previous discussion that the two had about his current academic standing and responded, "Wilson, a couple of weeks ago you told me that you were struggling to keep your grades up in a couple of classes; you mentioned that you were losing interest in your classes and in running. I wonder if the marijuana use has anything to do with this." Wilson responded that he is really not interested in quitting because the marijuana "calms my nerves." The staff member asked Wilson if he would be willing to talk to a counselor to address the anxiety and mentioned that the counseling center was a place where a student could explore his or her concern and talk to someone who could listen and help. "You have always mentioned that staying healthy and fit is important to you. The counselor might be able to help you get that back in your life again." The phone number of the counseling center was given to Wilson before he went back to his residence hall to study for an exam he would have the next day.

The day after Wilson returned from Colorado, he called the counseling center to set up an appointment for the following week. He mentioned it to the staff member, "Hey, I made that appointment. It will be nice to talk to someone, but don't expect me to stop doing what I need to do to calm my nerves." The staff member responded, "Wilson, I am glad to hear that you have an unbiased person to talk to!"

It is an unfortunate but entirely realistic probability that some students who are addicted to alcohol or drugs will overdose at some point (Berk, 2011; Connors

157

et al., 2013). In these extreme situations, it is often unclear as to what constitutes the best course of action and the student affairs professional will often have to exercise professional judgment. Still, there are some basic recommendations that should provide a framework for developing an effective response in these kinds of scenarios. First, the student affairs professional should do his or her best to stay calm (Berk, 2011). Saving a student's life is often dependent on the professional's ability to remain calm while taking the appropriate action in a rational manner (eDrug Rehab, 2015). Second, the professional should try to determine what substances the student may have consumed, as well as how much (Duke Student Wellness Center, 2016). This information could be vital when Emergency Medical Technicians or other first responders arrive on the scene. Third, the professional needs to assess the behavior and symptoms of the student who has potentially overdosed. For example, is the student breathing? Is he or she conscious? Can he or she respond verbally to questions? Being responsive is a very positive sign. If the student is responsive, the professional should try to keep him or her engaged in conversation until help arrives (eDrug Rehab, 2015). Fourth, it is essential to get help for the student as soon as possible. If the situation warrants, the professional should call 911 or take the student to an emergency room immediately. If there are other individuals present, their help can be solicited as individuals who are under the influence of drugs or alcohol can be difficult to manage (Robinson et al., 2015). When these extraordinary circumstances evolve, as they inevitably will from time to time on a college campus, it is important not be overly concerned about legal implications, especially when a student's life is at stake. Finally, the professional should keep the student warm and keep the area around him or her clear (Berk, 2011). The professional should also avoid being "proactive" in this kind of situation, especially if he or she does not have a working knowledge of the most appropriate course of action (i.e., he or she should not induce vomiting, submerge the student in cold water, try to get him or her to stand up and walk, etc.) (Fisher & Harrison, 2012). The role of the student affairs professional is simply to manage the situation as effectively as possible until more qualified personnel arrive (eDrug Rehab, 2015).

MULTICULTURAL CONSIDERATIONS

As helpers within educational institutions, student affairs professionals are in a position to proactively respond with sensitivity to the needs of our multicultural and diverse students. The personal, professional, ethical standards, and multicultural competencies, discussed in Chapter 2, move us beyond knowledge and awareness and demand that our awareness and knowledge be applied to affect our practice with students. When working with students in distress, cultural considerations must be taken into account as to not invalidate a student's experience and to understand some unique needs associated with a student's cultural identity and how and when to make referrals and report issues related to students in crisis.

In your helping role as a student affairs professional, you should gain a greater understanding of the lived experiences of others and subsequently how you can competently serve people of multiple cultures. Hurtado et al.'s (1999) campus racial climate framework offers insight into ways that colleges and universities can support a diverse learning environment. The five factors include historical legacy of inclusion/exclusion (e.g., the manner in which an institution has previously handled racial/ethnic diversity), compositional diversity (e.g., numerical representation), psychological (e.g., perceptions of racial/ethnic tension, prejudice, and discrimination), and behavioral (e.g., enactment of diversity on the campus).

Examining perceptions of diversity among students becomes relevant since these perceptions can affect a student's development, acculturation, adjustment, sense of belonging, and institutional commitment. Gaining perspectives from students can help student affairs professionals promote a positive climate for diversity.

VOICES FROM THE FIELD

Multicultural Considerations: Helping College Students in Distress

LaShonda B. Fuller

In my experience, the challenges most students of color suffer from, specifically African American students, create academic strife, emotional and psychological distress, and career identity issues that cause students, who may be first-generation college students or simply from underrepresented groups, not to believe that they can achieve at the college level and pursue their aspired career goals (Gibbons & Shoffner, 2004; Hartig & Steigerwald, 2007; Lippincott & German, 2007; McCarron & Inkelas, 2006; Ramos-Sanchez & Nichols, 2007).

Literature in the fields of school counseling, college counseling, college student development, and even family counseling are in agreement that first-generation college students (or students from multicultural backgrounds) consist of students whose parents have not attended college, are from an ethnic background, low socioeconomic status, female-headed household, and speak another language besides English; additionally, this population suffers from the lack of financial and parental support, college preparatory skills, self-efficacy and esteem issues, and survivor guilt (Bui, 2002; Gibbons & Shoffner, 2004; Hartig & Steigerwald, 2007; McCarron & Inkelas, 2006; Ramos-Sanchez & Nichols, 2007). According to some researchers, students carrying such baggage have experienced difficulty with high school academics and testing, have a lowered self-efficacy toward future endeavors (Choy, 2001; Lippincott & German, 2007; McCarron & Inkelas, 2006), high levels of psychological distress (Gibbons &

Woodside, 2014; Rosenthal & Wilson, 2008), depression and suicidal behavior (Hirsch, Webb, & Jeglic, 2011; Longmire-Avital & Miller-Dyce, 2015), and racial identity crises (Cole & Zhou, 2014; Schmidt, Piontkowski, Raque-Bogdan, & Ziemer, 2014). What we may not be considering is that pursuing college for such students is a Rites of Passage (ROP) experience. For the students of color who have little to no knowledge at all concerning the higher education process, a ROP focuses more on transitions within life and how the person masters emotional, spiritual, and physical tests and/or tasks (Pratt-Clarke, 2013). Most historically Black colleges and universities (HBCU) have been known to cultivate a ROP experience for students of color. Literature on students who have attended HBCUs share that students have reported HBCU's campus environments *promote cultural identity and connection with peers and faculty members*; whereas, students of color experiences at predominantly White institutions (PWI) have consisted of a lack of support by administration, faculty, and peers (Fries-Britt & Turner, 2002). The lack of support at PWIs has caused students to believe that in order to survive at a PWI, they must "assimilate into the White culture" (Fries-Britt & Turner, 2002, p. 319) or "act White in order to be academically successful ... by losing their ethnic identity" (Butler, 2003, p. 52). Based on this experience, this is where you, the student affairs professional, may experience your students of color in emotional distress with identity crises, overwhelmed and failing academically, or where you might notice a number of students of color dropping out to return home to work minimum-wage jobs (McCarron & Inkelas, 2006) because they feel trapped by the stressors of college life, lack support and a sense of self, feel discontentment with their adjustment to the college environment, and lack a feeling of connection to the campus (Gullan, Hoffman, & Leff, 2011).

I believe it is safe to say that students of underrepresented groups at PWIs might experience the same culture that does not support their ROP and college success. With this in mind, student affairs professionals must obtain awareness, knowledge, and skills in serving multicultural student populations (Hanna, Bemak, & Chi-Ying Chung, 1999; Patterson, 1996) by first answering the following questions that support five basic interpersonal qualities for facilitative relationship building: (1) Respect for the student, (2) Genuineness, (3) Empathic understanding, (4) Communication of empathy and genuineness to the student, and (5) Structuring role to assist students with success (adapted from Roger's 1957 counselor qualities for effective counseling as cited in Patterson, 1996 and modified for this section). To respond to the needs of a diverse student population, you must first possess cultural and diversity awareness. *What has history taught you about human relations?* You must take heed to knowledge of self and of your student population. *How have historical practices influenced how you view yourself and students you work with who are from different cultures?* You must then be authentic enough to identify if you have compassion and the desire to apply your awareness and knowledge to positively impact others from diverse backgrounds. *How can I use my privilege to advocate for students who are from diverse backgrounds for college success?* If you are unable to locate compassion for all students who differ from you; if you are unable to want to advance students who lack resources and confidence in becoming a contributing civilian in our country; if you maintain superiority and a privileged attitude that keeps you disconnected from your students of underrepresented groups and their cultural experiences, you will not be able to adequately serve them.

Helping Students From Underrepresented Groups

Once we are able to (1) identify our personal views and our biases of students from underrepresented groups; (2) achieve an attitude of self-forgiveness in the event that guilt is experienced because of our prejudices or past acts of discrimination; and (3) feel compassion for students and the desire to heal the disconnect, we should feel confident moving toward campus-wide advocacy. The following recommendations should assist you in your support and advocacy for students from underrepresented groups.

1. Do not wait for students to seek you out. Research supports that students of diverse groups do not seek specific services for their needs and when in distress may not feel comfortable talking about feelings of oppression or stress (Rosenthal & Wilson, 2008); therefore, be intentional about implementing outreach efforts to identify persons in need and provide support by screening students early on in campus orientations, mid-term periods, and regular advisory check-ins.

2. Be willing to help students of diverse groups understand that their discrepancies in learning are not isolated to just them and highlight their strengths of perseverance and resilience (Cole & Zhou, 2014; Schmidt et al., 2014) by developing a mentoring program that connects the student to peers and administrators who mimic their values. Student affairs professionals do not necessarily have to share race or cultural experiences but need to be able to demonstrate cultural awareness and sensitivity considering that students who have a positive connection to their ethnic identity and can foster developing relationships are healthy psychologically (Schmidt et al., 2014). This approach will help students in creating a connection to people and the campus environment for a better sense of belonging considering that social support is documented as necessary for students of diverse population's college success (Gibbons & Woodside, 2014; Longmire-Avital & Miller-Dyce, 2015; Schmidt et al., 2014).

3. Promote positive cultural and ethnic diversity by encouraging specific and universal values as a campus (Cole & Zhou, 2014; Hirsch et al., 2011; Schmidt et al., 2014). For example, under the presidential leadership of Sidney Ribeau (Higher Education Center, n.d.), Bowling Green State University's campus developed a committee that created core values the university wanted to identify activities and behaviors with that would also undergird campus attitudes toward serving students. These five core values that guided campus interactions and opportunities for diverse involvements were: Respect for One Another, Cooperation, Intellectual and Spiritual Growth, Creative Imaginings, and Pride in a Job Well Done. Universities must make respect for diversity a priority by offering opportunities for diverse

161

experiences without oversimplifying or overdramatizing the ideal of multicultural-ism and diversity.

College students of diverse backgrounds use of campus services is limited already (Rosenthal & Wilson, 2008). When working with students who represent ethnic iden-tities, student affairs professionals should be mindful that the key to their students' success is promoting a healthy racial/ethnic identity, a genuine support system, and awareness of and access to academic, financial, and mental health resources (Gibbons & Woodside, 2014; Longmire-Avital & Miller-Dyce, 2015; Rosenthal & Wilson, 2008; Schmidt et al., 2014) to cultivate an accepting campus.

International Students

When it comes to multicultural competence, international students should also be considered as student affairs professionals work to develop their understand-ing of multicultural competencies. According to the 2013 Open Doors Report, 40% more international students are now studying at higher education institu-tions in the United States compared to 10 years ago (Institute of International Education, 2013). With this growth comes transitions and with transitions come unique challenges that are not experienced by domestic students. Although inter-national students come from diverse cultural backgrounds and have differences in language, they experience similar acculturation challenges and "being an inter-national student" represents a common minority identity in the United States (Schmitt, Spears, & Branscombe, 2003; Thomas & Althen, 1989).

Furthermore, international students face various challenges when adapting to their new academic and social environment and culture, which may include difficulty with the English language and communication, developing friendships, and a lack of knowledge of the American culture (Johnson & Sandhu, 2007) and changes in food, finances, housing, and social support (Eustace, 2007). Inter-national students are faced with the challenge of adapting to a new educational system that often requires a different approach to studying and the acquisition of additional academic coping skills. Furthermore, international students often experience higher levels of discrimination and homesickness when compared to students from their host country (Poyrazli & Lopez, 2007). The acculturation process and adapting to a new culture presents challenges and stresses (Eustace, 2007) and facing these challenges can lead to acculturative stress, which refers to the negative consequences that result from contact between two distinctive cultural groups during the experiences of acculturation (Berry, 2005). The long-term outcomes of psychological acculturation include psychological adaptation, which concerns one's self-esteem, identity consolidation, well-being, and satisfac-tion, as well as sociocultural adaptation pertaining to one's cultural knowledge, social skills, interpersonal and intergroup relations, and family and community relations (Berry, 1997; Berry & Sam, 1997). There are consequences associated with the stress and challenges experienced by international students. For example, Constantine, Okazaki, and Utsey (2004) attributed acculturative stress to depression in international students. Additionally, Sümer, Poyrazli, and Grahame (2008) asserted that a lack of social connectedness and lower level of English proficiency predicted higher levels of depression and anxiety in international students; students with lower levels of social support reported higher levels of depression; and international students with lower self-rated English proficiency experienced greater levels of both depression and anxiety. Being mindful of the experiences that contribute to acculturative stress in international students, which may impact their academic success, social belonging, and psychological well-being, is a relevant task for student affairs professionals so that they can provide assistance and support to them.

Being a Culturally Competent Professional

To become more culturally responsive and respectful to the students you help, you must first make a commitment to take steps toward understanding and helping diverse students and communities in the campus community. An acquisition of "appreciation, knowledge and understanding of cultural groups, especially those individuals and community that have been historically underserved and underrepresented" (Pope, Reynolds, & Mueller, 2004, p. 85) is needed to address barriers to multiculturalism and to help culturally diverse students. Being culturally aware and recognizing how culture will affect the helping process will aid in developing an empathic understanding toward the students you help (Pedersen, 1991). Furthermore, "all helping relationships require effort, adaptation, and more than a little humility" (Smith et al., 2004, p. 13).

Culturally competent helpers adapt and adjust their helping practices to accommodate cultural differences so that they may better meet the needs and goals of culturally diverse individuals (Diller, 2015). For example, a student from a Japanese or the Middle East culture might be reluctant about telling his or her family about changing a major from the one the family thinks is best. You, as a helper in a higher education environment, must realize that "you are a product of cultural conditioning and are not immune from inheriting hot buttons and biases associated with culturally diverse groups in our society" (Sue, 2006, p. 39). Just because you believe that you are a caring person does not mean that you are somehow immune from social conditioning; ignorance of issues does not make them disappear (Diller, 2015). All of us belong to multiple groups which informs our perceptions, beliefs, attitudes, and behavior and this belief allows room for you to effectively work with students who differ from you (Patterson, 1996). As discussed in Chapter 2, you must be willing to self-explore and work toward multicultural competence.

163

CONCLUSION

In summary, effectively responding to students in distress and/or crisis can be difficult and at times, even daunting. Nonetheless, people who are not mental health professionals, such as student affairs professionals, can play a significant role in the awareness, prevention, and treatment of psychological disorders. Student affairs professionals must be aware and knowledgeable about psychological and behavioral issues impacting college students and how to address and properly respond to the needs of students. It is important for student affairs professionals to assess their attitudes toward psychological disorders, including suicide, which can be major barriers to students seeking help. In particular, being aware of one's own anxiety and bias toward suicide is essential to being able to help a suicidal person. Additional training in suicide intervention is strongly recommended for student affairs professionals. Furthermore, client confidentiality is required in most states by law and in most professional organizations by ethical code; counseling centers cannot share client information without permission but they can take information from faculty and staff that are concerned about students. Therefore, student affairs professionals should be aware of qualified mental health professionals and how and when to make referrals and report issues related to students in crisis. Beyond that, there must also be an understanding of some unique needs associated with diverse students' cultural identity and an awareness of considerations that should be taken into account when working with these students.

REFERENCES

Agliata, D., & Tantleff-Dunn, S. (2004). The impact of media exposure on males' body image. *Journal of Social and Clinical Psychology, 23,* 7–22.

American Psychiatric Association. (2013). *Diagnostic and statistical manual of mental disorders* (5th ed.). Arlington, VA: American Psychiatric Publishing.

Bair, C., Kelly, N., Serdar, K., & Mazzeo, S. (2012). Does the internet function like magazines? An exploration of image-focused media, eating pathology, and body dissatisfaction [Abstract]. *Eating Behaviors, 13,* 398–401.

Becker, C. B., Bull, S., Schaumberg, K., Cauble, A., & Franco, A. (2008). Effectiveness of peer-led eating disorders prevention: A replication trial. *Journal of Consulting and Clinical Psychology, 76,* 347–354.

Belangee, S. (2006). Individual psychology and eating disorders: A theoretical application. *The Journal of Individual Psychology, 62,* 3–17.

Bergh, C., Callmar, M., Danemar, S., Hölcke, M., Isberg, S., Leon, M., Lindgren, J., Lundqvist, Â., & Sodersten, P. (2013). Effective treatment of eating disorders: Results at multiple sites. *Behavioral Neuroscience, 127,* 878–889.

Berk, M. (2011). *Drug overdose signs and symptoms (the educated patient).* Seattle, WA: Amazon Digital Services.

Berry, J. W. (1997). Immigration, acculturation, and adaptation. *Applied Psychology: An International Review, 46*(1), 5–68.

Berry, J. W. (2005). Acculturation: Living successfully in two cultures. *International Journal of Intercultural Relations, 29*, 697–712. Retrieved from http://isites.harvard.edu/fs/docs/icb.topic551691.files/Berry.pdf

Berry, J. W., & Sam, D. L. (1997). Acculturation and adaptation. In J. W. Berry, M. H. Segall, & C. Kagitcibasi (Eds.), *Handbook of cross-cultural psychology: Social behavior and applications* (pp. 291–326). Needham Heights, MA: Allyn & Bacon.

Borzekowski, D., Schenk, S., Wilson, J., & Peebles, R. (2010). E-Ana and e-mia: A content analysis of pro-eating disorder web sites. *American Journal of Public Health, 100*, 1526–1534.

Bui, K. V. T. (2002). First-generation college students at a four-year university: Background characteristics, reasons for pursuing higher education, and first-year experience. *College Student Journal, 36*(1), 3–11.

Butler, S. K. (2003). Helping urban African American high school students excel academically: The roles of school counselors. *High School Journal, 87*, 51–57.

Cazar, S. (2015). *Substance abuse: The greatest how to on substance abuse treatment–Release yourself from substance abuse and drug abuse, regain total control of your life for eternity.* Seattle, WA: Amazon Digital Services.

Choy, S. (2001). *Students whose parents did not go to college: Postsecondary access, persistence, and attainment* (NCES Rep. No. 2001–126). Washington, DC: National Center for Educational Statistics.

Cleveland, H., & Harris, K. (2010). *Substance abuse recovery in college: Community supported abstinence (advancing responsible adolescent development).* New York, NY: Springer.

Cole, D., & Zhou, J. (2014). Do diversity experiences help college students become more civically minded? Applying Banks' multicultural education framework. *Innovative Higher Education, 39*, 109–121.

Connors, G. J., DiClemente, C. C., Velasquez, M. M., & Donovan, D. M. (2013). *Substance abuse treatment and the stages of change: Selecting and planning interventions* (2nd ed.). New York, NY: The Guilford Press.

Constantine, M. G., Okazaki, S., & Utsey, S. O. (2004). Self-concealment, social self-efficacy, acculturative stress, and depression in African, Asian, and Latin American international college students. *American Journal of Orthopsychiatry, 74*(3), 230–241.

Crow, S. J., Peterson, C. B., Swanson, S. A., Raymond, N. C., Specker, S., Eckert, E. D., & Mitchell, J. E. (2009). Increased mortality in bulimia nervosa and other eating disorders. *American Journal of Psychiatry, 166*, 1342–1346.

Dare, C., & Crowther, C. (1995). Psychodynamic models of eating disorders. In G. Szmukler, C. Dare, & J. Treasure (Eds.), *Handbook of eating disorders: Theory, treatment, and research* (pp. 293–308). Chichester, England: John Wiley and Sons.

De Silva, P. (1995). Cognitive-behavioural models of eating disorders. In G. Szmukler, C. Dare, & J. Treasure (Eds.), *Handbook of eating disorders: Theory, treatment, and research* (pp. 141–153). Chichester, England: John Wiley and Sons.

Diller, J. (2015). *Cultural diversity: A primer for the human services* (5th ed.). Stamford, CT: Cengage.

Duke Student Wellness Center. (2016). *Signs and symptoms of alcohol and drug abuse.* Retrieved from https://studentaffairs.duke.edu/duwell/information-parents-families/tips-talking-your-student/signs-symptoms-alcohol-and-drug-abuse

eDrug Rehab. (2015). *Overdose: Why it happens and what to do when it does.* Retrieved from www.edrugrehab.com/overdose-why-it-happens-and-what-to-do-when-it-does

Eisenberg, D., Golberstein, E., & Hunt, J. (2009). Mental health and academic success in college. B.E. *Journal of Economic Analysis & Policy*, *9*(1), Article 40.

Eisler, I. (1995). Family models of eating disorders. In G. Szmukler, C. Dare, & J. Treasure (Eds.), *Handbook of eating disorders: Theory, treatment, and research* (pp. 155–176). Chichester, England: John Wiley and Sons.

Eustace, R. W. (2007). *Factors influencing acculturative stress among international students in the United States* (Doctoral dissertation). Available from ProQuest Dissertations and Theses database (UMI No. 3291368).

Fairburn, C. (1981). A cognitive behavioural approach to the treatment of bulimia. *Psychological Medicine, 11,* 707–711.

Fairburn, C., & Garner, D. (1986). The diagnosis of bulimia nervosa. *International Journal of Eating Disorders, 5,* 403–419.

Fisher, G., & Harrison, T. (2012). *Substance abuse: Information for school counselors, social workers, therapists and counselors* (5th ed.). New York, NY: Pearson.

Freedenthal, K. (2013). *Suicide attempt survivors*. Retrieved from www.speakingofsuicide.com/2013/07/05/suicide-attempt-survivors/

Fries-Britt, S., & Turner, B. (2002). Uneven stories: Successful black collegians at a black and a white campus. *The Review of Higher Education, 25,* 315–330.

Gallagher, R. (2014). *National survey of college counseling centers*. Retrieved from www.collegecounseling.org/wp-content/uploads/NCCCS2014_v2.pdf

Gibbons, M. M., & Shoffner, M. F. (2004). Prospective first-generation college students: Meeting their needs through social cognitive career theory. *Professional School Counseling, 8,* 91–97.

Gibbons, M. M., & Woodside, M. (2014). Addressing the needs of first generation college students: Lessons learned from adults from low-education families. *Journal of College Counseling, 17,* 21–36.

Gordon, R. (2000). *Eating disorders: Anatomy of a social epidemic.* Malden, MA: Wiley-Blackwell.

Groesz, L., Levine, M., & Murnen, S. (2002). The effect of experimental presentation of thin media images on body dissatisfaction: A meta-analytic review. *International Journal of Eating Disorders, 31,* 1–16.

Gullan, R. L., Hoffman, B. N., & Leff, S. S. (2011). I do but I don't: The search for identity in urban African American adolescents. *Perspectives on Urban Education, 8*(2), 29–40.

Hanna, F. J., Bemak, F., & Chi-Ying Chung, R. (1999). Toward a new paradigm for multicultural counseling. *Journal of Counseling and Development, 77,* 125–134.

Hartig, N., & Steigerwald, F. (2007). Understanding family roles and ethics in working with first generation college students and their families. *The Family Journal: Counseling and Therapy for Couples and Families, 15,* 159–162.

The Higher Education Center for Alcohol and Other Drug Prevention. (n.d.). Sidney Ribeau, Presidential Profiles. Retrieved from www2.edc.org/cchs/plg/profiles/ribeau.pdf

Hirsch, J. K., Webb, J. R., & Jeglic, E. L. (2011). Forgiveness, depression, and suicidal behavior among a diverse sample of college students. *Journal of Clinical Psychology, 7*(9), 896–906.

Hogan, J., & Gabrielsen, K. (2002). *Substance abuse prevention: The intersection of science and practice.* New York, NY: Pearson.

Hoyt, W. D., & Ross, S. D. (2003). Clinical and subclinical eating disorders in counseling center clients: A prevalence study. *Journal of College Student Psychotherapy, 17,* 39–54.

Hurtado, S., Milem, J. F., Clayton-Pedersen, A., & Allen, W. (1999). *Enacting diverse learning environments: Improving the climate for racial/ethnic diversity in higher education institutions.* Washington, DC: ASHE-ERIC Higher Education Report Series: George Washington University Graduate School of Education.

Hysenbegasi, A., Hass, S. L., & Rowland, C. R. (2005). The impact of depression on the academic productivity of university students. *Journal of Mental Health Policy and Economics, 8*(3), 145–151.

Institute of International Education (IIE). (2013). *Open doors 2013: Report on international educational exchange.* New York, NY: Institute of International Education. Information and Data Tables. Retrieved from http://iie.org/Researchand-Publications/Open-Doors

Johnson, L. R., & Sandhu, D. S. (2007). Isolation, adjustment, and acculturation issues of international students: Interventions strategies for counselors. In H. D. Singaravelu & M. Pope (Eds.), *A handbook for counseling international students in the United States* (pp. 13–36). Alexandria, VA: American Counseling Association.

Joiner, T. (2009). *The interpersonal-psychological theory of suicidal behavior.* Retrieved from www.apa.org/science/about/psa/2009/06/sci-brief.aspx

Jordan, L. (2009). *I never thought addiction could happen to me: The 3 secret addictions that are shattering the lives of college students … and what to do about it.* Long Island City, NY: Madison Publishing.

Kobasa, S. C. (1982). Commitment and coping in stress resistance among lawyers. *Journal of Personality and Social Psychology, 42*(4), 707–717.

Krumrei, E. J., Newton, F. B., & Kim, E. (2010). A multi-institution look at college students seeking counseling: Nature and severity of concerns. *Journal of College Student Psychotherapy, 24*(4), 261–283.

Kuhn, C., & Swartzwelder, S. (2014). *Buzzed: The straight facts about the most used and abused drugs from alcohol to ecstasy.* New York, NY: W. W. Norton and Company.

Lazarus, R. S. (1974). Psychological stress and coping in adaptation and illness. *International Journal of Psychiatry in Medicine, 5*, 321–333.

Lippincott, J. A., & German, N. (2007). From blue collar to ivory tower: Counseling first generation, working-class students. In J. A. Lippincott & R. B. Lippincott (Eds.), *Special populations in college counseling: A handbook for mental health professionals* (pp. 89–98). Alexandria, VA: American Counseling Association.

Longmire-Avital, B., & Miller-Dyce, C. (2015). Factors related to perceived status in the campus community for first generation students at an HBCU. *College Student Journal, 49*(3), 375–386.

Lowes, J., & Tiggemann, M. (2003). Body dissatisfaction, dieting awareness and the impact of parental influence in young children. *British Journal of Health Psychology, 8*, 135–147.

Malecki, C. K., & Demaray, M. K. (2002). Measuring perceived social support: Development of the child and adolescent social support scale. *Psychology in the Schools, 39*, 1–18.

Malinauskas, B. M., Raedeke, T. D., Aeby, V. G., Smith, J. L., & Dallas, M. B. (2006). Dieting practices, weight perceptions, and body composition: A comparison of normal weight, overweight, and obese college females. *Nutrition Journal, 5*(11), 1–8.

McCarron, G. P., & Inkelas, K. K. (2006). The gap between educational aspirations and attainment for first-generation college students and the role of parental involvement. *Journal of College Student Development, 47*, 534–549.

167

Miller, W., & Carroll, K. (2010). *Rethinking substance abuse: What the science shows, and what we should do about it.* New York, NY: The Guilford Press.

Minuchin, S., Rosman, B., & Baker, L. (1978). *Psychosomatic families: Anorexia nervosa in context.* Cambridge, MA: Harvard University Press.

National Institute of Mental Health. (2014). *Eating disorders: About more than food.* NIH Publication No. TR 14–4901. Bethesda, MD: Author. Retrieved from www.nimh. nih.gov/health/publications/eating-disorders-new-trifold/eating-disorders-pdf_148810.pdf

Nelson, D. L., & Simmons, B. L. (2011). Savoring eustress while coping with distress: The holistic model of stress. In J. C. Quick & L. E. Tetrick (Eds.), *Handbook of occupational health psychology* (pp. 55–74). Washington, DC: American Psychological Association.

Neumark-Sztainer, D. (2005). *I'm, like, so fat!: Helping your teen make healthy choices about eating and exercise in a weight-obsessed world.* New York, NY: The Guilford Press.

Ousley, L., Cordero, E. D. & White, S. (2008). Fat talk among college students: How undergraduates communicate regarding food and body weight, shape and appearance. *Eating Disorders, 16*, 73–84.

Patterson, C. H. (1996). Multicultural counseling: From diversity to universality. *Journal of Counseling and Development, 74*, 227–231.

Pedersen, P. B. (1991). Multiculturalism as a generic approach to counseling. *Journal of Counseling & Development, 70*, 6–12.

Pope, R. L., Reynolds, A. L., & Mueller, J. A. (2004). *Multicultural competence in student affairs.* San Francisco, CA: Jossey-Bass.

Poyrazli, S., & Lopez, M. (2007). An exploratory study of perceived discrimination and homesickness: A comparison of international students and American students. *Journal of Psychology, 141*(3), 263–280.

Pratt-Clarke, M. (2013). A radical reconstruction of resistance strategies: Black girls and Black women reclaiming our power using transdisciplinary applied social justice ©, Ma'at, and rites of passage. *Journal of African American Studies, 17*, 99–114.

Quinnett, P. G. (2000). *Counseling suicidal people.* Spokane, Washington: The QPR Institute, Inc.

Quinnett, P. G. (2004). *Suicide: The forever decision.* New York, NY: Crossroad Publishing Company.

Ramos-Sanchez, L., & Nichols, L. (2007). Self-efficacy of first-generation and non-first generation college students: The relationship with academic performance and college adjustment. *Journal of College Counseling, 10*, 6–17.

Robinson, L., Smith, M., & Saisan, J. (2015). *Drug abuse and addiction.* Retrieved from www.helpguide.org/articles/addiction/drug-abuse-and-addiction.htm

Rodriguez, R., Marchand, E., Ng., J., & Stice, E. (2008). Effects of a cognitive dissonance-based eating disorder prevention program are similar for Asian American, Hispanic, and White participants. *International Journal of Eating Disorders, 41*, 618–625.

Rosenthal, B., & Wilson, W. C. (2008). Mental health services: Use and disparity among diverse college students. *Journal of American College Health, 57*(1), 61–66.

Ruiz, P., & Strain, E. (2011). *Lowinson and Ruiz's substance abuse: A comprehensive textbook* (5th ed.). Philadelphia, PA: Lippincott Williams and Wilkins.

Sanford, N. (1969). *When colleges fail: A study of the student as a person.* San Francisco, CA: Jossey-Bass.

Schmidt, C. K., Piontkowski, S., Raque-Bogdan, T. L., & Ziemer, K. S. (2014). Relational health, ethnic identity, and well-being of college students of color: A strengths-based perspective. *The Counseling Psychologist, 42*(4), 473–496.

Schmitt, M. T., Spears, R., & Branscombe, N. R. (2003). Constructing a minority group identity out of shared rejection: The case of international students. *European Journal of Social Psychology, 33,* 1–12.

Selye, H. (1974). *Stress without distress.* Philadelphia, PA: J. B. Lippincott.

Singal, J. (2015). *The myth of the ever-more-fragile college student.* Retrieved from nymag.com/science of us/2015/11/myth-of-the-fragile-college student.html

Smith, T. B., Richards, P. S., Granley, H. M., & Obiakor, F. (2004). Practicing multiculturalm: An introduction. In T. B. Smith (Ed.), *Practicing multiculturalism: Affirming diversity in counseling and psychotherapy.* Boston, MA: Pearson.

Smolak, L. (2011). Body image development in childhood. In T. Cash & L. Smolak (Eds.), Body image: A handbook of science, practice, and prevention (2nd ed., pp. 67–75). New York, NY: Guilford.

Stauffer, M. D. (2004). From Seneca to suicidology. In D. Capuzzi (Ed.), *Suicide across the life span: Implications for counselors* (pp. 3–37). Alexandria, VA: American Counseling Association.

Stice, E. (2001). A prospective test of the dual pathway model of bulimic pathology: Mediating effects of dieting and negative affect. *Journal of Abnormal Psychology, 110,* 124–135.

Stice, E., Marti, C. N., & Rohde, P. (2012). Prevalence, incidence, impairment, and course of the proposed DSM-5 eating disorder diagnoses in an 8-year prospective community study of young women. *Journal of Abnormal Psychology, 122,* 445–457.

Stice, E., Mazotti, L., Weibel, D., & Agras, W. (2000). Dissonance prevention program decreases thin-ideal internalization, body dissatisfaction, dieting, negative affect, and bulimic symptoms: A preliminary experiment. *International Journal of Eating Disorders, 27,* 206–217.

Stice, E., & Presnell, K. (2007). *The body project: Promoting body acceptance and preventing eating disorders facilitator guide.* New York, NY: Oxford University Press.

Stice, E., Rohde, P., Durant, S., & Shaw, H. (2012). A preliminary trial of a prototype internet dissonance-based eating disorder prevention program for young women with body image concerns. *Journal of Consulting and Clinical Psychology, 80,* 907–916. doi:10.1037/a0028016.

Sue, D. W. (2006). *Multicultural social work practice.* Hoboken, NJ: John Wiley & Sons.

Sümer, S., Poyrazli, S., & Grahame, K. (2008). Predictors of depression and anxiety among international students. *Journal of Counseling & Development, 86,* 429–437.

Suokas, J. T., Suvisaari, J. M., Gissler, M., Löfman, R., Linna, M. S., Raevuori, A., & Haukka, J. (2013). Mortality in eating disorders: A follow-up study of adult eating disorder patients treated in tertiary care, 1995–2010. *Psychiatry Research, 210,* 1101–1106.

Swanson, S. A., Crow, S. J., LeGrange, D., Swendsen, J., & Merikangas, K. R. (2011). Prevalence and correlates of eating disorders in adolescents: Results from the National Comorbidity Survey Replication Adolescent Supplement. *Archives of General Psychiatry, 68,* 714–723.

Thomas, K., & Althen, G. (1989). Counseling foreign students. In P. B. Pedersen, J. G. Draguns, W. J. Lonner, & J. E. Trimble (Eds.), *Counseling across cultures* (3rd ed., pp. 205–241). Honolulu, HI: University of Hawaii Press.

169

Thompson, J. K., Heinberg, L. J., Altabe, M. N., & Tantleff-Dunn, S. (1999). *Exacting beauty: Theory, assessment and treatment of body image disturbance.* Washington, DC: American Psychological Association.

Twenge, J. M., Gentile, B., DeWall, C. N., Ma, D., Lacefield, K., & Schurtz, D. R. (2010a). A cross temporal meta-analysis of the MMPI. *Clinical Psychology Review, 20,* 145–154.

Twenge, J. M., Gentile, B., DeWall, C. N., Ma, D., Lacefield, K., & Schurtz, D. R. (2010b). Birth cohort increases in psychopathology among young Americans, 1938–2007: A cross-temporal meta-analysis of the MMPI. *Clinical Psychology Review, 30*(2), 145–154.

University of Central Florida Counseling and Psychological Services. (2015). *Making a referral.* Retrieved from http://caps.sdes.ucf.edu/referral

Vartanian, L., Giant, C., & Passino, R. (2001). "Ally McBeal vs. Arnold Schwarzenegger": Comparing mass media, interpersonal feedback and gender as predictors of satisfaction with body thinness and muscularity. *Social Behavior and Personality, 29,* 711–723.

Wade, T. D., Keski-Rahkonen, A., & Hudson, J. (2011). Epidemiology of eating disorders. In M. Tsuang & M. Tohen (Eds.), Textbook in psychiatric epidemiology (3rd ed., pp. 343–360). New York, NY: Wiley.

White, H., & Rabiner, D. (2011). *College drinking and drug use (Duke series in child development and public policy).* New York, NY: The Guilford Press.

Wisotsky, W., Dancyger, I., Fornari, V., Katz, J., Wisotsky, W. L., & Swencionis, C. (2003). The relationship between eating pathology and perceived family functioning in eating disorder patients in a day treatment program. *Eating Disorders: The Journal of Treatment and Prevention, 11,* 89–99.

Zaider, T. I., Johnson, J. G., & Cockell, S. J. (2000). Psychiatric comorbidity associated with eating disorder symptomology among adolescents in the community. *International Journal of Eating Disorders, 28,* 58–67.

Chapter 7

Developing Your Helping Philosophy

Although student affairs practices "are based upon a variety of different philosophies" (MacKinnon & Associates, 2004, p. 8), the focus on the whole student has consistently been at the forefront. After examining 13 philosophical statements related to student affairs, Evans and Reason (2001) concluded that student affairs professionals' guiding principles include their responsibility to focus on the student as the primary focus on their work, creating supportive and responsive environments to ensure students' total development. Reynolds (2011) asserted, "Attending to the needs of the whole student has been embedded in the core values, philosophies, and literature of the student affairs profession from the very beginning" (p. 399). With the changing context of higher education, now more than ever, helping college students navigate the higher education system in a healthy and successful way in a safe environment is vital. The profession also highlights the importance of helping students in finding roles in relation to others that will make them feel valued, contribute to their feelings of self-worth, and contribute to a feeling of kinship with others (Young, 2003). To effectively help students develop and feel supported, student affairs professionals must be able to effectively use helping, advising, and counseling skills in various settings (Reynolds, 2009).

Anyone can help. Anyone can advise. However, in a professional setting, the process of helping and advising is carried out with careful intention (originating from awareness and knowledge base) and skill. You probably already figured out by now that in order to become skillful in something, you need to learn and study the skills and then you must practice them (over and over). Clarifying and understanding the intention behind what skills you use is a bit more complicated. The intention behind each act of professional helping should come from an integration of your own personal philosophy of helping and a theoretical framework.

Chances are you already have beliefs and thoughts about how others should be helped. In short, this is your personal philosophy of helping. You have beliefs about how others should be helped because of your own personal experiences, current knowledge, and values. Albeit it will grow and change, essentially this personal philosophy of helping will provide a framework from which to base your professional practice. This personal helping philosophy is a compass that provides navigation. It will serve as a roadmap for judgment, and therefore influences actions.

THINKING ABOUT MY PRACTICE

What experiences and beliefs influenced your interest in helping others?
What do you get out of helping others?
Why do you think people seek help?
How do you define good practice in helping others?

As a student affairs professional, a primary focus is obviously gaining essential skills that are the basis for informed and effective professional practice. However, beyond the skills attainment and development, you should draw from your natural helping abilities and the knowledge drawn from your life and professional experiences to build and transform your personal philosophical approach as a helping professional in higher education. Developing your personal philosophy for helping college students, which includes your view of students' behaviors, intentions, motivation, development, and relationships, also builds a framework for understanding and constructing your approach to helping, an essential component of moving toward skill development. For this process, we recommend focusing on the following areas: professional knowledge; personal awareness; and active practice, integration, and synthesis.

1. **Professional Knowledge:** You should study the values that guide the actions of professionals and good practices associated with student affairs. Be sure to refer to the professional standards of student affairs and the themes related to professional competencies (e.g., accountability, integrity, helping, equity, leadership, professionalism, and ethics) in working successfully with college students. The principles associated with effectiveness, ethics, values, and expectations in student affairs are outlined by professional organizations such as the American College Personnel Association (ACPA), the National Association of Student Personnel Administration (NASPA), and the Council for the Advancement of Standards (CAS). Focus on what you see as the purpose of your area of student affairs, relating to its values, core beliefs, and competencies.

2. **Personal Awareness:** You need to engage in a great deal of introspection, taking the time to learn who you are as an individual and a professional. In addition, you should become aware of how

you view the world and comprehend your beliefs (Watts, 1993). Identify your personal core values and beliefs, focusing on factors that contribute to your role as a student affairs professional (e.g., advocate, educator, leader, and helper). Reflect on how your personal values and beliefs complement the values and competencies of student affairs and contribute to your role as a helping professional in student affairs. Reflect on how some of your personal values and beliefs may potentially pose barriers to ethical and competent professional practice. Go beyond the superficial. As MacKinnon and Associates (2004) assert, "only by studying and applying deeply held assumptions and premises can a practitioner of student affairs hope to bring insight to a novel problem, a difficult student, or a new situation" (p. 7).

3. **Active Practice, Integration, and Synthesis:** Through work-related experiences and practices, you can try out various approaches, strategies, and techniques in working with students. Integrate the knowledge you have gained, practical experiences, and understanding of good professional practice and standards to develop your personal theory. It is expected that you will continue to grow and even transform your ideology and accordingly, your helping philosophy will change as you mature as a professional.

In the end, the helping philosophy is formed from perceptions and beliefs about how you believe things should be and why they should be that way. Furthermore, it encompasses many influences which may include but are not limited to your life experiences, family of origin, cultural experiences, socioeconomic status, and/or religions and spiritual beliefs. As we are not value-free beings, it is important for student affairs professionals to think about what is valued, how much emphasis is placed on these values, and how these values influence expectations and actions. Furthermore, examining, affirming, and validating your philosophy can enhance your professional and personal growth.

BUILDING YOUR FRAMEWORK AND APPROACH FOR HELPING

Recall the importance of approaching every opportunity to help with intention. That is, you enter the situation already with a sense of how you believe people in general are best helped. You carry out your help accordingly. However, as a professional helper, it is absolutely essential that the framework of your helping goes beyond just your personal experiences, values, and knowledge about life up until that point. After you a have a sense of what you believe about how others should be helped, it is important to begin applying theoretically based helping models within your professional practice. Without both a clear understanding of your helping philosophy and a theoretical framework, you will end up haphaz-ardly approaching your helping work with students. That is, without a well-tuned compass guiding your professional helping, you will rely primarily on your own experiences and personal opinions, all of which may be neither appropriate nor relevant to the student being helped.

So where do you start? If you have gotten to this point in the chapter, you already began working on step one, crystalizing your personal philosophy. The next step is to gain knowledge of counseling theory models and examine how these theories fit with your beliefs about college student development and needs. First, it will be helpful to understand what exactly a counseling theory is!

Theoretical counseling models provide a framework which can be used to describe and understand a person's thoughts, behaviors, and emotions and as a way to view these concepts from the perspective of a person's past, present, or future. As described by Hackney (1992), theory can be used to define the nature of the helping relationship, conceptualize the nature of the presenting problem(s), and define the resulting goals or desired outcomes and related interventions. Theoretical models provide logical direction and can assist in a practical manner by assisting the helper in focusing on relevant information and providing a framework for what to look for within a helping relationship (Boy & Pine, 1983). A theory is more than speculation, opinion, statement of position, or a point of view and is more than just a collection of prin-ciples, methods, or techniques. Rather, it is an organized set of ideas which can explain the largest amount of material of concern (Luciano, Granahl, & Hansen, 1986).

Although theoretical frameworks provide a limited utility in learning help-ing skills, understanding counseling theories can assist you as a student affairs practitioner in developing techniques to use in your work with students. While you will not be providing counseling, the counseling theory will help you conceptualize how and why any given student is behaving, thinking and feeling the way he or she is. Additionally, it will provide insight into problem development and maintenance, as well as best approaches for student support and applied intermediation. In essence, a theory is a context from which to understand and view human behavior that provides direction to the helper for best practice.

There are hundreds of theories; and you could spend a lifetime studying and practicing each one. Each theory has its own limited viewpoint (Fox, 2013) and unique "different kind of lens" through which to understand and help individuals (Bitter, 2014, p. 6). We suggest that you study two or three. You may start with the three that we briefly introduce in this chapter. Your next task is to read about any of them at greater length (see the multiple references provided). Dive deeper into understanding any given theory based upon whether the introductory concepts are similar to your own philosophy of helping.

COUNSELING THEORIES: APPROACHES AND APPLICATION

In review, a "theory serves as a conceptual framework and guide to interventions" (Halbur & Halbur, 2011, p. 11). Essentially, a theory provides a systematic approach to understanding someone's presenting concerns and struggles and helping the person work through them. Helpers decide on a theory to frame their work based upon how the theory best fits with their personal philosophy of helping. In this section, we briefly outline the primary tenets of three specific theories, including Cognitive Behavioral Theory, Choice Theory, and Individual Psychology (Adlerian Theory). We will suggest considerations related to how the theory may be applied to work with college students. The theories will not be presented in depth; however, the information can be used as you reflect on your helping philosophy.

Individual Psychology or Adlerian Theory

Adlerian theory was founded by Alfred Alder in the early 1900s. Adler actually was a member of Sigmund Freud's professional meetings and left because of his fundamentally different views of human nature. Adler's Individual Psychology is referred to as a personality theory, accounting for the developmental, social-psychological, and cognitive. Incidentally, much of the "positive psychology" trend that has boomed over the last few years derives from the basic principles of Adlerian psychology.

Individuals are believed to have unique personalities or *lifestyles* characterized by subjective beliefs, personal convictions, and attitudes (McCurdy, 2007; Powers & Griffith, 1987). This is often referred to as the indivisible whole of each person. How we deal with or face a problem is dependent on our lifestyle, or how we operate within the social field via basic convictions we have about ourselves, others, and the world. Our lifestyles are typically established by the age of eight. Not surprisingly, then, Adlerians place attention on various aspects of family of origin, or *family constellation*. Our birth order, for example, is one influence on our lifestyle. It provides insight about our earliest vantage points specifically related to how we assessed and viewed ourselves, others, and the world (Powers & Griffith, 1987).

My parents tell me (second author) the story about how I responded when my sister was born. Apparently, I was not happy (as I was the oldest, and before my sister Kim, the only). I misbehaved and threw tantrums shortly after she joined our family. Essentially, Kim's birth was a clear indication to me that I was not the one and only that I perceived to be. However, there was more to the story than a first born being dethroned by the second born. The narrative began years before I was even born. It took my parents seven years of many fertility struggles to eventually have me, their first child. Can you imagine eventually having your first child after seven years of anticipation, disappointment, and pain? They loved and appreciated my life so much that they captured hours of me sleeping on videotape! Needless to say that for two and a half years, I felt this intense love from both of my parents. Being the center of their attention was an understatement. Suddenly, though, it felt to me like my world came crashing down all around me. Even at the very young age of 2½ I felt the impact of having to share their attention. I could elaborate on my lifestyle development (personality development), including the many influences that shaped it, however, it is no coincidence that I pursued and achieved the successes in my life that I have thus far. I had to find a way to feel important.

Additionally, *family atmosphere*, as well as how the individual experienced problems, goals, frustrations, achievements, and obstacles within the family, will have an impact on one's lifestyle, or how he or she currently views self, others, and the world when positive experiences or challenges arise. Adlerians buy into the idea that we are treated how we expect to be treated; and these expectations have been formed at a young age and based on a multitude of experiences, much of which having occurred in our family of origin. When I was 2 (this was before my sister was born), I was severely bitten in the face by a dog to the point of necessitating plastic surgery, and months later fell off a toy truck which also required stitches on my forehead. However, my mother's way of dealing with feeling like a failure was to find a way not to feel that way. She got me in the backyard swimming pool and taught me how to swim across the diameter of the family pool by myself.

I hope you gleaned a couple of interesting dynamics from this story. First, my mother must have learned that failure indicates something to be overcome, rather than something that leads to immobility. Despite feeling defeated, she moved to action by doing something to overcome the feeling. She learned this from her own family of origin and this eventually became part of her lifestyle (personality). Then, through her actions she communicated to our family that:

- Hard times will come and it is okay to feel bad. Then get up off your knees (symbolic) and get back in the game.
- Never give up.
- You are not responsible for something that happens to someone that is out of your control.

Who she became and who I eventually became were highly influenced by our family systems. Adlerians would pay attention to how the individual's family system impacted who he or she is today.

Adlerians believe that people are self-determining and creative. We have choices about what to do or what not to do. We are not passive bystanders or victims of any given situation (Dewey, 1984). As the first optimists within the field of counseling psychology, Adlerians believe that "everything can also be different" (Adler, 1933, p. 7). This can be done by altering our *perceptions* of any given situation and choosing to do something different, even though it may initially feel uncomfortable. As you may recall, Adlerians believe that such perceptions of situations and other people are patterned from early life experiences. Consequently, a part of helping someone change his or her perceptions about a current situation will include consideration of the narratives developed across memory lane.

Let's go back to the example. What if my mother continued to perceive my injuries (as well as the injuries of everyone else that she was in contact with) as being related to something intrinsically wrong with her (a position she would have likely learned as a child in her own family of origin)? What might have been the impacts of this on me and others in my family? How might this have changed my own perceptions of myself, her, others, and the world? Depending on the interaction of other experiences, I may have grown up with the ultimate goal of always taking on the responsibility for events that I had no control over. I may have assumed that my injuries (and other personal life experiences) were someone else's to carry and so I may have gone through my life not caring what I did because, after all, someone else would take responsibility for the consequences. The goal, although quite mistaken in its nature, would be to get away with anything and everything. Or, because I assumed (perception) that when bad things happen to me, it will cause others to become depressed and disengaged and so I am better off dodging close relationships (mistaken goal). We can see that one behaves according to an ultimate purpose, and this purpose is molded and shaped by early life experiences, typically within the primary system the individual is a part of (i.e., one's family).

Another concept is that behavior can be categorized as useful or useless. Useful kind of behavior is cooperative and aimed at the common good (Dreikurs, Grunwald, & Pepper, 1982). If we are engaged in useful behavior, we are concerned with not only bringing good to ourselves, but also to others and the world. In short, useful behavior helps make the world a better place. Someone engaged in useless behavior, on the other hand, is interested in self and is neither interested in contributing to the good of others nor believes he has a place with others. A child who does not believe that he can find belonging or acceptance will engage in useless behavior, and thus may adopt four mistaken goals of behavior without even being aware of why (Dreikurs, 1957/1968). These four mistaken goals are attention seeking, power seeking, revenge seeking, and inadequate and assumed disability. Attention-seeking behaviors typically imply that the individual has felt discouraged. He or she will attempt to gain attention with perfectionistic behaviors (the classroom superstar), destruction (showing off, bully), and/or self-imposed disabilities (illogical fears). Rather than seeking to be collaborative or work nicely with others, one may engage in power-seeking behaviors. He or she wants to feel better about himself or herself and the situation, and so will

177

engage in a power struggle with others (more often authority figures). You may also encounter children engaged in a pattern of revenge-seeking behavior. They are interested in "getting back" (lying, stealing, or hurting others). Chances are that people who engage in revenge-seeking behavior have been hurt themselves somewhere along the line. The last mistaken goal, inadequacy or assumed disability, is the child's way of communicating the following: "Don't expect anything from me because I don't have anything to give." They are truly discouraged and have given up on themselves, as well as the hope that anyone else could help. Keep in mind that these four useless kinds of behaviors are typically noted in children. In adulthood, the behaviors may become more complex as other goals are being pursued (Sweeney, 2009). However, when you are working with a student, it is helpful to consider that his or her behaviors are all driven by either a conscious or unconscious goal that is likely similar to these four mistaken goals.

Chances are that if you are working with a student with behavioral concerns, that particular student has been behaving uselessly toward one particular mistaken goal since childhood. If you are going to help the student (and the persons he or she is involved with), it is imperative to contextualize what is happening, rather than simply focusing on changing the behavior. That is, attempting to motivate the individual to do something different will only go so far (or not far at all). There is a greater intention, if you will, of misbehaving and causing problems. For example, if you guess that a student is engaged in power-seeking behaviors, for example, you might dialogue with this student about the importance of her feeling powerful and good about herself. Perhaps it was important for her to experience power as a child in order to overcome a given challenge. You could therefore direct the conversation toward more socially appropriate behaviors that still allow her to experience feeling powerful. You both might even recreate her definition of power.

An additional tenet of Adlerian theory is that behavior is purposeful (referred to as theological) and is not driven by instincts (what Freud believed); however, often the intentions of our behavior are not conscious. We do what we do without really knowing why. Understanding why someone behaves the way he or she does requires understanding what this person values or what he or she is attempting to achieve. Based upon a review and understanding of the individual's lifestyle, insight is created about the purpose behind any given opinion, behavior, or feeling. Let's go back to the example. Because of many experiences in my family of origin that supported personal and intrinsic success, I am much of who I am today. However, let us say that had my mother responded differently to my injuries (experienced herself as the point of failure for my injuries), I as a consequence may have developed the mistaken belief that others are responsible for carrying the burdens of negative events in my life. For example, as a college student I could have been the student that even after multiple warnings and consequences for providing and keeping alcohol in my room, said, "I don't know what the problem is. It's not my fault my roommate got drunk. She should have stopped after one or two. I shouldn't be blamed for this. No one would have even known I had alcohol in the room if she didn't get drunk!" You wonder to yourself why this student cannot seem to grasp the seriousness of the situation. Note, the behavior has a greater purpose, since I mistakenly believe that others are responsible for my behaviors, I have no reason to take any responsibility for a bad choice.

Finally, Adlerians believe that every one of us is faced with five major life tasks, including work, friendship, love, spirituality, and self. The task of work is different for different age groups. For example, for college students, this task is met by moving through college successfully (i.e., getting good grades, participating in rewarding campus activities, etc.). The task of friendship also differs across age groups. For college students, successfully meeting this task might include maintaining healthy friendships, engaging in an intimate relationship where one practices being cooperative and respectful and manages mutual giving and taking (Sweeney, 2009). Meeting the task of love requires self-sacrificing, vulnerability (to a greater extent than one would expose with just an acquaintance), and good conflict resolution skills. The life task of spirituality involves finding meaning in one's relationship to God, the universe, or a higher power. The final task involves one's success in coping with self by maintaining and achieving self-esteem and a sense of self-efficacy. A good Adlerian helper will be able to walk any given individual through how well or how unsuccessfully one is meeting these life tasks. As a student affairs professional, you are certainly encouraged to ask students how well they believe that they are doing in meeting each of these life tasks.

How might you apply an Adlerian approach in a student affairs context?

- Listen. Focus on the real issue (Sherman & Dinkmeyer, 1987). Keep in mind that what you will initially see are symptoms (i.e., argument with a roommate). What is the real goal behind the symptom (i.e., to always be right)?
- Encourage. Encourage. Encourage. Help build the student's self-esteem and self-worth. Notice the exceptions to the behavior. What positive assets does the student have? What positive, useful behaviors has the individual taken part in? Consider some guidelines for providing encouragement (see Sweeney, 2009, p. 90):
    - Focus on what the student is doing rather than on how he or she is doing it (i.e., "Josey, you sought help from me. That took courage.");
    - Focus on the present rather than on the past or future (i.e., "I know that you are concerned about how to interact with your roommate next week. Let's just focus for a bit on how you are helping yourself feel better in this moment.");

- Focus on the effort more so than the outcome (i.e., "You made an effort to ask your roommate out for coffee despite what her response might be.");
- Focus on what is being done successfully versus what has been done not so successfully (i.e., "Josey, you have mentioned a few times that you struggle making friends, but I have heard you talk about how often you reach out to others who could use a place to belong. You certainly seem like you know how to pursue friendships!").

- When working with more than one student, engage them in role reversal. Ask them to act as if they are the other person with whom they are in conflict. Encourage them to consider what it feels like to be in the other's shoes.
- Help the student get involved in activities that he or she finds worthy. Encourage social belonging and social contributions.
- Teach conflict resolution steps such as (Sherman & Dinkmeyer, 1987, p. 283):
  - Show mutual respect to each other. Refrain from fighting or giving in;
  - Focus on the real issue and the goal behind the issue;
  - Seek to find areas of agreement; be open to doing something different;
  - Participate in mutual decisions.

As previously mentioned, the concepts of Adlerian theory account for multiple influences that impact who an individual is and what he or she does. It suggests that while our past experiences may influence us, we have the capacity to become not only aware of these influences, but also the power to do something different as we interact with others, the world, and ourselves. We are self-determining and by nature, we are born to belong to others and make positive differences in their lives.

Below is a list of recommended reading:

Adler, A. (1979). *Superiority and social interest.* New York, NY: W. W. Norton & Company.

Ansbacher, H. L., & Ansbacher, R. R. (1956). *The individual psychology of Alfred Adler.* New York, NY: Harper Torchbooks.

Dreikurs, R., & Soltz, V. (1991). *Children: The challenge.* New York, NY: Plume. (Original work published 1964)

Grunwald, B. B., & McAbee, H. V. (1999). *Guiding the family* (2nd ed.). New York, NY: Taylor & Francis.

Hoffman, E. (1994). *The drive for self.* Reading, MA: Addison-Wesley. (Adler's biography)

Sweeney, T. J. (2009). *Adlerian counseling and psychotherapy: A practitioner's approach* (5th ed.). New York, NY: Routledge. (Introduction and summary of major concepts)

Choice Theory/Reality Therapy

A Choice Theory perspective emphasizes that individuals behave in ways to meet basic and universal needs. Human behavior is believed to be guided by five basic universal needs, including survival or self-preservation, love and belonging, freedom, fun, and power (Glasser, 1998; Wubbolding, 2011). Survival and self-preservation is the most basic need and is guided by basic physiological behaviors needed to stay alive and healthy. Love and belonging is the need for being a part of a social group (i.e., family), connecting with others, and belonging. Power is a need to feel worth it, confident, and/or competent. Contrary to what it may sound like, meeting the basic need of power does not refer to experiencing power over others. Freedom or independence is one's desire for autonomy and freedom of choice. Fun is the need for relaxation and engagement in pleasurable activities. According to the theory, each of us has a varying degree of need satisfaction for each basic need. For example, on a scale of 1 to 10 (with 10 representing the highest need or importance), I can rate the *strength* (how much it is important to me) of each basic need:

- survival, 8;
- love and belonging, 10;
- power, 8;
- freedom and independence, 7;
- fun, 6.

In other words, I (second author) have a higher need to be connected with my family and friends than I have a desire or need to be engaged in something fun on my days off. Similarly, it is very important for me to experience self-confidence and competence (power). See Figure 7.1, which provides the *Strength and Satisfaction Rating Scale for Students* adopted from *Glasser's Choice Theory Rating Needs Scale*. Go ahead and complete the strength rating for each basic need (the first rating line for each basic need category).

Another concept of Choice Theory is referred to as the "quality world" or a symbolic picture album. Our quality worlds include symbolic pictures, if you will, of what we want in our lives. More specifically, as we take part in everyday life we assign values to relationships, beliefs, traditions, cultural rituals in an attempt to construct an idyllic depiction of a world in which we want to live (Wubbolding, 2011). For example, my quality world includes the following (although certainly not limited to): time spent with my husband, family, and dog; secure and trustworthy friends; successful experiences at work; connection and volunteer time at church; and enough time to enjoy boating, wine tasting, and exercise.

The behaviors we engage in, which according to Choice Theory are all choices, are parallel and align themselves with our quality world (Glasser, 1998; Wubbolding,

Needs and Their Definitions	STRENGTH AND SATISFACTION RATING SCALE
Love and Belonging: The need for interpersonal contact, working together with others, and the potential for developing long-term relationships and friendships. To feel wanted and approved of by classmates, as well as by authorities.	Need Strength 0 1 2 3 4 5 6 7 8 9 10 Need Satisfaction 0 1 2 3 4 5 6 7 8 9 10
Self-Worth/Power: The need for a sense of empowerment, competence, and opportunities for personal effectiveness in the school environment. A connection between one's personal sense of achievement and worthiness with similar experiences in the home, school, and community. Opportunities for leadership and management roles.	Need Strength 0 1 2 3 4 5 6 7 8 9 10 Need Satisfaction 0 1 2 3 4 5 6 7 8 9 10
Freedom: The need for autonomy, independence, and limited restrictions in the school environment and in the home. Opportunities for spontaneity and change in all areas of one's life.	Need Strength 0 1 2 3 4 5 6 7 8 9 10 Need Satisfaction 0 1 2 3 4 5 6 7 8 9 10
Fun and Enjoyment: The need for balance between work and pleasure. Sufficient opportunities for enjoyable and fun experiences within the context of school, home, and community.	Need Strength 0 1 2 3 4 5 6 7 8 9 10 Need Satisfaction 0 1 2 3 4 5 6 7 8 9 10
Survival and Health: Safe physical environment at home and school. An environment that is a supportive context for one's mental and emotional health. Family income that adequately provides for enhanced educational opportunities, personal self-care, leisure activities, and vacations.	Need Strength 0 1 2 3 4 5 6 7 8 9 10 Need Satisfaction 0 1 2 3 4 5 6 7 8 9 10

FIGURE 7.1 Choice Theory Career Rating Scale for Children and Adolescents

2000). *Total behavior*, as Glasser puts it, includes action, thinking, feeling, and physiology. All are choices. For example, since it is important to me (second author) to feel competent (i.e., basic need of power), my quality world includes pictures of successful work experiences. Thus, my total behavior includes this: *thinking* that I am competent enough to write; creating an outline and clearing out my schedule to write (*doing*); *feeling* positive and compassionate about what I am writing about; and getting a good night's sleep the night before and having a cup of coffee to help me focus (*physiological*). I can apply total behavior toward obtaining each "picture" in my quality world. When I do this, I have my life quite in balance! My needs are being satisfied, and I am choosing and engaging in behaviors to make that happen.

Let us be realistic. Our lives are not always in balance. At times, there is an inconsistency between what is desired (pictures in the quality world) and what is being experienced. Sometimes we have control over this and sometimes we do not. For example, a few weeks ago I (second author) had a lovely day planned with my niece. I woke to an expectant and unfortunate surprise: a four-day flu. There was nothing that I could do except to focus on my basic need of survival. Needless to say my need satisfaction of love and belonging, as well as fun, was not being met. Although my body was ill (*physiology*) and there was not much I could physically *do*, I told myself (*thinking*) that there would be other times to enjoy Anna. I began to *feel* appreciative of the times that I did have with her and the experience of health (which I normally experience). In my best attempt, I attempted to influence my entire experience through my total behavior; despite not exactly achieving total need satisfaction. Let us go back to the *Strength and Satisfaction Rating Scale for Students*. You should have rated your *need strength* for each basic need. Now, for each basic need, rate on a scale of 1 to 10 with 10 representing that you are completely satisfied with how you are currently meeting that need. For example:

- survival, 7, I am feeling fairly well except for a cough that I cannot seem to lose.
- love and belonging, 8, I have spent the last few days with good friends; however, I miss my family back home in Chicago.
- power, 10, I am actively engaged in co-writing this book and am excited about the information we are sharing with you.
- freedom and independence, 7, my vacation is coming to a close and I am anticipating less freedom with the upcoming work schedule.
- fun, 10, I have had lots of fun with friends over the last few days.

Reality Therapy is the conduit for applying Choice Theory. The therapy (or helping process) is used to assess one's basic need fulfillment, psychological well-being, behavior change, and life choices consistent with individual quality world pictures and need satisfaction (Wubbolding, Brickell, Imhof, Kim, Lojk, & Al-Rashidi, 2004). The desired outcome of this process is behavioral change toward a greater need satisfaction by helping people examine their wants and needs, evaluate behaviors, and make plans for fulfilling those needs (Glasser & Wubbolding, 1995). This application process is referred to as the WDEP system (Wubbolding, 2011).

The WDEP system is an acronym for Wants, Doing, Evaluation, and Plan. The first step includes assisting the individual in uncovering what goals and outcomes are being sought. That is, what does he or she want? Additionally, this step involves addressing what pictures the individual has in his or her quality world pictures, as well as his or her level of satisfaction across the five basic needs. You might encourage the student whom you are helping to complete the *Strength and Satisfaction Rating Scale for Students* adopted from *Glasser's Choice Theory Rating Needs Scale* (see Figure 7.1). Let us say that you are working with Josey, a student who is struggling with her roommate. Josey presents the following complaints: her roommate takes her things without asking; talks on the phone loudly when she is trying to sleep; and is sometimes unfriendly and rude when they are in a large group. You would ask Josey what she wanted. Chances are we all know what she would say. She wants to feel respected. She does not want her things to be taken without asking. And she wants to sleep. You could also ask her if she wants to pursue a friendship with this roommate. The answer to that question will likely inform you about the next best steps.

The D (Doing) is a discovery tool that helps the individual consider what he or she is actually doing that is consistent or inconsistent with the Wants. You might ask this student a series of questions:

- Have you talked to your roommate about any of this yet?
- When your roommate is rude to you around friends, what do you typically do?
- How do you manage sleeping when your roommate is on the phone?

The third step, or Evaluation, involves facilitating dialogue with the individual in the attempt to have him or her self-evaluate behavior that is effective or noneffective based on wants and needs. That is, are the behaviors (doing) getting the person what she wants? Let us go back to the student with the unfriendly roommate. Suppose you asked her some of the questions above and her response was: "I left her a note; and that did not seem to work. She never responded and keeps doing the same things over and over. When she is rude and unfriendly to me around people, I go out of my way to be kind to her. Sometimes it just feels like she is walking all over me. The last few times she was on the phone when I was trying to sleep, I put a pillow over my head. Surprisingly, that helped!" Your role in this third step will be to help the student dialogue about whether what she is doing is getting her what she wants (i.e., respect). Some evaluative questions and possible responses might include:

- You said that when you put a pillow over your head, that worked! So it sounds like that is one way of getting the sleep that you need despite her being loud. Is this working for you? *"Well, it actually is working. Although it makes me mad that she still does it, I guess I can let this go."*

■ When you work extra hard to be kind to her, you still feel like she is "walking all over you." Is that helping you get the respect that you said that you wanted? . . . And if not, is there something else that you might try to feel less walked on? *"Yea, I do not feel good in situations like this. I tell myself that I don't need to be treated like this. So no, it's not working to try to be her friend. In fact, I am beginning to wonder if she is the kind of friend I need in my life."*

■ I can see how you would have preferred to write a note to her. Sometimes that feels a whole lot better than verbally confronting someone. How is that working for you in terms of feeling heard and respected by her? *"Well, I really don't want to confront her verbally. I was never good at that. Can you help me?"*

By now you and the student will be actively engaged in a dialogue. You will be discussing what has worked, what does not work, and what some other possibilities are. It is time for the final component of the framework, the action plan (P). The individual, with the assistance of the helper, develops a plan of action both short term and long term to assist him or her in behavior changes working toward psychological balance and need satisfaction (Wubbolding, 2011). Proceeding with our example, this step may unfold like this:

■ Great! It sounds like you can continue putting the pillow over your head!

■ You know that you want to be respected and that you never have to feel disrespected. You are actually considering whether she would make a good friend to you. What do you think you want to do now? *"Well, I think for starters, I am not going to try so hard. I can ignore her, or I can decide to go out with other people!"* That sounds like a plan, why don't you try it and we can talk about how it worked the next time we meet?

■ I certainly will help you find a way to communicate that it is not okay with you for her to take your things without asking. Let's consider some possibilities. What do you think? (It is important to let the student create possibilities.)

In summary, questions consistent with the WDEP therapeutic framework are:

1. What do you *want*?
2. What are you *doing* to get what you want?
3. Is it working? (one's *evaluation* of what he or she is doing)
4. What is your *plan* now?

The goal of the process is to help people understand what wants and needs they are attempting to maneuver their behavior toward. The process involves helping them close the gap between what they want and what they have in the given moment (Wubbolding, 2000, p. 21).

VOICE FROM THE FIELD

Using Reality Therapy

Dr. Cynthia Palmer Mason

First, I consistently use Reality Therapy to help manage my day-to-day activities. I am goal oriented so the procedures for Reality Therapy work well for me. Regardless to whether I am making personal decisions or helping others to work through difficult situations, I follow the procedures. The acronym WDEP is used to describe the basic procedures of this approach whether used for individual, small group, or large group counseling sessions.

For instance, when I am making decisions each day, I decide initially what my goal is; next, I consider what I am doing to reach this goal. This is followed by a self-evaluation of whether or not what I am doing is leading me in the direction I want to go and if there is a reasonable chance for me to reach my goal without some changes. If I decide that I need to make changes—the next step is to consider what my options are, decide what I think will work best for me, and then proceed to decide on an action plan for change.

When working with high school students, my initial focus was on the counseling environment. My intention was to create a friendly, empathic atmosphere where students felt listened to, accepted, and safe. I always emphasized the fact that in all situations we have choices and we are responsible for the choices that we make.

I followed the Reality Therapy procedures by asking students how I could help them or what was going on in their lives. I listened patiently as they told their stories. After acknowledging their concerns, I usually asked them what they wanted to happen or what their goals were for their particular situations. After this discussion, I followed up by asking what students were doing with regard to their concerns. This led to the evaluation where students were asked if what they were doing was likely to solve their problems and usually the answer was "no." So, we started talking about options and when a decision was made about what would work best for each student, we proceeded to make a plan for change that the student was committed to. After reviewing the action plan we had decided on, I made comments to each student to show my support and also to encourage them as we were setting the next counseling appointment.

In two of the courses that I teach, I use role plays to help students get experience with this approach and I emphasize the importance of including group counseling because of the documented effectiveness of this format. I teach my students to apply the RT procedures to the four stages of group counseling identified by Corey in his book *Theory and Practice of Group Counseling*. A brief summary of what I do in each phase follows:

Initial Stage

The first stage of group development is the stage at which inclusion and identity are dealt with. Participants are wondering about their roles in the group, whether they will be accepted, and how they will fit. As the group leader, I help members to get beyond their anxiety by answering their questions and setting some boundaries. The next step is to ask students to explore their *wants:* what they want to get from the group experience, what possible benefits they see, and how they feel about being in the group. After this discussion, participants are asked to talk to each other in pairs or groups of three. They are asked to share their *wants* as much as is comfortable for them. No pressure is exerted and each dyad or triad makes a list for further discussion. Someone from each subgroup reads the list to the entire group. As leader, I facilitate a discussion of the aggregate of expectations, thoughts, and feelings of the participants. Questions for discussion usually include:

1. What are the common wants and expectations?
2. What are the common feelings and thoughts?
3. How much effort will it take to get the desired results from the group experience?

I prefer to use the activity *Who am I?* early in the group experience. The discussion of these data in the group process helps members to develop a feeling of belonging, a sense of inclusion, and the belief that there is something for me in this group because the other people are both similar to me in some ways and different from me in other ways.

Transition Stage

The second stage (transition) is usually *difficult* for the members as they deal with anxiety, resistance, and conflict. As leader, I help group members recognize and express their feelings; also, I point out power struggles and resistive behaviors. At this time, asking the participants about their levels of commitment and internal obstacles to progress is a useful activity that can be related to each level of *wants* in their list of priorities.

Working Stage

The third stage is the working stage and several elements can be described as most characteristic of this stage of group development. The first characteristic of this stage is that members establish the perception that they are able to work together after dealing with conflicts with each other and also challenging the legitimacy of the group leader's role. Another characteristic of this stage is that members usually experience a higher level of commitment; this can be to self-improvement, to solving problems, or a commitment to the group itself. This commitment to personal change fulfills the need for power and achievement and the commitment to the group enhances the feelings of belonging. A third characteristic of this stage is *cognitive restructuring*. During this stage a change in thinking behaviors occurs as the members conduct an honest and sometimes searching inventory and evaluation of the effectiveness of their behaviors, the attainability of their wants, and the depth of their commitments to change. My role as group leader in this stage is to facilitate the interdependence of group members, to build a sense of cohesion, and to help members elevate their levels of commitment.

Consolidation and Termination Stage

In the final phase (Consolidation and Termination Stage), group members are usually enthusiastic about having completed the group experience and having made changes, and at the same time, they feel anxious and fearful because the familiar support group will cease to exist. My efforts during this stage are aimed at allowing participants to discuss, without criticism, their feelings of sadness, fear, anxiety, hope for the future, and pride in what they have accomplished. At this time, I directly ask members to provide feedback to each other as a final gesture of friendship.

At this point, participants are asked to summarize their progress. Encouraged by direct questioning, the participants evaluate their progress. They are encouraged and helped to develop plans to maintain their effective behaviors and also to cope with the urge to choose the old, less effective alternatives.

For example, in connecting theory to practice, these questions could be useful when working with a student who is experiencing anxiety about his or her academic major or future career, dealing with student conduct issues, and expressing uncertainty about college life.

How might you apply a Choice Theory approach in a student affairs context?

- Help the student understand himself or herself better. Identify the student's need strengths and how well these needs are being met. Have the student complete the *Strength and Satisfaction Rating Scale for Students*. If one basic need is short of being fully met, help the student identify ways in which he or she can meet it.
- Use the WEDP Plan. Ask questions that could engage a student in discussions and the process of clarifying purpose and aspirations, self-evaluation, evaluating the current situation, identifying a path to reach goals, and committing to change as well as following through.
  - Help the student focus on what she or he wants. Some appropriate questions might include:
    - □ What do you want by the end of this semester?
    - □ How important is it to you to end the semester with a B average GPA?

- ☐ What are your short-term and long-term professional goals?
- ☐ What do you want out of relationships with your friends, your partner?
- ☐ How do you see a balance in your life?
- ☐ How do you want to spend your free time?
- ■ Help the student understand what she or he is doing to get what is wanted. Some questions may include:
    - ☐ What kind of study habits are you engaged in?
    - ☐ What are you doing to maintain the GPA that you want?
    - ☐ What are you doing to keep your professional and personal record clean?
    - ☐ Are you hanging out with people who help you get what you want?
    - ☐ How are you monitoring your drinking?
    - ☐ What are you doing to maintain balance in your life?
    - ☐ How many hours of sleep are you getting?
- ■ Help the student self-evaluate. Is what he or she is currently engaged in total behavior that lends itself to getting what is wanted?
    - ☐ Are the study habits helping you maintain the GPA that you want?
    - ☐ How will posting pictures of parties on Facebook impact your professional career?
    - ☐ How are the people you are hanging around with helping you get what you want now and what you eventually want?
    - ☐ Are your drinking habits getting in the way of being able to focus on your academics?
    - ☐ Could you be gaming too much on the weekends?
    - ☐ Do you need more than 5 hours of sleep at night to function at your best the next day?
- ■ Create a plan. The plan can be anything related to the following (note, the list is not exhaustive):
    - ☐ Effective identification and use of campus resources to help a graduate student who did not have any issues achieving satisfactory grades in undergraduate courses, but is now struggling and wants to get better grades or have better study habits.
    - ☐ Steps toward getting involved with campus/clubs group.
    - ☐ Creating and following through on a study plan for any given week.

The concepts of Reality Therapy can be incorporated in a variety of situations when working with students on issues related to relationships, goal setting, and focusing on what is in their control. The here-and-now nature of Reality Therapy aids both the helper and helpee in reaching a solution-focused, efficient approach to addressing any given concern.

Below is a list of recommended reading.

Glasser, W. (1998). *Choice theory: A new psychology of personal freedom*. New York, NY: HarperCollins Publishers.

Glasser, W. (2003). *Psychiatry can be hazardous to your mental health*. New York, NY: HarperCollins.

Glasser, W., & Glasser, C. (2000). *Getting together and staying together*. New York, NY: HarperCollins Publishers.

Wubbolding, R. (2000). *Reality therapy for the 21st century*. Philadelphia, PA: Brunner Routledge.

Cognitive Behavioral Theory

A cognitive behavioral approach focuses on identifying and changing illogical and distorted thinking that leads to and/or serves as a catalyst for disturbing behavior and feelings (Beck, 1995). Similar to Choice Theory, little emphasis is placed on the historical root of a problem, but rather on the present and on resolving the particular problem. Attention is on what Beck referred to as the "cognitive triad" (Weishaar, 1993), which includes (a) cognitive distortions (often referred to as irrational beliefs); (b) cognitive deficits; and (c) an overall negative view of self, the world, and the future.

Examples of cognitive distortions that we all have engaged in are listed below. (See Bitter, 2014, pp. 387–388; Ellis, 1994, pp. 19–22.)

- Musturbating: absolute shoulds, demands, musts, and necessities that a person puts on himself or herself. For example, Josey would be musturbating if she believed that she needed to be friends with everyone she met.
- Overgeneralization: if I do good things then I am a good person; if I do things that seem to harm myself and others, I am a bad person. Such generalizations could be applied to others as well. For example, Josey never mentioned how many times her roommate took her things without asking. Josey would be overgeneralizing if she said, "She is not a good friend, and she should not be trusted" based upon the roommate only taking a pencil once because she needed it for an exam.
- Awfulizing: a kind of overgeneralization in the negative; perceiving unfortunate qualities or events as completely awful and terrible. Josey would be awfulizing her roommate ignoring her during the one outing if you heard her say things like, "The whole night was a complete disaster. My roommate refused to even acknowledge that I was part of the group"

when she previously told you that she went to her favorite restaurant and sat next to a new friend.

- Arbitrary inference: conclusion made about something without supporting evidence. Josey decides that her roommate does not like her based upon the experience of one outing. (We never did ask Josey how many times she has experienced her roommate's "rudeness." What if the roommate was having a bad day?)

- Selective abstraction: taking something out of context, distorting the details and/or while ignoring other facts. Josey never mentioned that her roommate brought her soup the other day when she was sick, or the time her roommate held a birthday party for her a few months ago.

- Magnification and minimization, making more or less out of the facts or events presented: Josey would be magnifying her roommate's "rudeness" by stating, "She is always so rude" when in fact the roommate was rude to her on one occasion. If the friend was nice to her during the following outing, Josey would minimize it by saying, "Well, it was my birthday. She had to be nice."

- Personalization: a kind of arbitrary reference; taking something personal that in fact has limited evidence to be personally related. When Josey was out with her group of friends, the roommate mentioned that she started thinking about the importance of keeping friends that help her become a better person and slowly disengaging from so-called friends who do not. Josey would be personalizing what she heard if she assumed that she was one of the friends that her roommate was trying to disengage from (i.e., even though the roommate invited her to go on the outing).

- Dichotomous thinking: all or nothing, always or never, totally good or totally bad thinking. This kind of thinking would be present if Josey's roommate was "rude" to her once, and yet her response was, "My roommate will never be a good friend."

- Labeling and mislabeling: attributing traits to self or others based upon limited facts or detail. We certainly do not know for sure if Josey's roommate is a rude person. All we know is that Josey perceived her behavior as rude on at least one occasion. Let us say that we asked Josey to describe other times when the roommate was rude. Josey would be mislabeling her if she responded, "Well I can only remember once. And I don't care if she was having a bad day, she is a rude, ignorant and a very bad friend!"

- Mind reading: a kind of arbitrary reference; assuming one knows what someone else is thinking or will do. Josey would be mind reading her roommate if she said, "She didn't have to say it. I know that she thought I was acting hyper that day. She was rolling her eyes at me in her head."

These distortions originate from *schemas*, or core beliefs that have developed over time (i.e., family of origin, life experiences, culture, society) about what we believe should be (Weishaar, 1993). Our schemas orient ourselves to others, the world, and actually back to ourselves. Sometimes they get us in trouble, namely, by leading to distorted thoughts. A good cognitive behavioral therapist can help clients consider and revisit their cognitive schemas. You, as the student affairs professional, can help get the process rolling.

The goal of the approach is to help individuals feel better by relieving anxious and depressive symptoms. This can be done by using a few cognitive behavioral techniques. First, you can help a student identify the cognitive pattern that is contributing to feeling unhappy and anxious. Consider Albert Ellis's ABC theory of self-disturbing (Ellis, 2001). Adversities (A) can interfere with happiness and functionality; (B) is defined as "believing-emoting-behaving" (p. 19) in response to the adversity, which eventually leads to consequences (C), which can be unhealthy and self-defeating or healthy and self-helping. Achieving healthy and self-helping consequences requires one to engage in "Rational Bs" while vigorously acting and feeling against "Irrational Bs." You help the student spend some time considering what negative beliefs are therefore impacting his or her feelings and behaviors which are eventually leading to negative consequences. Feel free to recreate the following chart as you dialogue with the student about his or her current process.

Situation or Event	Automatic Thought	Cognitive Distortion	Emotion	Challenging Self-Statement	Alternate Response

For example, in the case of Josey, one example might be:

Situation or Event	Automatic Thought	Cognitive Distortion	Emotion	Challenging Self-Statement	Alternate Response
Roommate talked more to the others than me during last outing.	She is rude and does not like me.	Arbitrary inference	Hurt	This is one incident. Maybe she thought I could handle not getting all the attention.	Talk to her about it; or let it go and see what happens during the next outing.

Student affairs professionals who use a cognitive behavioral approach can help students slow down their thinking and behaving enough to examine the process that occurs over seconds, but can have an hour- to week-long impact. While the approach is a here-and-now one, it also helps highlight one's lifelong patterns of distorted thinking that continue to lend themselves to patterns of behavior and feeling that do not work too well. For example, this approach can help students stop and change distorted thoughts to help improve behaviors and to feel better. This could be applied across an array of problems, including study habits, relationship concerns.

How might you apply a Cognitive Behavioral approach in a student affairs context?

- Walk the student through the chart. Help the student dispute irrational and distorted beliefs. Ask the student to keep the chart journal outside of your meetings.
- Consistently communicate that irrational beliefs can be changed! Help the student consider alternatives.
- Convey that an optimistic view of self, the world, and others will help the student achieve personal and professional goals.
- Underscore the evidence that contradicts cognitive distortions (Beck, 1995).
- Teach stress management strategies.
- Help the student work on his or her self-acceptance. You can do this by offering him or her unconditional other-acceptance (Ellis, 2001).
- Dialogue with the student about how to take life's stressors less seriously by stressing the notion that most stressors pass. (Be sure, though, to do this with empathy.)
- Encourage the student to consider how he or she will approach new situations.

Below is a list of recommended reading:

Bandura, A. (1969). *Principles of behavioral modification*. New York, NY: Holt, Rinehart, & Winston.
Beck, A. T. (1979). *Cognitive therapy and the emotional disorders*. New York, NY: International Universities Press.
Beck, A. T. (1988). *Love is never enough*. New York, NY: Harper & Row.
Beck, J. S. (1995). *Cognitive therapy: Basics and beyond*. New York, NY: Guilford Press.
Beck, J. S. (2005). *Cognitive therapy for challenging problems: What to do when the basics don't work*. New York, NY: Guilford Press.
Ellis, A. (2001). *Overcoming destructive beliefs, feelings and behaviors*. Amherst, NY: Prometheus Books.

CONCEPTUALIZING AND COMPOSING YOUR HELPING PHILOSOPHY

Inherent in developing your helping philosophy is articulating your conceptualization of why you believe college students need support and how does this support look. If someone asked you to explain your philosophy of helping

193

college students, what would you say? What would capture the essence of your belief about helping? The process of developing your helping philosophy begins with introspection, openness, and self-examination. As a student affairs professional, it is beneficial to conduct an exploration of your personal beliefs, values, and obligations and how these are interrelated to your personal life and professional practice. As you compose your personal philosophy, consider the following questions:

- What is the role of student affairs on a college campus?
- What is the role of student affairs in a student's development?
- How can student affairs contribute to supporting students with developing a purpose? How is this related to your idea of a person's purpose in life?
- What do you believe a student can contribute to society upon completion?
- What is the purpose of helping college students? Why do you believe what you believe?
- As a student affairs practitioner, what is your role in a student's matriculation? What are your professional obligations to students? Why?
- What should a successful student look like once he or she graduates from an institution of higher education?
- What do you consider to be your natural helping behaviors? How do you integrate these with how you function as a student affairs professional?
- What experiences shape your view of helping?
- How do you view helping in student affairs?
- Looking back at your experiences, who or what approaches have the greatest impression on you, and why?
- What is your view of an individual's ability to change? What is your view of human motivation?
- When helping college students, what would frustrate you in terms of a student's progress toward a set goal or resolution of an issue/concern? What is acceptable/not acceptable to you?

It is understandable that developing a personal philosophy for helping could be challenging due to the integration of your personal life experiences, view of student development, and personal as well as professional beliefs. The process, nonetheless, is an essential component of enhancing your professional helping skills as you begin the process of building your framework, orientation, and approach based on your values, personality, awareness, and intention. Building your framework and approach for helping, as well as "understanding how you view yourself, others, and the world around you is the first step in placing theory into a practical realm" (Halbur & Halbur, 2011, p. 13).

194

The purpose of this chapter is to provide you with just a few theoretical spring-boards, if you will, that will move you to pursue additional study. With additional knowledge of any of the given models, you should feel comfortable in eventually applying the concepts. In the meantime, let us now focus on writing the first draft of your personal philosophy for helping college students. Take time to reflect and engage in self-understanding and move toward applications and techniques. Remember, as you evolve as a professional and have more experiences, this philosophy will more than likely change.

CONCLUSION

In summary, self-awareness is essential in any helping profession and it is prudent for a helping professional to have a helping philosophy to guide his or her work. Engaging in activities that assist you in gaining insight into your personal helping style and developing a helping philosophy can make you a better student affairs professional. However, you must be intentional. Developing and adopting a help-ing philosophy is an ongoing process and a part of creating your professional iden-tity as you become more confident in developing your techniques and in meeting the needs of students.

REFERENCES

Adler, A. (1933). *Der Sinn des Lebens* [Social interest: A challenge to mankind]. Leipzig, Germany: Rolf Passer.

Beck, J. S. (1995). *Cognitive therapy: Basics and beyond.* New York, NY: Guildford Press.

Bitter, J. R. (2012). [Alfred Adler's] On the essence and origin of character: An introduc-tion. In J. Carlson & M. P. Maniacci (Eds.), *Alfred Adler revisited* (pp. 89–97). New York, NY: Routledge.

Bitter, J. R. (2014). *Theory and practice of family therapy and counseling* (2nd ed.). Belmont, CA: Brooks/Cole.

Boy, A. V., & Pine, G. J. (1983). Counseling: Fundamentals of theoretical renewal. *Counsel-ing and Values, 27*, 248–255.

Corey, G. (2016). *Theory and practice of group counseling* (9th ed.). Boston, MA: Cengage.

Dewey, E. A. (1984). The use and misuse of emotions. *Journal of Adlerian Theory, Research, and Practice, 40*(2), 184–195.

Dreikurs, R. (1968). *Psychology in the classroom: A manual for teachers* (2nd ed.). New York, NY: Harper & Row. (Original work published 1957).

Dreikurs, R., Grunwald, B. B., & Pepper, F. C. (1982). *Maintaining sanity in the classroom* (2nd ed.). New York, NY: Harper & Row Publishers.

Ellis, A. (1994). *Reason and emotion in psychotherapy* (rev.). New York, NY: Kensington. (Original work published 1962).

Ellis, A. (2001). *Overcoming destructive beliefs, feelings and behaviors.* Amherst, NY: Pro-metheus Books.

Evans, M. J., & Reason, R. D. (2001). Guiding principles: A review and analysis of philo-sophical statements. *Journal of College Student Development, 42*(4), 359–377.

Fox, R. (2013). *Elements of the helping profession: A guide for clinicians* (3rd ed.). New York, NY: Routledge.

Glasser, W. (1998). *Choice theory: A new psychology of personal freedom*. New York, NY: Harper Perennial.

Glasser, W., & Wubbolding, R. (1995). *Current psychotherapies* (5th ed.). Itasca, IL: F.E. Peacock Publishers.

Hackney, H. (1992). *Differentiating between counseling theory and process*. Ann Arbor, MI: ERIC Clearinghouse on Counseling and Personnel Services. (ED347485).

Halbur, D. A., & Halbur, K. V. (2011). *Developing your theoretical orientation in counseling and psychotherapy* (3rd ed.). Boston, MA: Pearson.

Luciano, L., Granahl, G., & Hansen, J. C. (1986). *Methods of family therapy*. Englewood Cliffs, NJ: Prentice-Hall.

MacKinnon, F. J. D., & Associates. (2004). *Rentz's student affairs practice in higher education* (3rd ed.). Springfield, IL: Charles C. Thomas Publishing.

McCurdy, K. G. (2007). Making love or making love work: Integrating the crucial Cs in the games couples play. *The Journal of Individual Psychology, 63*(3), 279–293.

Powers, R. L., & Griffith, J. (1987). *Understanding lifestyle: The psycho-clarity process*. Chicago, IL: American Institute of Adlerian Studies.

Reynolds, A. L. (2009). *Helping college students: Developing essential support skills for student affairs practice*. San Francisco, CA: Jossey-Bass.

Reynolds, A. L. (2011). Counseling and helping skills. In J. H. Schuh, S. R. Jones, & S. R. Harper (Eds.), *Student services: A handbook for the profession* (5th ed., pp. 399–412). San Francisco, CA: Jossey-Bass.

Sherman, R., & Dinkmeyer, D. (1987). *Systems of family therapy: An Adlerian integration*. New York, NY: Brunner/Mazel.

Sweeney, T. J. (2009). *Adlerian counseling and psychotherapy: A practitioner's approach* (5th ed.). New York, NY: Routledge.

Watts, R. E. (1993). Developing a personal theory of counseling: A brief guide for students. *TCA Journal, 21*(1), 103–104.

Weishaar, M. E. (1993). *Aaron T. Beck*. Thousand Oaks, CA: Sage.

Wubbolding, R. E. (2000). *Reality therapy for the 21st century*. New York, NY: Routledge.

Wubbolding, R. E. (2011). *Reality therapy*. Washington, DC: American Psychological Association.

Wubbolding, R. E., Brickell, J., Imhof, L., Kim, R., Lojk, L., & Al-Rashidi, B. (2004). Reality therapy: A global perspective. *International Journal of Reality Therapy, 26*(3), 219–228.

Young, R. B. (2003). Philosophies and values guiding the student affairs profession. In S. R. Komives & D. B. Woodard (Eds.), *Student services: A handbook for the profession* (pp. 89–106). San Francisco, CA: Jossey-Bass.

Chapter 8

Helping Yourself
Self-Care and Personal Well-Being

The student affairs profession, like most helping professions, can be demanding, challenging, and emotionally taxing. Particularly in light of today's competitive postsecondary education environment, there are increasing demands on student affairs professionals (Burkhard, Cole, Ott, & Stoflet, 2005) and accordingly, the responsibilities of student affairs professionals create a high personal demand in terms of time, talent, and energy (Carpenter, 2003). However, even as student affairs work becomes more complex, work should not become a student affairs professional's whole life (Renn, Jessup-Anger, & Doyle, 2008). Working in student affairs can be rewarding in so many ways; however, balancing the constancy of demands and the integration of many roles and duties can be time-consuming and can lead to feeling overwhelmed, uncertain, and pressured. Sandeen and Barr (2009) noted that because student affairs professionals are at times subject to conflicting demands, work long hours, are objects of public criticism and are often not thanked for what they do, they are physically and emotionally exhausted by the end of any semester or academic year. As a consequence of trying to meet these demands, expectations, and circumstances, a student affairs professional can suffer the consequences of poor work–life balance; that is, the feeling an individual has when he or she devotes more energy in one area while neglecting other areas (Chick, 2004).

The challenge is to find a balance between the personal life and the professional life. However, as Guthrie, Woods, Cusker, and Gregory (2005) concluded, "student affairs work holds particular challenges for attaining balance, most particularly the '24/7' nature of the work, the involvement in the 'informal life of the college,' and the demands of a helping profession" (p. 125). Therefore, "finding time for family and/or friends, personal renewal, wellness, and other priorities while juggling the demands of a job that requires a 24/7 commitment is more of a goal than an achievement" (Beeny, Guthrie, Rhodes, & Terrell, 2005, p. 137). If a balance of caring for oneself and caring for others is not found, over time, there could be consequences such as stress and burnout.

A CONSEQUENCE OF NOT HAVING A BALANCE

By virtue of student affairs professionals' roles and responsibilities, serving as a caregiver is customary. In helping students, however, we can sometimes forget to help ourselves. According to Corey and Corey (1998), "no one is immune from the cost of caring for others" (p. 321) and they recommend that it is best for helping professionals, such as student affairs professionals, to understand the external realities that likely produce stress for them and their contribution to their stress by how they perceive and interpret reality.

Richard Lazarus (1966) described stress as a condition or feeling experienced when a person perceives that "demands exceed the personal and social resources the individual is able to mobilize" (p. 4). Therefore, due to instinctive, innate response mechanisms and perceptions, an individual's capacity to manage psychological stress rests on his or her ability and available resources to cope with life's circumstances and relationships, which can lead to psychological distress, primarily experienced as symptoms of depression and anxiety (Mirowsky & Ross, 2003; Pearlin, Lieberman, Menaghan, & Mullan, 1981). Left unattended and managed, stress can have a psychological and physical effect upon individuals and impair daily functioning. In other words, stress can take a toll on those who help others and they should take account of their resources to cope, "recognizing and understanding the stress process and its extreme consequences—physical, mental, or emotional burnout—is a professional necessity for people who work with people" (Peters, 1985, p. 139).

Working effectively with college students in their development requires an emotional investment and it is impossible for student affairs professionals not to be personally affected (Figley, 1995). Without proper self-care, the nature of work for student affairs professionals can cause them to be vulnerable to more than just stress. They are also at risk of developing burnout and compassion fatigue (Figley, 2002; Maslach, 1982). Student affairs professionals, as helping professionals, are especially susceptible to burnout because of the heavy time and emotional demands, responsibilities, and uncertainties they encounter by working with others (Peters, 1985).

Experiencing burnout goes beyond feeling stressed. The term *burnout* was first introduced by Herbert Freudenberger (1974), defining it as "to fail, wear out, or become exhausted by making excessive demands on energy, strength, or resources," (p. 159) and attributed it to the constant pressures of working with emotionally needy and demanding individuals. Burnout is characterized by symptoms of emotional exhaustion, depersonalization, and reduced feelings of personal accomplishment (Kahill, 1988). There is also a unique form of burnout, referred to as compassion fatigue, which is considered a natural consequence of a helping relationship due partly to the empathy required (Figley, 1995), involving being preoccupied with the concerns, distressing experiences, and problems of

198

those being helped. It is almost like the helper cares too much. Helping begins to feel like a huge physical and emotional chore. The helper may even wonder whether the work is worth it. In short, the helper loses any sense that he or she is actually making a difference. The experience of burnout and/or compassion fatigue can also include feeling depressed or anxious, eventually taking a toll on one's health and interactions with others.

For student affairs professionals, it is important to not focus on the care of students at the expense of their own well-being. Gentry (2002) urges "Making best use of available resources to establish respite and sanctuary for ourselves, even in the most abject of circumstances, can have an enormous effect in minimizing our symptoms and maximizing our sustained effectiveness" (p. 47). To enhance effectiveness, personal wellness and self-care are necessary for student affairs professionals, which requires both introspection and action.

THINKING ABOUT MY PRACTICE

What gives you energy? What motivates you?

Who is in your support system that you can trust and talk to during times of stress, lethargy, or difficulty?

What skills do you have or can develop to manage anxiety effectively? What skills do you possess to help you tackle new and unexpected challenges?

What can you do to empty your mind of negative thoughts so that you can be productive in your personal and professional life?

How much does work invade your personal life? How can you ensure a balance between work life and personal life?

What are your stumbling blocks, if any, to self-care?

PERSONAL WELLNESS AND SELF-CARE

Personal wellness inherently involves self-care, described as "an integral part of multiple aspects of a person's life, including health and wellness" (Collins, 2005, p. 264), which can assist a helping professional with coping with daily stressors. It involves learning how to manage personal and work-related stress, making healthy decisions, participating in behaviors that help maintain equilibrium in daily life, and drawing boundaries when necessary (Shallcross, 2013). Understanding how to cope during stressful or uncertain times and finding time for personal wellness are integral for a helping professional's success. Myers, Sweeney, and Witmer (2000) defined wellness as,

a way of life oriented toward optimal health and well-being, in which body, mind, and spirit are integrated by the individual to live life more fully within the human and natural community. Ideally, it is the optimum state of health and well-being that each individual is capable of achieving.

(p. 252)

A key question to ask yourself: What are you capable of achieving to ensure your well-being? How often have you said that you will wait until you have the time to engage in an activity that relaxes you or you will do something relaxing once you take care of the many things in your busy life? The inability to cope success-fully with the many demands of working in student affairs may impact emotional, intuitive, and physical health as well as professional efficiency and effectiveness. As with any helping profession, student affairs professionals can be inclined to enter into interactions in which they can lose track of their needs in assisting another, making it difficult to set limits when viewing himself or herself as the only person who can solve the problem, provide the answer, or complete the task (Manning, 2001). Although it might sound cliché, it is best to take care of yourself first or you will simply have nothing left to care for others. Have you ever thought about why the flight attendant instructs passengers to please put on their own oxygen mask before assisting others? A metaphor offered by Berry (2012) is to think of your self-care as how we interact with our cell phones:

Cell phone batteries have to be recharged and there are three ways to do this: (1) wait until the battery is completely run down and live without power until a recharge can occur; (2) listen when the phone is bleating at you for attention and start recharging then; or (3) recharge regularly to always have power.

(p. 6)

Similar to the cell phone battery, you can choose to charge yourself "after all of your energy is depleted; when your body, mind, and spirit are screaming for attention; or in a proactive way that looks for balance between energy depletion and restoration" (Berry, 2012, p. 6). The bottom line is to find a way to engage in activities to renew yourself when needed. Integrating self-care, whether in small or large ways, can help a student affairs professional deal with the potential emo-tional and physical consequences associated with student affairs work. Self-care can help create balance and can contribute to good physical and mental health and improved quality of life (Pope & Vasquez, 2005). However, since the nature of working in student affairs brings about numerous demands and expectations related to the care of others, student affairs professionals can miss the opportu-nity to be proactive in caring for themselves and finding a balance that works for them. An appropriate balance between power, position, personal life, and policies must be found for a healthy life balance (Manning, 2007). Beyond the personal benefit of a student affairs professional's personal well-being, there is a communal aspect as well. Carpenter (2003) asserted that it is advantageous for student affairs professionals to get appropriate exercise, pay attention to health needs, and attend to needs for recreation and renewal since students need their optimal effort.

Corey and Corey (1998) recommend that helping professionals avoid or reduce stressors, alter stress-inducing behavior patterns, and develop coping resources. A student affairs professional who is tired, tense, or stressed out for long periods of time clearly cannot do his or her best work and " . . . mental and physical relaxation and rest are necessary" (Carpenter, 2003, p. 585). For the purpose of self-care and general wellness, student affairs professionals should learn to be aware of their mind and body to be better prepared to take care of themselves as they take care of others. In the end, whether through exercising, having dinner with friends, reading a good book, or watching a movie, self-care activities need to bring contentment and fulfillment. Additionally, these activities need to be scheduled in the weekly calendar!

Student affairs professionals should take the same advice that is often given to students related to taking care of themselves and prioritizing, ensuring they are always at their best in terms of our ability to be in a helping role. By engaging in self-care, student affairs professionals can better assist students and the campus community as "the ultimate obligation of a profession is to self" (Carpenter, 2003, p. 585). Finding a balance that works best can seem a bit elusive, which is why it takes proactive planning and sincere effort to achieve that balance. In addition, identifying stressors and gauging the impact they can have are necessary in finding a proper balance.

So how do you engage in self-care? Are you aware of your self-care needs and triggers? Have you created a strategy for self-care?

PERSONAL STRATEGY FOR SELF-CARE

It's time to reflect and create your intended strategy for self-care (mental, physical, spiritual/emotional, and environmental) in order to maintain your optimal level of functioning as a helping professional, avoid burnout, and deal with stress. A self-care plan can strengthen your ability to do your work in a healthy and balanced way (Gentry, 2002). Use the following guiding questions to frame your responses as you compose your personal strategy for self-care.

- Outline the potential consequences to your professional career, students, and others if your self-care is neglected.
- What signs and symptoms help you realize that you may be experiencing burnout or too much stress? In other words, what do you consider to be the warning signs?
- How will you address your warning signs? What are your current and future wellness strategies? What can you do better in your life to manage your stress and maintain health? Be specific about the current strategies

that have been beneficial to you thus far in successfully managing stress, maintaining health, and creating a sense of balance/wellness in your life.

- How will you continue to practice effective self-care to avoid burnout and compassion fatigue in the future?
- Who in your life promotes wellness or takes care of you and how do you let them do that? Who is in your social support network?
- What are your resources for wellness? List at least five resources to which you have access that can help promote all areas of wellness and prevent stress (e.g., local classes, websites, professional organizations, etc.).

To guide your thinking, use the following Personal Wellness Plan Worksheet, developed by Dr. Cheryl Pence Wolf based on *The Indivisible Self: An Evidenced-Based Model of Wellness* by Myers and Sweeney (2005).

Refresh Your Mind, Rejuvenate Your Body, Renew Your Spirit

PERSONAL WELLNESS PLAN

Name: _____

Start date: _____ **End date**: _____

People who are successful at making lifestyle changes create a plan of action. You may use this worksheet to identify wellness goals that you would like to achieve over the next several months; the five areas are based on the Indivisible Self wellness model. Review the areas and decide where you would like to make improvements. Create an action plan and identify specific activities that you would like to participate in and list your goals in measurable terms (e.g., have coffee with a friend every Saturday morning, exercise for 30 minutes three times each week). You are encouraged to track your progress throughout your active wellness period.

Creative Self: thinking, emotions, control, work, positive humor

What would you like to have more/less of to improve your creative self (e.g., mentors, studying, bibliotherapy/book discussions, workshops, art, creativity, energy, attitude shifts, counseling, competence, confidence, satisfying work, job security, feeling appreciated, fun, humor)?

Action Plan

Coping Self: leisure, stress management, self-worth, realistic beliefs

What would you like to have more/less of to improve your coping self (e.g., leisure activities, daily relaxation, hobbies, biofeedback, coping, setting limits, time and energy

management, avoiding bad habits/addictions, counseling, self-acceptance, realistic goals, avoiding unrealistic expectations) ?

Action Plan

Social Self: *friendship, love*

What would you like to have more/less of to improve your social self (e.g., social or intimate relationships, parties, potlucks, happy hours, networking, mentors, study groups)?

Action Plan

Essential Self: *spirituality, gender identity, cultural identity, self-care*

What would you like to have more/less of to improve your essential self (e.g., values, virtues, or service that provides meaning, purpose, peace, and enrichment to your life and to others, prayer, meditation, compassion, gender or cultural support, self-care)?

Action Plan

Physical Self: *exercise, nutrition*

What would you like to have more/less of to improve your physical self (e.g., physical activities, exercise, stretching, balanced diet, limiting sugar, salt, and alcohol, vitamins/supplements, maintaining a healthy weight, blood pressure, cholesterol, and other levels)?

Action Plan

Present Weight: _____   Goal weight: _____

Present Blood Pressure: _____   Goal BP: _____

Present Cholesterol/HDL levels: _____   Goal levels: _____

Physical Activity and Exercise: _____   Goal activity: _____

Last Physical Exam: _____   Next exam: _____

Commitment to Self

I make the commitment to implement these wellness goals to the best of my ability.

Signature   Date

Factors and definitions taken from Myers and Sweeney (2005). *The Five Factor WEL Inventory.* Greensboro, NC: Authors.

Definitions of Wellness Scales on the 5F-WEL

Wellness: The sum of all items on the 5F-WEL; a measure of one's general well-being or total wellness.

Creative Self: The combination of attributes that each of us forms to make a unique place among others in our social interactions and to positively interpret our world.

- **Thinking:** Being mentally active, open-minded; having the ability to be creative and experimental; having a sense of curiosity, a need to know and to learn; the ability to think both divergently and convergently when problem solving; the capacity to change one's thinking in order to manage stress; the ability to apply problem-solving strategies in resolving social conflicts.

- **Emotions:** Being aware of or in touch with one's feelings; being able to express one's feelings appropriately; being able to enjoy positive emotions as well as being able to cope with negative emotions; having a sense of energy; avoiding chronic negative emotional states.

- **Control:** Beliefs about your competence, confidence, and mastery (i.e., "I can"); belief that you can usually achieve the goals you set out for yourself; being able to exercise individual choice through imagination, knowledge, and skill; having a sense of planfulness in life; being able to be direct in expressing one's needs (assertive).

- **Work:** Being satisfied with one's work; having adequate financial security; feeling that one's skills are used appropriately; feeling that one can manage one's workload; feeling a sense of job security; feeling appreciated in the work one does; having satisfactory relationships with others on the job; being satisfied with activities in work and play which one chooses to perform; having a playful attitude toward life tasks; the ability to cope with stress in the workplace.

- **Positive Humor:** Being able to laugh at one's own mistakes and the unexpected things that happen; the ability to laugh appropriately at others; having the capacity to see the contradictions and predicaments of life in an objective manner such that one can gain new perspectives; enjoying the idiosyncrasies and inconsistencies of life; the ability to use humor to accomplish even serious tasks.

Coping Self: The combination of elements that regulate our responses to life events and provide a means for transcending their negative effects.

- **Leisure:** Activities done in one's free time; satisfaction with one's leisure activities, importance of leisure, positive feelings associated with leisure; having at least one activity in which "I lose myself and time stands still"; ability to approach tasks from a playful point of view; having a balance between work and leisure activities; ability to put work aside for leisure without feeling guilty.

- **Stress Management:** General perception of one's own self-management or self-regulation; seeing change as an opportunity for growth rather than as a threat to one's security; ongoing self-monitoring and assessment of one's coping resources; the ability to organize and manage resources such as time, energy, setting limits, and need for structure.
- **Self-Worth:** Accepting who and what one is, positive qualities along with imperfections; acceptance of one's physical appearance; affirming the value of one's existence; valuing oneself as a unique individual.
- **Realistic Beliefs:** Understanding that perfection or being loved by everyone are impossible goals, and having the courage to be imperfect; the ability to perceive reality accurately, not as one might want or desire it to be; separating that which is logical and rational from that which is distorted, irrational, or wishful thinking; controlling the "shoulds," "oughts," "dos," and "don'ts," which tend to rule one's life; avoiding unrealistic expectations or wishful thinking.

Social Self: Social support through connections with others in our friendships and intimate relationships, including family ties.

- **Friendship:** Social relationships that involve a connection with others individually or in community, but which do not have a marital, sexual, or familial commitment; having friends in whom one can trust and who can provide emotional, material, or informational support when needed; not being lonely; being comfortable in social situations; having a capacity to trust others; having empathy for others; feeling understood by others; having relationships in which nonjudgmental caring is experienced; being comfortable with one's social skills for interacting with others; being involved in one or more community groups.
- **Love:** The ability to be intimate, trusting, and self-disclosing with another person; the ability to give as well as express affection with significant others; the ability to accept others without conditions, to convey nonpossessive caring which respects the uniqueness of another; having at least one relationship that is secure, lasting, and for which there is a mutual commitment; having concern for the nurturance and growth of others; experiencing physical and emotional satisfaction with one's sexual life; having a family or family-like support system characterized by shared spiritual values, the ability to solve conflict in a mutually respectful way, the ability to solve problems together, commitment to one another, healthy communication styles, shared time together, the ability to cope with stress, and mutual appreciation.

Essential Self: Our essential meaning-making processes in relation to life, self, and others.

- **Spirituality**: Personal beliefs and behaviors that are practiced as part of the recognition that we are more than the material aspects of mind and body. Dimensions include belief in a higher power; hope and optimism, worship, prayer, and/or meditation; purpose in life, love (compassion for others); moral values; and transcendence, or a sense of oneness with the universe.
- **Gender Identity**: Satisfaction with one's gender; feeling supported in one's gender; transcendence of gender identity (i.e., ability to be androgynous).
- **Cultural Identity**: Satisfaction with one's cultural identity; feeling supported in one's cultural identity; transcendence of one's cultural identity (i.e., cultural assimilation).
- **Self-Care**: Taking responsibility for one's wellness through self-care and safety habits that are preventive in nature; such habits include obtaining timely medical care, wearing a seat belt; limiting the use of prescribed drugs and avoiding the use of illegal drugs; avoiding the use of tobacco; abstaining from or very moderately using alcohol; getting adequate sleep; minimizing the harmful effects of pollution in one's environment.

Physical Self: The biological and physiological processes that constitute the physical aspects of our development and functioning.

- **Exercise**: Engaging in sufficient physical activity to keep in good physical condition; maintaining flexibility in the major muscles and joints of the body through work, recreation, or stretching exercises; regular exercise and not overdoing it are important guidelines.
- **Nutrition**: Eating a nutritionally balanced diet, three meals a day including breakfast, consuming fats, cholesterol, sweets, and salt sparingly; maintaining a normal weight (i.e., within 15% of the ideal) and avoiding overeating.

Factors and definitions taken from Myers and Sweeney (2005). *The Five FactorWEL Inventory*. Greensboro, NC: Authors.

© Cheryl Pence Wolf. For questions, contact Dr. Cheryl Pence Wolf, Principal Investigator, at cheryl.wolf@wku.edu. This was developed as part of a research study at the University of Florida and was sponsored by CSI Beta Chapter. Partial funding for this research was provided by a grant from the Chi Sigma Iota Counseling Academic and Professional Honor Society International.

CONCLUSION

Each of us deserves to lead a satisfying, meaningful life and the students you support deserve the best from you. To offer your best, you should be intentional in your actions to pay attention to and take care of your physical, mental, and emotional health. Self-care is invaluable and your ability to assist students is connected to your ability to deal effectively with the multiple aspects of your life. Try to remember that you are not Superman or Superwoman; in fact, they even had a support network in the Justice League to assist them in times of need. Stress affects us all, including those who enjoy helping others, so no one is immune. Step back and take stock. Be proactive and take meaningful measures, starting with the development of a personal strategy for self-care followed by purposeful action.

REFERENCES

Beeny, C., Guthrie, V. L., Rhodes, G. S., & Terrell, P. S. (2005). Personal and professional balance among senior student affairs officers: Gender differences in approaches and expectations. *College Student Affairs Journal, 24*(2), 137–151.

Berry, J. O. (2012). *My clients, my students, my patients, myself: Self-care advice for caring professionals.* Center for Learning and Leadership/UCEDD, University of Oklahoma Health Sciences Center, OU College of Medicine. Retrieved from www.ouhsc.edu/thecenter/products/documents/self-care_web.pdf

Burkhard, A. W., Cole, D. C., Ott, M., & Stoflet, T. (2005). Entry-level competencies of new student affairs professionals: A Delphi study. *Journal of Student Affairs Research and Practice, 42*(3), 545–571.

Carpenter, D. S. (2003). Professionalism. In S. R. Komives & D. B. Woodard (Eds.), *Student services: A handbook for the profession* (4th ed., pp. 573–592). San Francisco, CA: Jossey-Bass.

Chick, E. (2004). *Fundamentals of work-life balance.* Alexandria, VA: American Society for Training and Development.

Collins, W. L. (2005). Embracing spirituality as an element of professional self-care. *Social Work and Christianity, 32*(3), 263–274.

Corey, M. S., & Corey, G. (1998). *Becoming a helper* (3rd ed.). Pacific Grove, CA: Brooks/Cole Publishing.

Figley, C. (Ed.). (1995). *Compassion fatigue: Coping with secondary traumatic stress disorder in those who treat the traumatized.* New York, NY: Brunner-Routledge.

Figley, C. (2002). *Brief treatments for the traumatized: A project of the green cross foundation.* Westport, CT: Greenwood.

Freudenberger, H. J. (1974). Staff burnout. *Journal of Social Issues, 30*(1), 159–165.

Gentry, J. E. (2002). Compassion fatigue: A crucible of transformation. *Journal of Trauma Practice, 1*(3/4), 37–91.

Guthrie, V. L., Woods, E., Cusker, C., & Gregory, M. (2005). Portrait of balance: Personal and professional balance among student affairs educators. *College Student Affairs Journal, 24*(2), 110–128.

Kahill, S. (1988). Interventions for burnout in the helping professions: A review of the empirical evidence. *Canadian Journal of Counselling Review, 22*(3), 331–342.

Lazarus, R. S. (1966). *Psychological stress and the coping process.* New York, NY: McGraw-Hill.

Manning, K. (2001). Infusing soul into student affairs: Organizational theory and models. *New Directions for Student Services, 95*, 27–35.

Manning, K. (2007). Ethic of care for new student affairs professionals: Keeping them out of the trenches. *Student Affairs Leader, 35*(19), 6.

Maslach C. (1982). *Burnout: The cost of caring.* Englewood Cliffs, NJ: Prentice Hall.

Mirowsky, J., & Ross, C. E. (2003). *Social causes of psychological distress* (2nd ed.). New Brunswick, NJ: Aldine Transaction.

Myers, J. E., & Sweeney, T. J. (2005). The indivisible self: An evidence-based model of wellness. *Journal of Individual Psychology, 61*, 234–245.

Myers, J. E., Sweeney, T. J., & Witmer, J. M. (2000). The wheel of wellness counseling for wellness: A holistic model for treatment planning. *Journal of Counseling & Development, 78*, 251–266.

Pearlin, L. I., Lieberman, M. A., Menaghan, E. G., & Mullan, J. T. (1981). The stress process. *Journal of Health and Social Behavior, 22*, 337–356.

Peters, M. (1985). Burnout: The modern malady of helping. In D. Avila & A. Combs (Eds.), *Perspectives on helping relationships and the helping professions* (pp. 139–154). Newton, MA: Allyn & Bacon.

Pope, K. S., & Vasquez, M. J. T. (2005). *How to survive and thrive as a therapist: Information, ideas, and resources for psychologists.* Washington, DC: American Psychological Association.

Renn, K. A., Jessup-Anger, E. R., & Doyle, S. J. (2008, Fall). *Top ten tips for new professionals from the National Study of New Professionals in Student Affairs.* The Eighth Vector, Newsletter of the ACPA Standing Committee for Graduate Students and New Professionals, Washington, DC.

Sandeen, A., & Barr, M. (2009, June 15). Stress and the student affairs professional. *Student Affairs Leader, 37*(2), 6–7.

Shallcross, L. (2013, January). Who's taking care of Superman? *Counseling Today, 55*(7), 42–46.

About the Authors

Monica Galloway Burke is an Associate Professor in the Department of Counseling and Student Affairs at Western Kentucky University. Prior to her 17 years of experience as a faculty member and practitioner in Student Affairs and Higher Education, she worked in the field of mental health. She also serves as the Assistant to the Chief Diversity Officer at Western Kentucky University. Dr. Burke earned a Bachelor of Arts degree in Psychology from Tougaloo College and a Master of Science degree in Counseling Psychology and a Doctor of Philosophy degree in Educational Administration and Supervision from the University of Southern Mississippi. She has published in several peer-reviewed journals and contributed chapters to various books. Additionally, Dr. Burke has conducted numerous workshops and presentations at the international, national, regional, and state levels.

Jill Duba Sauerheber is a Licensed Professional Clinical Counselor and a National Certified Counselor. She is EMDR certified, is Reality Therapy Certified, has completed levels 1–3 of the Gottman Couples Therapy Method, and holds a Certification of Study in Adlerian Psychology. She is a Professor in the Department of Counseling and Student Affairs at Western Kentucky University and maintains a small private practice. She has published over 55 journal articles, book chapters, and edited two books addressing areas related to Adlerian psychology, couples counseling, psychopathology, and religious factors in counseling and academic gatekeeping. Dr. Duba has conducted over 45 national and international presentations and over 60 regional and state presentations related to similar topics. She is currently serving as president of the North American Society of Adlerian Psychology.

Aaron W. Hughey is a Professor in the Department of Counseling and Student Affairs at Western Kentucky University, where he oversees the graduate degree program in Student Affairs in Higher Education. Before joining the faculty in 1991, he spent 10 years in progressive administrative positions, including five years as the Associate Director of University Housing at WKU. He was also head of the department of Counseling and Student Affairs for five years before returning to the faculty full-time in 2008. Dr. Hughey has degrees from the University of Tennessee at Martin, the University of Tennessee at Knoxville, Western Kentucky University, and Northern Illinois University. He has authored (or co-authored) over 50 refereed publications on a wide range of issues including leadership and student development, standardized testing, diversity, and educational administration. He regularly presents at national and international conferences and consults extensively with companies and schools. He also provides training programs on a variety of topics centered on change management.

Karl Laves is a Licensed Counseling Psychologist. He is a Qualified Instructor with the QPR Institute, one of the more established suicide awareness and prevention organizations in America. He is the Associate Director of the WKU Counseling and Testing Center and has taught undergraduate and graduate courses for the Psychology Department and the Counseling and Student Affairs Department at WKU. He has presented on a variety of topics at state and regional conferences and has provided mandated suicide awareness and prevention training for public school faculty for the last five years. He has provided individual therapy and crisis response to the WKU campus for over 20 years and has consulted with faculty and departmental staff on suicide prevention and postvention.

VOICES FROM THE FIELD

Contributing Authors

Susan E. Belangee, PhD, LPC, NCC, ACS, specializes in the treatment of eating disorders from the Adlerian psychology model. Currently, she is in private practice near Atlanta, GA, teaches online courses for Adler Graduate School in Minneapolis, MN, and is an instructor for the International Committee of Adlerian Summer Schools and Institutes (www.icassi.net). Her experience includes college counseling and college student development as well as training master's level students pursuing degrees in Student Affairs. Susan is actively involved in the North American Society of Adlerian Psychology (www.alfredadler.org), serving in numerous leadership positions since 2000.

Imelda N. Bratton is an Assistant Professor in the Department of Counseling and Student Affairs at Western Kentucky University where she is the Program and Clinical Coordinator of the School Counseling Program and Co-Director of the Talley Family Counseling Center. She is a Professional School Counselor, Licensed Professional Clinical Counselor, Registered Play

Therapist-Supervisor, and National Certified Counselor. She has over 15 years of experience working in inner-city and rural communities as a bilingual school counselor and professional counselor in addition to 10 years of experience in higher education. Her areas of interests relate to integrating play therapy, sandtray and expressive arts in teaching, counseling, and supervision experiences. She is currently serving as President of the Kentucky Association of Counselor Education and Supervision and President-Elect of the Kentucky School Counselor Association.

Colin Cannonier is a former first-class cricketer and central banker who began his career as a country economist in the Eastern Caribbean. He is currently an Assistant Professor of Economics at Belmont University. His research interests include health economics, economic demography, applied economics, public policy, and labor economics. He has a PhD in economics from Louisiana State University.

Lacretia Dye is an Assistant Professor in the Department of Counseling and Student Affairs at Western Kentucky University. As a Licensed Professional Clinical Counselor and a National Certified Counselor, Dr. Dye serves her local, regional, and national community with Heart, Mind, and Body Wellness. She regularly gives workshops with parents, teachers, students, and community professionals in the areas of ancestral healing, shamanic healing, yoga and drumming therapy, trauma-releasing activities in counseling, urban school counseling, and self-care. She has also published and presented at national and international conferences on these topics. Dr. Dye is also a Certified Yoga Calm Instructor and Trainer, Adult Yoga Instructor (RYT-200), and a licensed Professional School Counselor. She is currently conducting research on mindful yoga and student well-being.

LaShonda B. Fuller is an Assistant Professor of Counseling at Chicago State University located in Chicago, Illinois, and has served as a Counselor Educator for five years. Dr. Fuller is an advocate for human development across the lifespan through her business, Truth UnTold Enterprises, LLC, blogging, and self-help book, *In Search for Love and Freedom: What I Lost Along My Way*, and work in private practice with Eustress Therapy and Wellness Center on the Southside of Chicago. Training future clinical and school counselors, African American females and group counseling, and bullying in academia are of special interest to Dr. Fuller.

Cynthia Palmer Mason is a Professor in the Department of Counseling and Student Affairs at Western Kentucky University. She is a Certified NCATE Board Examiner (BOE), Glasser Scholar, Reality Therapy Certified (RTC), has CT/RT Supervisor Certification, and a CT/RT Faculty Endorsement by the William Glasser Institute. She received her doctorate in Educational

Administration and Instruction from the University of Kentucky. Dr. Mason holds memberships in the American Counseling Association, Association for Counselor Education and Supervision, Association for Multicultural Counseling and Development, Kentucky Counseling Association, Kentucky School Counselors Association, and the William Glasser Institute.

Monique U. Robinson-Nichols is the Associate Dean for Students and Equity, Diversity and Inclusion, Peabody College at Vanderbilt University, where she is responsible for various aspects of campus diversity efforts and student and academic affairs areas such as recruitment, admissions, first-year student and transfer orientation, and graduation activities. Prior to Vanderbilt University, she was the Director of Student Life and Diversity Initiatives at Volunteer State Community College (VSCC) in Gallatin, Tennessee.

Fred E. Stickle is a Professor at Western Kentucky University where he teaches courses related to marriage and family counseling. He also maintains a private practice. Dr. Stickle has over 40 years of experience in teaching and has been active in his counseling practice for approximately 33 years. He received his BS degree from Cedarville University where he majored in Social Science Secondary Education and completed his graduate study in counseling at Wright State University (MS) and Iowa State University (PhD).

Cheryl Wolf is an Assistant Professor in the Department of Counseling and Student Affairs at Western Kentucky University. She is a Licensed Professional Counselor Associate (LPCA), Nationally Certified Counselor (NCC), Certificated Professional in Human Resources (PHR), Certified Clinical Hypnotherapist (CHt), and a Certified Global Career Development Facilitator (GCDF) where she helps individuals through counseling and career development. Her research interests include career development, career meaning, wellness, and multicultural spirituality. She has published 17 academic journal articles, book chapters, and other peer-reviewed publications and has conducted 18 national, regional, and state presentations related to her research interests. She is currently serving as treasurer-elect of the Southern Association for Counselor Education and Supervision.

Index